Financial Management
in Academic Libraries:
Data-Driven Planning and Budgeting

Robert E. Dugan
and Peter Hernon

Association of College and Research Libraries
A division of the American Library Association
Chicago, Illinois 2018

The paper used in this publication meets the minimum requirements of American National Standard for Information Sciences–Permanence of Paper for Printed Library Materials, ANSI Z39.48-1992. ∞

Cataloging-in-Publication data is on file with the Library of Congress.

Printed in the United States of America.

22 21 20 19 18 5 4 3 2 1

Contents

Preface

An important aspect of librarianship, regardless of the type of library, relates to financial management, which essentially deals with the management of the budget and expenditures as libraries engage in planning and demonstrate their accountability, effectiveness, efficiency, and sustainability. Complicating matters, academic library budgets might range from hundreds of thousands of dollars to millions of dollars. Everyone who engages in library management oversees a fraction of that amount or, as directors, they are responsible (accountable) for the entire amount and for all expenditures. Camila A. Alire and G. Edward Evans underscore that "understanding institutional finances and how and where funds come from and are spent is important to academic libraries."[1] So too is an understanding of the budget process from a library perspective. Anyone wanting to become a library manager, from middle management upward, must be knowledgeable about the management of academic library budgets, from the planning stage through stages for implementation, reporting, and conducting audits. Such a person also needs familiarity with data collection, the use of metrics (input, output, throughputs, and outcomes), the ability to relate the use of the data gathered to improved performance and organizational efficiency, and automated management information systems.

In its first eight chapters, *Financial Management in Academic Libraries: Data-Driven Planning and Budgeting* covers the various stages and topics involved in managing budgets: planning, the types of budgets used in academic institutions, the overall budgeting process as well as a specific process in program budgeting, managing a budget during the fiscal year and its aftermath, and providing reports on the budget. A ninth chapter introduces general concepts, which ensures that readers understand the context for financial management in academic libraries (e.g., the financial management cycle, a system model, and the importance of accountability). The final, or tenth, chapter elevates the discussion from financial management to financial leadership, the articulation of a detailed vision, and the realignment of the budget with the promises specified in that vision statement. The values addressed are ones that, we believe, all academic library leaders should possess. They should align these critical values with financial matters and demonstrate a context for them.

Some time-honored best practices are included; these may help new middle managers as they gain experience with managing budgets. The application of data is evident throughout the book, such as our showing what data are needed for planning and preparing the budget, dealing with expenditures as outputs, and understanding how costs for programs and services are calculated. Data are also applied for benchmarks and best practices. The tables and figures in the book represent actual applications, and most of them are replicable in an academic library environment. Text boxes add clarity to the discussion, while chapter exercises enable readers to form groups and to work together in answering the questions.

Similar to our other coauthored works, this one takes both a practitioner and a more theoretical perspective. One of the authors, Robert E. Dugan, relates his many years of experience in managing academic library budgets. Both of us have taught at the master's and doctoral levels, and one of us, Peter Hernon, created and maintained a doctoral program, managerial leadership in the information professions, and made the connections between financial management and financial leadership (see chapter 10). We have also delivered webinars and workshops for new library middle managers.

The audience for *Financial Management in Academic Libraries* includes middle managers and those in higher management positions wanting a review of key issues. Both groups might regard this work as a companion to *Managing with Data*,[2] which shows readers how to extract, use, and interpret data available from ACRL*Metrics*, an online service that provides access to the data from the ACRL/ARL annual survey (1998 to 2014), ACRL's annual survey (2015 to present), the National Center for Education Statistics (NCES) academic library statistics (2000 to 2012), the Integrated Postsecondary Education Data System (IPEDS) annual Academic Libraries component (2014 to present), plus select IPEDS metrics for libraries (2004 to present).[3] Other audiences include individuals aspiring to be managers and students in management courses in schools of library and information science.

The readers of this book will see the connection between financial management and accountability, effectiveness, efficiency, and sustainability. Among the different units of an academic institution, the library has an advantage in that its managers can link these concepts to the library's infrastructure, namely its staffing, collections, services, and technology. Planning and the budget focus on these components and enable everyone in the library to work to achieve organizational sustainability over time.

Notes

1. Camila A. Alire and G. Edward Evans, *Academic Librarianship* (New York: Neal-Schuman, 2010), 119.
2. Peter Hernon, Robert E. Dugan, and Joseph R. Matthews, *Managing with Data* (Chicago: ALA Editions, 2015).
3. Ibid.

Bibliography

Alire, Camila A., and G. Edward Evans. *Academic Librarianship.* New York: Neal-Schuman, 2010).

Hernon, Peter, Robert E. Dugan, and Joseph R. Matthews. *Managing with Data: Using ACRLMetrics and PLAmetrics.* Chicago: ALA Editions, 2015.

Chapter 1

Planning

The basis for budgeting is planning, where the goals and objectives specified in a library's long-term plan are aligned with the plans of the organizational levels above it, such as a division (e.g., academic affairs) and the institution. Briefly, a plan at any organizational level identifies the goals that will be pursued, the courses of action to adopt to attain those goals through measurable objectives, and the allocation of organizational resources from the budget to attain those goals.

The plan accounts for a library's unique identity and enables it to function within the institution as a customer-focused organization that develops information services intended to meet stakeholder needs and expectations and to shape the customer experience. The plan also serves as a basis for marketing services to nonusers who comprise potential customers (these might be students and faculty members who are unaware of the services and support available and who might be willing to use such services and take advantage of that support).

There are critical concepts central to the creation of a plan. First, the plan explains the purpose of the library, its capabilities, and the processes for moving the library from where it is to where it wants to be by a specified time. The plan lays out a predetermined course of action and commits resources, mostly through budgeting, to accomplish that course of action. The planning process should include all levels of library management and staff, as well as customers, actual and potential, who will be affected by the plan as it is implemented. Finally, the planning process results in a written document. If done well, the plan becomes the library's internal and external guide to action rather than an overlooked document collecting dust and serving little, if any, purpose other than showing that the library has a plan.

Why Plan?

In addition to the requirement of most institutions that their organizational units have a plan, there are other reasons for a library to develop and implement a plan. First, planning provides a sense of direction for the future—a long-term view that advocates for services. Second, the library should plan for change rather than becoming a victim of unplanned change. Libraries plan to offset uncertainty by anticipating future change. Many resources are available for academic libraries to learn about expected future trends, including reports and articles from the Association of College and Research Libraries (ACRL) and from organizations such as EDUCAUSE (see table 1.1). Third, planning involves staff in decision making as they participate in the planning process, giving them shared ownership of library's operations. Fourth, a plan helps management coordinate different library functions and departments in a consistent and logical way. Fifth, a plan guides the budget and expenditure processes.

Table 1.1
Resources Available for Academic Libraries to Learn about Expected Future Trends

Organization	What	Website
Association of College and Research Libraries (ACRL)	Every other year (even), the ACRL Research Planning and Review Committee produces a review of the trends and issues affecting academic libraries in higher education.	Appears in the June issue of College and Research Libraries News; http://crln.acrl.org/index.php/crlnews
Association of College and Research Libraries (ACRL)	Every other year (odd), the ACRL Research Planning and Review Committee publishes a scan of the higher education environment with a focus on implications for academic libraries.	http://www.ala.org/acrl/sites/ala.org.acrl/files/content/publications/whitepapers/EnvironmentalScan2017.pdf (2017 edition)
The New Media Consortium	NMC Horizon Report: Library Edition, an annual report.	https://www.nmc.org/publication-type/horizon-report
Ithaka S+R	US Library Survey (about every three years; latest is 2016).	http://www.sr.ithaka.org/publications/us-library-survey-2016
American Library Association	Center for the Future of Libraries	http://www.ala.org/transforminglibraries/future
EDUCAUSE	A nonprofit association and a community of IT leaders and professionals committed to advancing higher education; has a topic section on libraries and technologies.	https://library.educause.edu/topics; then select Libraries and Technologies

Lastly, a plan provides a means to demonstrate accountability to the multiplicity of library stakeholders. From a financial management perspective, the inputs (the allocation of the budget and the resulting numbers) must align with the outputs (the volume of use made). It is possible to connect how much was expended and for how many units as managers discover if the application of resources resulted in the expected volume of use. For example, if an objective is to strengthen the library's existing general biology collection to support undergraduate students, four important questions arise:

1. How much was budgeted?
2. How much was expended?
3. How many resources were purchased?
4. Did the purchased resources *strengthen* the general biology collection?[1]

Library managers can review the measurable objectives specified in the plan and evaluate the extent to which they were attained. To do this, they might compare the evidence gathered to the standards and guidelines issued by professional associations or accrediting organizations. An example is ACRL's 2017 *Standards for Libraries in Higher Education* Principle on Collections, which states, "Libraries provide access to collections sufficient in quality, depth, diversity, format, and currency to support the research and teaching mission of the institution."[2] The library may provide data to support this performance indicator by conveying customer satisfaction with library resources, the ratio of the collection by format (print and electronic), and the ratio of successful searches for library resources to all searches conducted.

Factors in Planning

Plans incorporate the perspective of those closest to carrying out the operations in the individual units and departments. Additionally, managers ensure that the information necessary to produce the plan proceeds upward from the bottom of the hierarchy. The information from all levels is compiled and forms the plan for the whole organization. Proceeding this way ensures that the entire organization benefits from the plan.

The more relevant and comprehensive the information on which the plan is based, the better the results from the planning process will be. Planning focuses on the systematic collection of data about the library and its services: the use of these services, information about day-to-day operations and functions, staff activities and workflows, and use of spaces and equipment. To collect such data, the library relies on its integrated library system, internal data gathering (e.g., gate counts, the number of reference questions asked, the number of books loaned through interlibrary loan), vendor-provided reports, surveys, staff observation, and user comments.[3] Many of the data can be compiled into a management information system for basic analysis.[4]

Information is also collected about the internal and external environments that affect the library. Internally, the library can gather data on activities and processes, such as how long it takes to reshelve a print volume in the stacks and the associated staff costs. Externally, data can be collected about the expected cost increases for collection contents such as serials and collection-related needs such as cataloging records. Collecting and compiling data can be used for analytical studies of services, operations, and functions of the various parts (or the whole) of the organization.

The perspectives of those working in, using, and supporting the library constitute a final planning factor. These perspectives inform both the library's long-term and short-term planning efforts. Each stakeholder, whether a user or a nonuser, has perceptions concerning the quality of the library and its services. An immediate perspective on quality comes from those closest to the library (staff and frequent, known users), but their views may differ widely. Next are the perspectives of faculty and students in the academic programs who use the library and its services less frequently or not at all. The varied perspectives extend upward and through the institutional hierarchy; they include views from divisions such as student affairs and financial services. Members of the institution's governing board also have perspectives about the library. Additionally, planners learn about the library from groups such as alumni, local and regional government officials, and those working in businesses and community organizations.

Planning Techniques

Many techniques are available to help libraries create long- and short-term plans. Libraries should have both types of plans. A long-term plan is an organized and extended view of the library, charting its course for three to five years. This plan addresses the strategic directions for the entire library. A short-term plan, often for a year at a time, serves as the annual operations plan for achieving the goals, objectives, and strategic directions of the long-term plan. An annual budget is an example of a short-term plan that is aligned with the long-term plan.

This section briefly discusses some types of plans and factors to address in planning. These are standards and guidelines, forecasting, management by objectives, total quality management, and strategic planning.

Standards and Guidelines

Standards and guidelines are not plans, but they provide a means of framing services because they are measurable and directly related to goals. They convey critical information to review and incorporate as libraries develop or revise their long-term plans. They also offer metrics by which one judges something as authentic, good, or adequate. Professional groups and associations such as the American Library Association (ALA) and ACRL oftentimes create standards and guidelines. Program accreditors such as the American Bar Association (ABA) and the Association to Advance Collegiate Schools of Business (AACSB) and regional accrediting organizations such as Southern Association of Colleges and Schools Commission on Colleges (SACSCOC) also develop standards and guidelines applicable to institutions and their components, including libraries.

Examples of academic library standards and guidelines are those developed by ACRL. The first edition of the college library standards was published in 1959; subsequent editions were published in 1975, 1986, and 1995. Historically, standards were *prescriptive*, first recommending a predetermined level of inputs (e.g., number of books) and later adding general outputs (e.g., a library should expend *X* number of dollars per student). As the discipline of library and information science matured, standards and guidelines eschewed prescriptive metrics designed to demonstrate library accountability through institutional and user-centered efficiency and effectiveness. With the 2000 edition of the *Standards for College Libraries*, ACRL departed from prescriptive standards. These new *Standards* included basic statistical inputs used for traditional aspects of evaluation, engaged in outcomes assessment, and provided methods to analyze library outcomes and operations.[5]

ACRL's 2011 *Standards for Libraries in Higher Education* are designed to guide academic libraries in advancing and sustaining their role as partners in educating students, achieving their institutions' missions, and positioning libraries as leaders in assessment and continuous improvement on their campuses. These *Standards*, which differ from previous versions by articulating expectations for library contributions to institutional effectiveness, provide a comprehensive framework using an outcomes-based approach, with evidence collected in ways most appropriate for each institution.[6] The core of these standards is the section titled "Principles and Performance Indicators," which recounts nine principles and their related performance indicators applicable to all types of academic libraries.[7]

Table 1.2 is an example of an academic library aligning its collection development objective with the 2011 *Standards*. The mapping process starts with listing the collection development functions from the library's strategic plan (column 1), the inputs (column 2), and the outputs (column 3). ACRL's collection-related quality measures from the document are listed in the column 4. The last column (5) indicates the library's derived metrics. ACRL's performance indicators from the *Standards* are listed at the bottom of the table.

Table 1.2

Mapping Collection Development to ACRL *Standards for Libraries in Higher Education*, 2017

Column 1: Functions	Column 2: Inputs	Column 3: Outputs
acquire info resources	funding allocated	expenditures
• special collection	linear feet shelving available	• by format
• reserves	collection	• by accounting index
• general collections, databases, and reference	• total print volumes held (books, bound serials)	• collection

Column 1: Functions	Column 2: Inputs	Column 3: Outputs
• GovDocs	• titles held	• number of print volumes added
• CML (branch library)	• number of current serial subscriptions by format	• number of titles added
• ECC (branch library)	• number of monographs by format	• number of serial subscriptions added by format
• digital collections projects	• number of subscribed databases	• number of microforms added
• acquire resources through consortia collection development	• number of microforms	• number of government publications added
	• number of government publications	• number of items in audiovisual formats, by format, added
support internal financial system for collections	• number of items in audiovisual formats, by format	• number of maps added
• order and renew resources	• number of maps	• number of e-books added
• maintain order and receive files	• number of items in special collections	usage of library resources
• track orders; resolve problems and claims	number of subject specialists	• collections (e.g., circulation, reserves)
• process invoices and renewals	number of items to catalog	• collection use by call number
	number of items to process	• databases funded through library and state
prepare materials for access and use	number of items to bind by format	subscription database usage
• provide bibliographic access (e.g., OCLC & Aleph)	number of items to be shelved	• number of electronic queries / searches
• (add, withdraw, correct, maintain catalog)	planned number of items to weed	• number of full-text articles successfully downloaded
• process materials (physical)		in-library use of materials
• repair materials / bind		number of accreditations supported
• manage supplies		number of program reviews supported
		number of bibliographic records
collection management		number of items prepared
• maintain stacks		• cataloged
• weed		• processed
• preserve		number of items
		• withdrawn by format
		• weeded [not the same as withdrawn]
		• preserved/treated
		number of items bound
		user can access collections from all user locations

Column 4: Quality Measures / ACRL 2017 Standards	Column 5: Metrics
collection strength, measured in programs and disciplines	user satisfaction with library resources
• percentage of titles included in Bowker Book Analysis System	• users find the library resources they need
• impact of weeding on collection quality	ratio of collection by format (print, electronic)
volumes held by program / discipline	• holdings by collections
• volumes held by call number as a proxy	• annual expenditures
• aligned with curricula and institutional strengths	• [example] electronic serial titles to print serial titles
overall collection age	volumes and students
collection use by call number	• volumes held per FTE student
supports accreditation	• volumes added per year per FTE student

user satisfaction with library resources	volumes and faculty
• users find the library resources they need	• volumes held per FTE faculty
accuracy of expenditures	• volumes added per year per FTE faculty
number of financial errors	usage information from ILL is used for collection development
passes audit	percentage of availability of information resources on and from off campus
accuracy of cataloging	average cost per resource added
accuracy of processing	collection expenditures
• bar code on correct item	• serial expenditures as percentage of total library materials expenditures
accuracy of shelving/reshelving an item	• monograph expenditures as percentage of total library materials expenditures
	• e-book expenditures as percentage of monograph expenditures
	collection expenditures per student
	• library materials expenditures per FTE undergraduate student
	• library materials expenditures per FTE graduate student
	ratio of collections expenditures that are acquired through consortia
	average cost per current serial subscription
	ratio of successful searches for library resources to all searches
	percentage of empty linear feet
	average time to catalog by type
	average time to process by type
	average time to bind
	average time to withdraw an item
	average time to shelve an item
	• by item type

ACRL Performance Indicators
4. Discovery: Libraries enable users to discover information in all formats through effective use of technology and organization of knowledge.
4.1 The library organizes information for effective discovery and access.
5. Collections: Libraries provide access to collections sufficient in quality, depth, diversity, format, and currency to support the research and teaching mission of the institution.
5.1 The library provides access to collections aligned with areas of research, curricular foci, or institutional strengths.
5.2 The library provides collections that incorporate resources in a variety of formats, accessible virtually and physically.
5.3 The library builds and ensures access to unique materials, including digital collections.
5.4 The library has the infrastructure to collect, organize, provide access to, disseminate, and preserve collections needed by users.

Standards issued by regional accrediting organizations are critical for library planning. An example is the standards from the Southern Association of Colleges and Schools Commission on Colleges, a regional accreditor that monitors, evaluates, and accredits educational institutions in the states of Alabama, Florida, Georgia, Kentucky, Louisiana, Mississippi, North Carolina, South Carolina, Tennessee, Texas, and Virginia. Its *Principles*, current through 2017,[8] include these directly discussing library services:

2.9 The institution, through ownership or formal arrangements or agreements, provides and supports student and faculty access and user privileges to adequate library collections and services and to other learning/information resources consistent with the degrees offered. Collections, resources, and services are sufficient to support all its educational, research, and public service programs. (**Learning resources and services**)

...

3.8 **Library and Other Learning Resources**

3.8.1 The institution provides facilities and learning/information resources that are appropriate to support its teaching, research, and service mission (**Learning/information resources**)

3.8.2 The institution ensures that users have access to regular and timely instruction in the use of the library and other learning/information resources (**Instruction of library use**)

3.8.3 The institution provides enough qualified staff—with appropriate education or experiences in library and/or other learning/information resources—to accomplish the mission of the institution (**Qualified staff**).[9]

Forecasting

Forecasting is a process of making projections and predictions based on assumptions about the future. Projections are based on a systematic review, while predictions are opinions based on facts. Methods used in forecasting include using opinion polls and surveys, applying a Delphi process,[10] graphically plotting future trends based on experience, reporting numerical data, and engaging in environmental scanning. Planners also search for best practices in other organizations through benchmarking studies.[11] Scenario planning generates multiple forecasts of future conditions followed by an analysis of how to respond to each scenario.[12]

Management by Objectives

Management by objectives (MBO) establishes organizational goals and objectives and aligns them to individual personnel over a stated period of time, usually a year. The objectives must be measurable, have time limits, and require specific and realistic actions. MBO, a form of participatory management, involves everyone, to an extent, in the management process by ensuring that planning is part of the personnel evaluation process. This means that managers communicate and negotiate with personnel concerning their responsibilities in meeting stated objectives.

A typical MBO process includes identifying, setting, and validating the objectives; determining the steps for implementation during the year; and then reporting on the progress for meeting each objective. Meeting the objectives should be part of personnel evaluation. As an example, a stated objective might be to expend the funds allocated for collections development to within the cost of a postage stamp. The team members responsible for the collections' financial management would be evaluated on the extent to which they met this objective.

Total Quality Management

Total quality management (TQM) emphasizes quality. Library personnel work as teams as they develop and deliver high-quality services. TQM's mantra is getting things done right the first time. A major constraint to widespread application of TQM is that the systems for collecting and reporting data may become overwhelmingly complex.

Strategic Planning

The strategic planning process is the most common planning process that libraries use. Central to this process is a strategic plan, which lays out goals, objectives, actions taken, and progress in meeting those objectives. Personnel responsible for financial management (the library's senior and middle managers) determine the specific objectives the library will pursue during the next fiscal year and the action steps to accomplish those objectives; they also allocate the financial resources to achieve an objective. The quality of such planning addresses the performance level needed to determine financial effectiveness (the accomplishment of objectives) and organizational efficiency (the efficient use of resources) during the fiscal year.

The strategic planning process, which consists of a cluster of decisions and actions that managers take to help an organization reach its goals, includes several basic steps. An early step is to identify members of the planning team. Academic institutions may hire an external planning consultant or may use an internal team comprised of members of the faculty, members of an organizational unit familiar with planning, or a combination of these methods. Planning team members determine who else should be involved in the process, how they are to contribute, and when their involvement will further the effort. It is a best practice to involve as many stakeholders as possible, including library staff, users, and the library's advocates and critics. A time-contiguous step is to learn what kind of, and how much, support can be expected from the institution, such as release time from day-to-day responsibilities for those designated to manage the planning process.

The planning team coordinates the collection of data from internal and external sources. Important data collection and analysis activities help to determine what various stakeholders need and expect from the library, including how they use the library both physically and remotely. While library staff and users have different needs, both should be surveyed because most of the objectives and the supporting activities to be implemented from the strategic plan will (or should) be directed toward meeting identified user needs and expectations, as well as enhancing the customer experience.

Once the data have been collected, the planning team undertakes internal and external scans to understand better the environment into which the library is moving. Self-analysis studies or reviews conducted by the library (e.g., using focus group interviews, an analysis of increasing or decreasing gate counts, and a review of incoming e-mail messages from stakeholders[13]) may reveal the library's strengths and weaknesses and trends over time. This review centers on the organizational culture, beliefs, ethos, values, or assumptions that guide the library's service goals. The planners also analyze the gap between customer expectations of library services and their satisfaction with the current delivery of those services they use. Methodologies for studying gap analysis include, among others, customer surveys and interviews.[14]

A critical part of strategic planning is often referred to as a SWOT analysis (strengths, weaknesses within the organization, opportunities, and threats from outside the organization). The external part of the analysis—an environmental scan—involves a review of political issues from the institution's governance bodies and their attitude toward the library; economic forces, such as general economic conditions and trends; social forces, including the norms and values of the local culture; and technological forces, such as anticipated changes in information technologies.

The planning team identifies and determines relevant standards or guidelines from the institution's regional accreditor as well as documenting the compliance needs of program accrediting organizations. These standards or guidelines may address the library's infrastructure (staffing, collections, facilities, and technologies) required to either gain or sustain accreditation.

The internal and external analysis leads to a concise understanding of the organization, whom it serves, and how it serves them. This work results in a data-informed strategic plan for improving programs and services within the library's physical and financial capabilities. The library's planning team reviews the organization's vision and mission statements and proposes changes that uniquely identify the library, the strategic goals and objectives, and the measurable and necessary action steps as well as the budget required to fulfill the objectives.[15] The draft document should be widely available to stakeholders for review and comment. Once the director approves the draft, it is sent to the appropriate institutional authority or authorities responsible for oversight of, and accountability from, the library. Depending on the hierarchical structure, the approval official may be a provost, a president, or a chancellor.

The approval process informs the hierarchy of the library's strategic directions and priorities, and its expectations, and it gains acceptance for the resources needed to achieve the long- and short-term objectives and actions. Once approved, the objectives and action steps can be budgeted and implemented. Performance metrics for each objective and their activities are compiled, compared, evaluated, and reported at least annually. Feedback provided during the implementation, accompanied by the reports and evaluation of progress, informs the next short-term plan and the eventual revision of the long-term plan. Adjustments might be made as objectives are accomplished and as priorities shift.

Major Components of a Long-Term Strategic Plan

The long-term strategic planning document reminds library decision makers to accomplish what is specified in the short-term planning and budgeting document. In other words, the objectives are reported in the long-term plan, and the short-term plan provides the basis for tackling them year by year. The library does not accomplish the long-term plan all at once.

The major parts of the long-term plan include the following:

- **Mission statement.** A mission statement portrays the library's identity: what it is doing and the services it provides its users and stakeholders. The statement may also address the library's critical values and principles, such as ensuring access to collections needed to support learning and research, and expected student learning outcomes, such as critical thinking. The library's goals and objectives support this stated mission.
- **Vision statement.** A vision statement is a declaration of the library's hoped-for future. An example is that the library will serve as an institutional gateway for all needed information. While less important for planning and budgeting than the mission statement, the vision statement declares the library's intentions and can serve as a focus for library advocacy and transformational change. Stakeholders are more interested in learning about the library's vision than its current mission. The reason is that the vision sets the foundation for how the future library will be perceived (see chapter 10).[16]
- **Goals.** Goals are broad areas that libraries want to achieve or change, such as empowering users to become self-sufficient, lifelong learners and effective evaluators of information. Goals should be challenging and outlive the lifetime of the long-term plan, but they should be realistic and ultimately achievable with the availability of better-than-expected resources such as funding.

- **Objectives.** Objectives are action-oriented, measurable initiatives that explain how the goals will be supported and user services improved. Objectives can be created for the library's infrastructure, services, programs and programming, and partnerships and collaborations, as well as for its management. A mnemonic is SMART objectives, which are specific, measurable, and budgetable; achievable; realistic; and timely. Further, an evaluative process can be applied to measure the progress toward achieving an objective.

Box 1.1, an example of a three-year strategic plan, includes mission and vision statements, two goals, and seven objectives. These aspects of a strategic plan, which are designed to be simple for the library's stakeholders to review, can be displayed on the library's public website and handed out as a one-page document. Additionally, library staff should be familiar with the strategic plan and be able to explain it whenever stakeholders inquire.

Box 1.1
Strategic Plan (University of West Florida Libraries)*

Mission Statement
The UWF Libraries' purpose is to provide information-related resources and services to support the University of West Florida's learning, teaching, research, and community service missions. It intends to inspire the total individual, encouraging personal, social and intellectual growth, and lifelong learning through the acquisition of information and knowledge.

Vision
The Libraries will be an innovative, inspiring, and vital component in the academic life of the University.[1]

Enhance the User Experience: Foster Environments through which Staff Provide Resources, Services and Programs Supporting Learning, Teaching and Research

Objective 1.0 Develop and manage relevant intellectual content, balanced across appropriate information formats, to support teaching, research, and service regardless of geographic location.
Objective 2.0 Provide assistance to users seeking information, and for using the library and its resources, services and programs.

*Source: University of West Florida Libraries, "Strategic Plan, July 1, 2014–June 30, 2017," revised September 2, 2014, http://libguides.uwf.edu/c.php?g=215171&p=1420488.

Objective 3.0   Coordinate a comprehensive information literacy program that provides opportunities to demonstrate student learning outcomes in support of academic achievement, career success, and lifelong learning.

Objective 4.0   Support access to resources and productivity by deploying and managing information technologies including workstations, the online integrated library system, and the libraries' website.

Objective 5.0   Create and manage a flexible, safe, functional, and inviting physical environment that supports all forms of learning, discovery, exchange and instruction.

Enhance Institutional Effectiveness

Objective 6.0   Provide administrative structure and support to manage and achieve the strategic objectives of UWF and the UWF Libraries.

Objective 7.0   Demonstrate the Libraries' value to the institution and other stakeholders.

Note

1. It merits mention that a university constantly changes. New degrees are offered, new student learning outcomes emerge, and, for public institutions, new challenges from the governor and state legislature develop.

- **Activities/action steps.** Although the plan's objectives may not change from year to year, the activities or steps to meet an objective's intention are most likely annually based. Action steps specify how the objective will be achieved and who is responsible. They also establish a time line for implementation and identify the resources that are expected to be budgeted. Expected performance metrics for each activity are identified; these metrics can be compiled, compared, evaluated, and reported during and after implementation.

  The activities supporting the first objective of the strategic plan (box 1.1) are contained in box 1.2. These activities can be budgeted and their expenditures calculated.

Box 1.2

Objective 1 and Activities (University of West Florida's Strategic Plan)

Objective 1.0. Develop and manage relevant intellectual content, balanced across appropriate information formats, to support teaching, research, and service regardless of geographic location.
- Maintain a curriculum-supportive circulating monographs collection of 500,000 print volumes (85 percent of total available linear shelf feet of 48,613).

+ Prepare materials for access and use.
  * Provide bibliographic/intellectual access to holdings in various collections through cataloging and metadata creation.
  * Process materials.
  * Repair materials/bind.
  * Manage supplies used in processing.
- Provide 25 percent of the libraries' monograph collection in digital format by 2017.
- Quantify the characteristics of the collection (e.g., collection age) via the libraries' integrated library system.
- Participate in relevant shared collection development efforts at the state level.
- Preserve rare or unique items in danger of being lost.
- Assess monograph holdings using the Bowker Book Analysis System and dedicate a portion of the book allocation to strengthen our collection to 40 percent of the Bowker standard.
- Continually review current electronic database and serial subscriptions for relevance and cost-effectiveness as well as evaluating new products for purchase consideration.
  + Evaluate use statistics, including price per use.
  + Review print serial subscriptions and replace with online subscriptions when feasible.
- Undertake collection management activities at the Pace Library that will strengthen library resources and make them more useful.
  + Maintain stacks.
  + Weed.
  + Inventory collection.
  + Repair catalog records to ensure discovery.
  + Withdraw discarded materials from catalog.
- Support the internal financial management system for collections.
  + Allocate funds based upon MIS data.
  + Order and renew resources.
  + Establish contact with faculty to encourage order submission.
  + Consult ILL data to identify titles to add to collection.
  + Maintain order and receive files
  + Track orders; resolve problems and claims.
  + Process invoices and renewals.
  + Streamline ordering process.

- **Appendices.** Most long-term plans include appendices that support the plan. Examples of documents found here include historical information, customer surveys and the detailed analysis of their findings, and current policies and procedures. The appendices are also a good place to include input and output metrics and data such as on past expenditure trends, collection development, staffing, and service outputs.

  One potential document to include in an appendix is a crosswalk of how the objectives and action steps from the library's strategic plan align with the strategic goals (directions), objectives, and activities expressed in institutional strategic plans. Table 1.3 represents part of a comprehensive crosswalk.

Table 1.3
Objective 1: Selected Portions of Crosswalk to University Strategic Plans (University of West Florida)

UWF STRATEGIC PRIORITIES 2012–2107 (Institutional Level)	
Strategic Direction 1: Enhanced Student Access, Progression, and Learning and Development	
Strategic Direction 2: Distinctive Teaching, Scholarship, Research, and Professional Contributions	
Strategic Direction 3: Values Partnerships: Community Engagement and Service	
Strategic Direction 4: Sustained Institutional Excellence	
ACADEMIC AFFAIRS STRATEGIC MASTER PLAN 2012–2017 (Division Level)	
Academic Goal 1: TEACHING: To develop and promote teaching that optimizes learning and personal transformation.	Academic Goal 5: QUALITY: To support, sustain, and reward high-quality academics.
Academic Goal 2: RESEARCH: To build a vibrant culture of research.	Academic Goal 6: VISIBILITY: To improve internal and external communication of academic programs and achievements.
Academic Goal 3: COMMUNITY ENGAGEMENT: To engage in mutually beneficial collaborations that advance academic programs and outreach.	Academic Goal 7: GROWTH: To promote reasonable and sustainable growth.
Academic Goal 4: INNOVATION: To create a culture of academic innovation.	Academic Goal 8: 21st–CENTURY SKILLS: To ensure current programs are 21st–century relevant.

University Libraries' Objectives	Libraries' Action Steps	Library Performance Measures	Alignment With University (U) and Academic Affairs (AA) Priorities And Goals	Supportive Library Objective
Library Objective 1.0 Develop and manage relevant intellectual content, balanced across appropriate information formats, to support teaching, research, and service regardless of geographic location.	- acquire information resources + by function (e.g., general collections, reserves, reference, and Professional Studies Library [PSL]) + acquire resources through consortia collection development - collection management + maintain stacks + weed + preserve	- user satisfaction + users find the library resources they need	1.3. Improve student persistence and timely progression to degree attainment. (U) 4.1. Create an environment and implement initiatives that encourage and support innovation. (AA) 5.2. Support and develop traditional and innovative undergraduate and graduate programs, and invest strategically in programs that will establish The University of West Florida as preeminent, distinctive, and unique. (AA)	The libraries contribute to retention by providing student-centered services and effectively managing a strong academic support program through its infrastructure.

University Libraries' Objectives	Libraries' Action Steps	Library Performance Measures	Alignment With University (U) and Academic Affairs (AA) Priorities And Goals	Supportive Library Objective

	- acquire information resources
	  + by function (e.g., general collections, reserves, reference and PSL)
	  + acquire resources through consortia collection development
		- volumes held by program / discipline
		  + volumes held by call number as a proxy
		  + aligned with curricula and institutional strengths
			2.1.
			Respond to the changing needs of the region, state, and nation by investing strategically to support innovative instruction and high-quality, relevant, and distinctive academic and research programs. (U)
			
			2.1.
			Increase student engagement in research, scholarship, and creative activities as high-impact learning experiences. (AA)
			
			5.2.
			Support and develop traditional and innovative undergraduate and graduate programs, and invest strategically in programs that will establish The University of West Florida as preeminent, distinctive, and unique. (AA)
				The libraries' programs and services (e.g., access and availability; information literacy; just-in-time services) provided through the infrastructure address the needs of the region and help our students to align with the region's needs.

	- acquire information resources
	  + by function (e.g., general collections, reserves, reference, and PSL)
	  + acquire resources through consortia collection development
		- volumes held by program / discipline
		  + volumes held by call number as a proxy
		  + aligned with curricula and institutional strengths
		- overall collection age
			2.3.
			Build a vibrant culture of scholarship and research that aligns with UWF's strengths and capacities and supports UWF's mission, vision, and values. (U)
			
			1.2.
			Define and promote high-quality teaching in relation to service and research in the evolving mission of the University. (AA)
			
			5.2.
			Support and develop traditional and innovative undergraduate and graduate programs, and invest strategically in programs that will establish The University of West Florida as preeminent, distinctive, and unique. (AA)
				The libraries promote teaching and library faculty scholarship and research in their efforts to support students.

Strategic Finance and Planning

Strategic finance is an internal organizational and institutional process of aligning resources with the institution's mission and strategic plan. Jane V. Wellman, as executive director of the Delta Project on College Costs of the Association of Governing Boards of Universities and Colleges, advocates that institutions and their organizational units consider costs when undertaking a strategic finance process.[17]

Strategic finance begins by addressing four questions that can be applied in an academic library's long- and short-term planning processes. First, what is the library *good* at (the mission statement)? Second, what do students and faculty *want* (the market)? Third, how can the library combine the mission and market in a way that remains true to the mission statement and generates use and value (referred to as the margin)? Fourth, what was the most successful action that the library has taken to create or revise programs or services based on the mission/ market/ margin focus? What did the library do *well* that returned *value* to the stakeholders?

Budgeting allocates resources to objectives and the aligned activities. Strategic finance, on the other hand, identifies costs for the objectives and actions, emphasizing a focus on outputs over inputs. As a process, it seeks to understand the library's critical success factors, to learn what drives use of the library, and to calculate those costs. For example, a critical success factor may be the current expenditure ratios among staffing, collection development, and other direct costs. Another factor might be the cost of answering a reference question. Additionally, how much activity can be added without increasing the cost of a service? Can productivity be improved without increasing its per-unit cost?

Table 1.4 is an example of calculating expenditures for a library's collection development objective. Column 1 lists the collection development activities, while the supportive functions in column 2 are cost drivers. Department staff are listed by activity and function in column 3; their percentage of time spent on the activity or function is in column 4. Staff wages and benefits are listed in column 5, and the estimated staff costs in column 6 (column 5 multiplied by column 4) provide the related activity or function cost per staff person involved. At the bottom of the table are the non-personnel costs. If asked how much it costs this library to undertake collection development, the response is $1,564,517.

Table 1.4
Strategic Finance Expenditure for Objective 1: Collections (University of West Florida Libraries)

Column 1: Activity Supporting This Objective	Column 2: Functions Supporting This Activity	Column 3: Department/ Staff	Column 4: Time Spent	Column 5: Staff Costs	Column 6: Estimated Costs
acquire info resources	special collection	SpecColl / Info Spec	35%	$46,496	$16,274
		SpecColl / Librarian	20%	$95,975	$19,195
	reserves	Circ / Reserve Coord.	60%	$38,053	$22,832
	general collections, databases, and reference	Ref / MG	15%	$95,433	$14,315
		Ref / SJ	20%	$84,679	$16,936
		Ref / HF	10%	$38,455	$3,845
		Ref / BM	10%	$77,350	$7,735
		Ref / CT	15%	$82,164	$12,325
		Ref / KS	30%	$65,833	$19,750
	PSL	PSL / Head	4%	$43,686	$1,747
		PSL / Asst.	3%	$38,627	$1,159
	ECC	ECC / Head	2%	$100,669	$2,013
	digital collections projects	IT / Server Admin	5%	$64,588	$3,229
	acquire resources through consortia collection development				
internal financial system for collections	order and renew resources	Ref / SJ	25%	$84,679	$21,170
		Admin / JS	60%	$39,809	$23,885
	maintain order and receive files	Admin / JS	18%	$39,809	$7,166
	track orders; resolve problems and claims	Admin / JS	18%	$39,809	$7,166
	process invoices and renewals				

Column 1: Activity Supporting This Objective	Column 2: Functions Supporting This Activity	Column 3: Department/ Staff	Column 4: Time Spent	Column 5: Staff Costs	Column 6: Estimated Costs
	assist with preparation, payment, and limited purchase orders	Admin / Fiscal Spec.	10%	$32,948	$3,295
prepare materials for access and use	provide bibliographic access (e.g., OCLC & ILS)	SpecColl / Info Spec	45%	$46,496	$20,923
	(add, withdraw, correct, maintain)	SpecColl / Librarian	20%	$95,975	$19,195
		Cataloging / Head	65%	$81,913	$53,243
		Cataloging / AM	70%	$46,753	$32,727
		Cataloging / AF	90%	$48,477	$43,629
		Cataloging / DM	65%	$51,442	$33,437
		Circ / Reserve Coord.	10%	$38,053	$3,805
		Ref / SJ	5%	$84,679	$4,234
		Serials / DB	85%	$30,124	$25,605
		PSL / Head	4%	$43,686	$1,747
		PSL / Asst.	2%	$38,627	$773
	process materials (physical)	Circ / Database Maint.	10%	$39,731	$3,973
		Circ / Equip. Coord.	5%	$46,716	$2,336
		Cataloging / AF	1%	$48,477	$485
		Cataloging / AM	5%	$46,753	$2,338
		PSL / Asst.	6%	$38,627	$2,318
		ECC / Head	3%	$100,669	$3,020
		ECC / Tech	33%	$32,811	$10,828
	repair materials / bind	Circ / Accts Coord.	5%	$42,072	$2,104
		ECC / Tech	1%	$32,811	$328
	manage supplies	ECC / Tech	5%	$32,811	$1,641

Column 1: Activity Supporting This Objective	Column 2: Functions Supporting This Activity	Column 3: Department/ Staff	Column 4: Time Spent	Column 5: Staff Costs	Column 6: Estimated Costs
collection management	maintain stacks	Circ / Stacks Manager	35%	$36,015	$12,605
		PSL / Asst.	9%	$38,627	$3,476
		Ref / ER	20%	$41,755	$8,351
	weed	Cataloging / DM	15%	$51,442	$7,716
		PSL / Head	3%	$43,686	$1,311
		ECC / Head	3%	$100,669	$3,020
	preserve				
Subtotal, Personnel					$509,204
OTHER COSTS					
6294: Collections					$1,026,261
70010/11 Postage/ Freight					$279
70154 OCLC Charges ILL and Illiad					$9,737
70165 Other Contractual Services					$3,774
70301 Office Supplies (collection processing)					$12,674
70551 Educational Supplies					$2,587
Subtotal, Non-personnel					$1,055,313
TOTAL					$1,564,517

Key questions from the strategic finance process support planning. First, the question "Where are we now?" is a reality check that asks

- Are appropriate metrics in place to understand the current environment of the library?
- Is the focus on outputs?
- Are we using data to tell the story?
- Are decisions made based on appropriate data?

Second, the question "Where are we going?" is related to the library's strategic plan and asks

- Is there a shared understanding of a sustainable future?
- Are the library's goals and objectives clearly stated and communicated to stakeholders?

Third, the question "What will it take to get there?" involves resource alignment and asks

- Are resources aligned with strategic goals?
- Have all reallocation opportunities been explored?
- Are opportunities for cost reduction and an increase in productivity being (or have they been) implemented?

And, finally, the question "How will we know when we have arrived?" asks

- Are metrics being monitored and adjustments to the plan being made?
- Are appropriate communication tools in place?

Answers to these questions inform and improve library budgeting and decision making. Reliable data place past budget allocations and expenses, as well as the current environment, such as trends and demographics (e.g., students, faculty, academic programs offered, and degrees awarded), in context. Once cost drivers are identified, the cost of the outputs is determined. A library manager engaged in strategic finance focuses more on what the numbers mean than on the numbers themselves. Metrics, such as "value of usage" or "the expenditures for consortia results in realized economies of scale," can be derived to help the library tell its financial story.

Conclusion

Planning enables libraries to prepare for the near future, align their programs and services with customer needs and expectations, and monitor progress in reaching what is specified in the plan's objectives. Planning also helps to demonstrate that libraries are dynamic places that cannot be characterized as warehouses of books and periodicals. It shows that libraries play a critical role in helping institutions achieve their future—libraries align their mission and vision statements with those of the institution. Planning also demonstrates how libraries are accountable for what they promise in plans and how they meet their responsibilities effectively and efficiently.

Exercises

1. How could a library use ACRL's *Standards for Higher Education* in a strategic planning process?
2. Discuss the role of regional accrediting organizations in library planning.
3. Suggest a structure and format for a library's strategic plan.

(Answers to these questions can be found in the appendix at the back of the book. We encourage different library managers to work together, perhaps with staff members, to answer each question and to discuss the results.)

Notes

1. *Strength* refers to improvement of the collection. Collection strengths are measurable through a conspectus or another book analysis system.
2. Association of College and Research Libraries, *Standards for Libraries in Higher Education* (Chicago: Association of College and Research Libraries, October 2011), 9, http://www.ala. org/acrl/standards/standardslibraries.
3. For choices of data collection, see Peter Hernon and Joseph R. Matthews, *Listening to the Customer* (Santa Barbara, CA: Libraries Unlimited, 2011).
4. See Peter Hernon, Robert E. Dugan, and Joseph R. Matthews, *Managing with Data* (Chicago: ALA Editions, 2015).
5. Association of College and Research Libraries, "Standards for College Libraries: The Final Version, Approved January 2000," *College and Research Libraries News* 61, no. 3 (March 2000): 175–82.
6. Association of College and Research Libraries, *Standards for Libraries in Higher Education*, 5–8.
7. Ibid., 9–14.
8. The draft replacement document maintains the same points.
9. Southern Association of Colleges and Schools Commission on Colleges, *The Principles of Accreditation*, 5th ed. (Decatur, GA: Southern Association of Colleges and Schools Commission on Colleges, 2012), 20, 31, http://www.sacscoc.org/ pdf/2012PrinciplesOfAcreditation.pdf.
10. A systematic method that involves structured interaction among a group of experts on a subject. Typically, experts answer questions and justify their answers in at least two rounds, with the opportunity between rounds for changes.
11. See Peter Hernon, Robert E. Dugan, and Danuta A. Nitecki, *Engaging in Evaluation and Assessment Research* (Santa Barbara, CA: Libraries Unlimited, 2011), 108.
12. See Peter Hernon and Joseph R. Matthews, *Reflections on the Future of Academic and Public Libraries* (Chicago: ALA Editions, 2013).
13. These e-mail messages might be complaints or compliments about the library or suggestions for the library.
14. See Peter Hernon, Ellen Altman, and Robert E. Dugan, *Assessing Service Quality*, 3rd. ed. (Chicago: ALA Editions, 2015).
15. The team may refer to the existing statements and revise them to update language or address a new climate. For example, it might recommend dropping accessibility to college and replacing it with affordability and graduation. Most of the time, the team revises the mission and vision statements and passes them along to the director and other senior managers.
16. See Hernon and. Matthews, *Reflections on the Future*.
17. Jane Wellman and Rick Staisloff, "Strategic Finance Workshop," University of West Florida, Pensacola, FL, February 25, 2011. See Association of Governing Boards of Universities and Colleges, *Strategic Finance for Colleges and Universities, A New Consulting Service from AGB*, brochure (Washington, DC: Association of Governing Boards of Universities and Colleges, n.d.), http://agb.org/sites/default/files/legacy/u3/StrategicFinanceBrochure.pdf.

Bibliography

Association of College and Research Libraries. "Standards for College Libraries: The Final Version, Approved January 2000." *College and Research Libraries News* 61, no. 3 (March 2000): 175–82.

———. *Standards for Libraries in Higher Education.* Chicago: Association of College and Research Libraries, October 2011. http://www.ala.org/acrl/standards/standardslibraries.

Association of Governing Boards of Universities and Colleges. *Strategic Finance for Colleges and Universities, A New Consulting Service from AGB.* Brochure. Washington, DC: Association of Governing Boards of Universities and Colleges, n.d. http://agb.org/sites/default/files/legacy/u3/StrategicFinanceBrochure.pdf.

Hernon, Peter, Ellen Altman, and Robert E. Dugan. *Assessing Service Quality: Satisfying the Expectations of Library Customers*, 3rd. ed. Chicago: ALA Editions, 2015.

Hernon, Peter, Robert E. Dugan, and Joseph R. Matthews. *Managing with Data: Using ACRLMetrics and PLAmetrics.* Chicago: ALA Editions, 2015.

Hernon, Peter, Robert E. Dugan, and Danuta A. Nitecki. *Engaging in Evaluation and Assessment Research.* Santa Barbara, CA: Libraries Unlimited, 2011.

Hernon, Peter, and Joseph R. Matthews. *Listening to the Customer.* Santa Barbara, CA: Libraries Unlimited, 2011.

———. *Reflections on the Future of Academic and Public Libraries.* Chicago: ALA Editions, 2013.

Southern Association of Colleges and Schools Commission on Colleges. *The Principles of Accreditation: Foundations for Quality Enhancement*, 5th ed. Decatur, GA: Southern Association of Colleges and Schools Commission on Colleges, 2012. http://www.sacscoc.org/pdf/2012PrinciplesOfAcreditation.pdf.

University of West Florida Libraries. "Strategic Plan, July 1, 2014–June 30, 2017." Revised September 2, 2014. http://libguides.uwf.edu/c.php?g=215171&p=1420488.

Wellman, Jane, and Rick Staisloff. "Strategic Finance Workshop." University of West Florida, Pensacola, FL, February 25, 2011.

Chapter 2

General Concepts

Just So We Are on the Same Page

In the context of this monograph, an academic library is a customer-focused organization that develops information services to meet the needs and expectations of the community it serves. Complicating matters, a library may also serve as a social setting, provide an educational support service, advance student learning, create and maintain digital content, engage in publishing services, and assist faculty in their scholarly pursuits. The library is basically an open social system with specific goals for meeting its stated mission. Libraries interact with the larger educational, economic, social, and cultural environments through their underlying values that support sources and services for the societal and educational good upon which higher education depends (see table 2.1).

Financial managers must understand and accommodate the library's infrastructure (staff, collections, technologies, and facilities) and continuous changes to it. Staff are becoming more function-specialized with new positions and responsibilities necessary to support present-day services as well as new ones that are emerging. Collections have certainly changed as the formats for presenting information and knowledge have been transformed, as has publishing itself. Libraries have long used modern technologies; for example, academic libraries were among the first to install photocopy and fax machines and adopt CD-ROMs.

Table 2.1

Core Values of Librarianship

The foundation of modern librarianship rests on an essential set of core values that define, inform, and, guide professional practice. These values reflect the history and ongoing development of the profession and have been advanced, expanded, and refined by numerous policy statements from the American Library Association. The selections in this table are taken from the *ALA Policy Manual* (American Library Association, http://www.ala.org/aboutala/governance/policymanual). Please note that many of these statements express the interrelationship among these values.

Access	All information resources that are provided directly or indirectly by the library, regardless of technology, format, or methods of delivery, should be readily, equally, and equitably accessible to all library users.
Confidentiality/ Privacy	Protecting user privacy and confidentiality is necessary for intellectual freedom and fundamental to the ethics and practice of librarianship.
Democracy	A democracy presupposes an informed citizenry. The First Amendment mandates the right of all persons to free expression, and the corollary right to receive the constitutionally protected expression of others. The publicly supported library provides free and equal access to information for all people of the community the library serves.
Diversity	We value our nation's diversity and strive to reflect that diversity by providing a full spectrum of resources and services to the communities we serve.
Education and Lifelong Learning	ALA promotes the creation, maintenance, and enhancement of a learning society, encouraging its members to work with educators, government officials, and organizations in coalitions to initiate and support comprehensive efforts to ensure that school, public, academic, and special libraries in every community cooperate to provide lifelong learning services to all.
Intellectual Freedom	We uphold the principles of intellectual freedom and resist all efforts to censor library resources.
The Public Good	ALA reaffirms the following fundamental values of libraries in the context of discussing outsourcing and privatization of library services. These values include that libraries are an essential public good and are fundamental institutions in democratic societies.
Preservation	The Association supports the preservation of information published in all media and formats. The Association affirms that the preservation of information resources is central to libraries and librarianship.
Professionalism	The American Library Association supports the provision of library services by professionally qualified personnel who have been educated in graduate programs within institutions of higher education. It is of vital importance that there be professional education available to meet the social needs and goals of library services.
Service	We provide the highest level of service to all library users…. We strive for excellence in the profession by maintaining and enhancing our own knowledge and skills, by encouraging the professional development of co-workers, and by fostering the aspirations of potential members of the profession.

Social Responsibility	ALA recognizes its broad social responsibilities. The broad social responsibilities of the American Library Association are defined in terms of the contribution that librarianship can make in ameliorating or solving the critical problems of society; support for efforts to help inform and educate the people of the United States on these problems and to encourage them to examine the many views on and the facts regarding each problem; and the willingness of ALA to take a position on current critical issues with the relationship to libraries and library service set forth in the position statement.

Source: American Library Association, "Core Values of Librarianship," accessed July 28, 2017, http://www.ala.org/advocacy/intfreedom/statementspols/corevalues.

Now academic libraries lead the migration from print to electronic formats and the development of open institutional repositories to house and widely share intellectual works and scholarly activities. While academic libraries have historically served as the physical center, as well as the heart, of the institution, they now emphasize users and use of spaces in the physical facilities. In sum, understanding the components of the infrastructure and how they support services and programs guides planning and budgeting.

Systems Model

The components of a simple system model, as shown in figure 2.1, include the following:
- inputs, the resources used to conduct an activity, such as funds and personnel
- processes, the activities undertaken using the inputs
- outputs, the results from implementing the activities
- outcomes, the impacts resulting from the outputs
- evaluative feedback, the information and data about the outputs or outcomes that managers use to review the inputs and make improvements

Figure 2.1
Systems Model

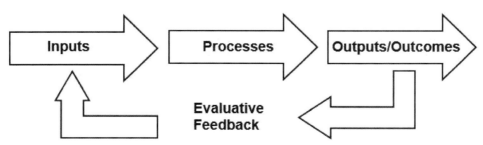

One of the most important reasons to apply this model to libraries is to affirm where evaluation fits in and to ensure, for instance, that an output is not confused with a process. For example, if it takes sixty minutes for a student assistant to reshelve a cart of books (output) and that seems longer than expected, it may be that the book carts used have an above-average capacity (process). The usefulness of this model is the evaluative feedback loop. Planners and managers use the information and data gathered from reviewing actual outputs and outcomes to consider how they might alter the inputs and the processes to improve an outcome: to align the output better with the activities specified in the short-term plan that support a strategic objective. For example, an output might be the acquisition of ten monographs on marine biology for undergraduate biology majors. However, the analysis shows that, while these ten titles strengthened the collection, the acquisition was insufficient to meet the intended collection depth target set in that year's action steps. Consequently, for the next fiscal year, the library must budget adequate funds (inputs) to purchase additional titles to improve the output or outcome of meeting the objective's collection strength target.

Accountability

The stakeholders responsible for funding and supporting higher education institutions are increasingly holding these institutions accountable for the funds, time, and other resources allocated and expended. Increased accountability has resulted in heightened attention to measures of institutional effectiveness and efficiency.

The culture of accountability—one committed to demonstrating a commitment to effectiveness and efficiency—is passed down through the institution to its organizational units. Users or nonusers might ask if the benefits they receive from using library services equal or exceed the cost; students, for example, are charged through the tuition they pay or, in the case of an institution, the funds allocated to the library. The issue is sometimes phrased as "Why do we need a library when it is all on the Internet?" For the library, financial efficiency is demonstrated through identifying costs for services, such as the cost to borrow an item on interlibrary loan (ILL), and transparently communicating to stakeholders the actions the library is taking to decrease or contain costs. Effectiveness, for instance, is demonstrated by assessing the changes in student knowledge, skills, and abilities from their contact with the library's programs and services. Value is another indicator of effectiveness. An example is the value of ILL to a faculty member's scholarly productivity. Central to the culture of accountability is how well the library shares its outcomes with stakeholders.[1]

A Financial Management Cycle

Most librarians know that a fiscal year is the twelve months during which a budget is expended. After one fiscal year ends, another begins. A financial management cycle is much longer. The month of September provides an example of three cycles running simultaneously (see table 2.2). The current fiscal year is underway as the funds allocated for the planned day-to-day operations and collection development are expended. A financial audit of the previous year, which ended on June 30, may be underway to verify and complete an accurate reporting of expenditures. And the institution and the library will begin short-term planning for the forthcoming fiscal year, which will start the following July 1.

Table 2.2 depicts a three-calendar-year perspective of the components of the financial management cycle, coded to four fiscal years (based upon July–June). There are at least two components occurring each month, and all three components may occur within a month twice or three times a calendar year depending on the institution's financial activities already underway. The point is that, while a fiscal year is a twelve-month period, a financial management cycle occupies parts of three fiscal years.

Table 2.2

Financial Management Calendar FY2018–FY2021 Based on Calendar Years

FY2018	FY2019	FY2020	FY2021
	Calendar 2018	Calendar 2019	Calendar 2020
January	FY2018 operations underway	FY2018 external institutional audit underway	FY2019 external institutional audit underway
	Library submits FY2019 budget via institutional forms	FY2019 operations underway	FY2020 operations underway
		Library submits FY2020 budget via institutional forms	Library submits FY2021 budget via institutional forms
February	FY2018 operations underway	FY2018 external audit report	FY2019 external audit report
	Library meets with academic affairs budget office FY2019	FY2019 operations underway	FY2020 operations underway
		Library meets with academic affairs budget office FY2020	Library meets with academic affairs budget office FY2021

Month			
March	FY2018 operations underway	FY2019 operations underway	FY2020 operations underway
	Library meets with institutional budget office FY2019	Library meets with institutional budget office FY2020	Library meets with institutional budget office FY2021
April	FY2018 operations underway	FY2019 operations underway	FY2020 operations underway
	Institution prepares and submits final budget request FY2019	Institution prepares and submits final budget request FY2020	Institution prepares and submits final budget request FY2021
May	FY2018 operations underway	FY2019 operations underway	FY2020 operations underway
	Institutional FY2019 budget proposed to Board of Trustees	Institutional FY2020 budget proposed to Board of Trustees	Institutional FY2021 budget proposed to Board of Trustees
June	FY2018 operations underway	FY2019 operations underway	FY2020 operations underway
	Board of Trustees approves FY2019 budget	Board of Trustees approves FY2020 budget	Board of Trustees approves FY2021 budget
July	FY2018 end of the year reporting	FY2019 end of the year reporting	FY2020 end of the year reporting
	FY2019 fiscal year begins; budget allocated	FY2020 fiscal year begins; budget allocated	FY2021 fiscal year begins; budget allocated
	FY2019 operations begin	FY2020 operations begin	FY2021 operations begin
August	FY2018 end of the year reporting	FY2019 end of the year reporting	FY2020 end of the year reporting
	FY2019 operations underway	FY2020 operations underway	FY2021 operations underway
September	FY2018 institutional audit underway	FY2019 institutional audit underway	FY2020 institutional audit underway
	FY2019 operations underway	FY2020 operations underway	FY2021 operations underway
	Planning for FY2020 budget submission	Planning for FY2021 budget submission	
October	FY2018 institutional audit underway	FY2019 institutional audit underway	FY2020 institutional audit underway
	FY2019 operations underway	FY2020 operations underway	FY2021 operations underway

	Planning for FY2020 budget submission	Planning for FY2021 budget submission	
November	FY2018 institutional audit report	FY2019 institutional audit report	FY2020 institutional audit report
	FY2019 operations underway	FY2020 operations underway	FY2021 operations underway
	Institution sends through FY2020 budget request via forms	Institution sends through FY2021 budget request via forms	
December	FY2018 external institutional audit underway	FY2019 external institutional audit underway	FY2020 external institutional audit underway
	FY2019 operations underway	FY2020 operations underway	FY2021 operations underway

Basic Steps

A financial management cycle includes three parts: preparation and approval of the budget, implementation of the budget, and reporting and auditing the budget. The first step encompasses the following:

- The institutional hierarchy releases the budget guidelines to the organizational units for them to use in preparation and submission of their annual budgets. The guidance may include instructions for expected increases or decreases in allocations and whether new staff positions will be hired.
- The library's preparation of the budget is based on the budget categories to be requested with justification for the amounts of funding. The preparation should
  - involve staff in the budget preparation; the staff oftentimes represent the functional units in the library's organizational chart, with information flowing upward through the hierarchy.
  - use the objectives and action plan from the long-term planning document to align resources needed to create a one-year short-term budget plan.
  - ensure the rationale for the budget identifies the programs and services needed, how much funding is required, and why the programs and services are needed for the requested dollar amount.
- The library submits the budget request per the institution-issued guidelines.
- The library may have an opportunity or opportunities to explain and defend its budget request in face-to-face meetings with administrators in the hierarchy. These meetings are excellent opportunities to inform stakeholders and market the library, its services, and its programs.

- The budget is approved, and the allocation information is forwarded to the library. This oftentimes occurs at least a month before the fiscal year begins.

With the second step, implementation of the allocated budget, the following components prevail:

- With the beginning of the fiscal year, the library receives its budgeted allocation. Depending on the institution, the allocation may be for the entire fiscal year, or it may be released throughout the fiscal year on a monthly or quarterly schedule.
- The library implements the allocated budget per the submitted budget.
- The library monitors scheduled expenditure reports from the institution and reconciles differences.

In the final step, reporting and auditing, the following occur:

- The fiscal year has ended.
- The library reconciles the final expenditure reports from the institution with its internal reporting.
- The library prepares its annual expenditures reports. The library's reports may include narrative for context.
- The annual reports are submitted as part of an institutional responsibility for accountability.
- The institution may require a financial audit of library expenditures to determine if funds were expended as reported. This audit may be conducted by an internal audit office or contracted with an external audit firm.
- The financial audits may lead to no adverse findings or to findings that the library must improve one or more specific internal controls concerning the expenditure and reporting of funds allocated.
- The financial audits may lead to the institution undertaking a program audit to determine if the funds were used as intended in the budget request, as allocated, and as reported after the fiscal year closed.

Management Information Systems

Many academic libraries use an internal information system to organize information and data collected throughout the organization. With this evidence, managers review and analyze what the library does, noting what occurs over time and ensuring there is continuous improvement in both effectiveness and efficiency. A spreadsheet serves as the simplest management information system (MIS). Outputs from the MIS, including financial information, are used for internal reporting and when responding to the numerous surveys received by the library and the institution throughout the year.

Table 2.3, an example of an internal MIS, shows a worksheet from a ten-year summary expenditures spreadsheet. Expenditures for each fiscal year are compiled from individual fiscal year spreadsheets into this summary. This library uses three major expenditure categories (staff salaries with fringe benefits, collections [information resources], and other operating). The table also displays the breakdown of expenditures for collection components (one-time purchases, recurring purchases, databases, and other collections-related costs such as document delivery). The spreadsheet then calculates the percentage (ratio) of total expenditures for these expenditure categories for the ten-year period. The data could be charted; however, the library graphed only the FY2016 ratio of the three categories as a data visualization to be shared with stakeholders.

Other General Concepts

Financial managers need to know about some other general concepts. People oftentimes use the terms *budgets* and *expenditures* interchangeably. These are not the same; budgets are inputs, whereas expenditures are outputs. Most of a library financial manager's work is concerned with expenditures rather than budgets. Second, a financial manager needs to be comfortable with creating and using spreadsheets and to understand simple formulas for performing calculations (sum and percentages are the most common). More advanced spreadsheet functions can be learned through resources available via the Internet, such as instructional videos and answers to questions.[2] Third, much of a manager's interactions with the financial management documents, including plans, budgets, and expenditures, will be (or will become) routine. A manager's first foray into financial management may seem daunting; as with anything, the learning curve declines with practice. Lastly, creating and managing budgets is scalable; once you get the hang of them, you can manage larger and more complex budgets.

Conclusion

These general concepts will help middle managers understand their library's context for financial management. Academic libraries have an advantage in the institution in that a known infrastructure facilitates planning and budgeting. Perhaps the two most important aspects of this chapter for middle managers to understand, once they view a library in terms of its infrastructure and see how any one part of the infrastructure impacts the other parts, are the systems model (figure 2.1) and management information systems. The systems model moves from inputs to outputs and outcomes, with the interpretation framework consisting of planning documents such as a strategic plan. The feedback stage reminds managers that they

Table 2.3

MIS Example

UWF: Management Information Statistics

	FY2008	FY2009	FY2010	FY2011	FY2012	FY2013	FY2014	FY2015	FY2016	FY2017
TOTAL EXPENDED FROM ALL FUNDS	$3,970,829	$3,397,327	$3,432,467	$3,625,699	$3,339,937	$3,440,556	$3,688,782	$3,668,699	$3,800,913	$3,878,763
Total of Salaries, Wages, and Fringe	$2,387,231	$2,142,817	$2,128,627	$2,103,775	$1,920,807	$2,011,221	$2,134,740	$2,148,871	$2,244,735	$2,257,737
Total Library Operation (non-personnel)	$1,583,598	$1,254,510	$1,303,840	$1,521,924	$1,419,130	$1,429,336	$1,554,042	$1,519,828	$1,556,178	$1,621,026
Information Resources	$1,262,982	$1,016,736	$973,972	$990,315	$1,004,639	$1,079,914	$1,132,714	$1,177,967	$1,218,793	$1,304,517
Other Operating	$320,616	$237,774	$329,868	$531,609	$414,491	$349,421	$421,329	$341,861	$337,385	$316,510
Select Information Resources										
monographs and other one-time acquisitions	$349,240	$138,128	$126,324	$89,208	$69,753	$94,424	$173,178	$154,244	$166,121	$175,587
print serials, microforms, e-journals, and e-books	$482,417	$428,886	$387,807	$386,725	$303,866	$275,072	$268,896	$275,202	$284,915	$286,244
databases (packages, aggregators)	$431,170	$449,722	$435,250	$514,383	$629,901	$709,973	$690,427	$748,423	$764,500	$840,301
document delivery (commercial)	$155	$0	$24,591	$0	$1,119	$446	$213	$99	$1,201	$928

Major Library Expenditures Categories Expressed in Percentages

	FY2008	FY2009	FY2010	FY2011	FY2012	FY2013	FY2014	FY2015	FY2016	FY2017
As a percentage of total expenditures										
Salaries	60.1%	63.1%	62.0%	58.0%	57.5%	58.5%	57.9%	58.6%	59.1%	58.2%
Information resources	31.8%	29.9%	28.4%	27.3%	30.1%	31.4%	30.7%	32.1%	32.1%	33.6%
Other operating	8.1%	7.0%	9.6%	14.7%	12.4%	10.2%	11.4%	9.3%	8.9%	8.2%

Major Library Expenditures Categories	**FY2017**
Salaries	58.2%
Information resources	33.6%
Other operating	8.2%

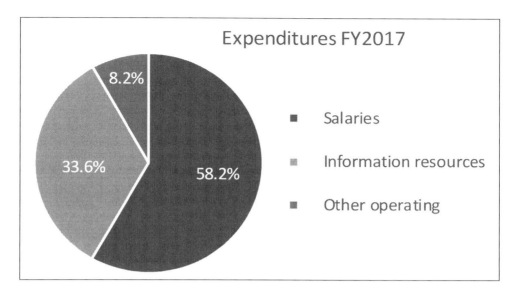

should collect meaningful evidence to review and improve the effectiveness and efficiency of library operations and services.

An automated MIS is easy to create and maintain, as Hernon, Dugan, and Matthews note.[3] That system might be created with the assistance of Counting Opinions (SQUIRE) Ltd., a Toronto, Canada, company that provides a platform to incorporate the ACRL*Metrics* dataset. Libraries might include their own evidence and add input and output metrics as well as data created by libraries they consider as peers; managers can use the ACRL*Metrics* dataset to examine data from peer libraries. They can use the evidence compiled to monitor their progress in meeting objectives, and they can display relationships among the evidence visually, perhaps through dashboards. Additionally, they can use the MIS to generate reports for their stakeholders.

Exercises

1. How does the infrastructure align with the system model?
2. What is the shortest time period for a financial management cycle?
3. Besides serving as a compilation of expenditures, what other benefits does an internal management information system provide?

(Answers to these questions can be found in the appendix at the back of the book. We encourage different library managers to work together, perhaps with staff members, to answer each question and to discuss the results.)

Notes

1. See Peter Hernon, Robert E. Dugan, and Danuta A. Nitecki, *Engaging in Evaluation and Assessment Research* (Santa Barbara, CA: Libraries Unlimited, 2011), 179–98.
2. A search engine will help a manager to learn advanced functions. First, a manager determines what he or she wants to do, such as create a chart. In the search engine text box, search for "create spreadsheet charts," and if the manager uses a specific application (e.g., Excel), that should be included in the search phrase. If you are looking for video instruction, add "videos" to the end of the search phrase. Help will also come from questions and answers posted by spreadsheet users. Replace "videos" in the search phrase with "blogs" to find this type of assistance.
3. Peter Hernon, Robert E. Dugan, and Joseph R. Matthews, *Managing with Data* (Chicago: ALA Editions, 2015).

Bibliography

Hernon, Peter, Robert E. Dugan, and Joseph R. Matthews. *Managing with Data: Using ACRLMetrics and PLAmetrics.* Chicago: ALA Editions, 2015.

Hernon, Peter, Robert E. Dugan, and Danuta A. Nitecki. *Engaging in Evaluation and Assessment Research.* Santa Barbara, CA: Libraries Unlimited, 2011. 179–98.

Chapter 3

Types of Budgets

A budget is an estimation of revenue or income and expenses over a set time period, which is often twelve months; such a time period is referred to as a fiscal year. A July through June fiscal year is common, but the starting and ending month and day vary by institution. Most of the revenue for an academic library is intra-institutional budget transfers, also known as budget allocations, for planned expenditures. Academic libraries may receive additional revenue from fines and fees, sales of surplus property or book sales, interorganizational transfers (e.g., chargebacks,[1] funded or sponsored research grants, and memberships from those wanting to use the library who are not currently faculty, students, or staff—for example, alumnae or community members in a geopolitical area). Against this background, this chapter describes some types of budgets that library managers may encounter.

Budgets

Budgets are political documents because they express the library's policy decisions about priorities for the delivery of services and programs. They are also a commitment with funding authorities that these services and programs will be provided as requested and approved; the library promises to do the right thing as a steward. Additionally, budgets facilitate the process of evaluating how successfully programs and services address the objectives expressed in planning documents.

However good the intention, libraries are in a difficult position with budgets compared to for-profit organizations because libraries largely depend on institutional sources for funding and are unable to adjust the price of goods and services to reflect the costs for acquiring, processing, organizing, storing, and disseminating information resources. For example, there are annual increases to the costs to acquire or otherwise license information content; these increases oftentimes are publicly blamed on inflation. These passed-along increases usually exceed the increases in the library's annual allocation. It is difficult to maintain, never mind strengthen, collections when cost increases that exceed funding allocations continuously erode a library's buying power. Libraries cannot adjust the price that users pay to match the increased costs passed on from third-party services.

Budgets can be used to predict and justify the financial resources needed to support the day-to-day operations of the library throughout a fiscal year. Many managers view budgets as a "tool of constraint." However, as managers gain experience, they come to see budgets as spending plans to financially execute the strategic plan; the budgets serve as a blueprint on how to use organizational resources to achieve goals and objectives efficiently and to make an impact on library users. As such, budgets are more than numbers because they reflect the library's mission, goals, plans, and intentions for providing services and programs.

There are two basic budgets: operational and capital. The most common is the year-to-year operational budget with recurring income and expenses. Libraries depend on operational budgets to fund the day-to-day expenses that support the infrastructure, in this case, staff, collections, and technologies. These budgets also include funds for staff travel and benefits, association memberships, cataloging and ILL expenses, licenses for library-specific software to create online library research guides, and "other direct costs" (e.g., supplies). They may provide funding for facilities-related costs (e.g., minor repairs).

Capital budgets cover extraordinary acquisitions or services with life spans of more than one year and beyond a dollar amount set by the institution. Capital budgets are most often associated with building renovations or major repairs (e.g., a roof). Capital projects include the replacement or upgrade of an integrated library system or acquiring and installing equipment and furniture for public areas. An institution may also assign books to capital costs if a single title exceeds a predetermined level, such as $500.

Types of Budgets

This section highlights the various types of operational budgets that middle managers may encounter.

Lump Sum Budgets

A lump sum budget is the simplest budget; the library receives a "lump" of funds from the institution. There are no budget categories applied (e.g., staff, collections, equipment, and supplies). This lack of organization of the budget into expense categories offers the most flexibility, and library managers favor this type of budget because this lack of organization lacks many constraints or limits. There are, however, downsides to lump sum budgets. The lack of categories makes it difficult to align the allocated funds to the library's goals and objectives. Additionally, the lack of budget categories can lead to financial mismanagement because expense priorities are not planned. For example, staff costs may be underfunded to build collections. Internal accounting systems may not closely track funds because there is a need to reconcile only the total funds annually expended.

Line-Item Budgets

A line-item budget is the most common form of budget due to its simplicity. Funds are allocated in horizontal titled categories (lines). Categories can be as broad as just staff, library resources, and general expenses, but they could become narrower based on institutional practice (e.g., staff delineated into specific budget lines for professional or faculty librarians, professional staff [the position requires a certain level of education and degree], and staff). Line-item annual budgets are often based on the previous year's budget allocations, and increases in the lines are incremental, such as cost-of-living increases. Because of their historical and incremental nature, line-item budgets are easy to prepare.

In some institutions, the totaled sum of the categories is the most important budget and expense factor; managers may unilaterally increase or decrease allocations between budget lines within categories and even between budget categories without approval and within institutional limits. This is true if the bottom line is not overexpended at the end of the fiscal year. For example, realized salary savings from vacancies may be reallocated to collections if they are within the institution-accepted limits (e.g., cannot transfer more than 10 percent of a category without approval, or cannot transfer more than $5,000 between categories). Although critics find that line-item budgets are no longer effective due to the need for more rigorous accountability, this budget type is still actively used.

Table 3.1 is an example of a simple annual line-item budget. The rows (line item by function) are budget categories that include professional travel (Univ Libraries Admin); student assistants for a specific library public service area (Univ Libraries Reserve); day-to-day operations budgets (Library Admin and FWB-Library Ctr—two rows); the collections budget for all formats (Library-Regular Books), which includes databases; and a special line-item budget for the Library Textbook Project. The columns show the funding allocation of the line-item budget for its categories.

Rate refers to salaries without fringe benefits, and *Total Salary* is sum of Rate plus the fringe benefits. By subtracting Rate from Total Salary, the fringe benefits budgeted can be calculated. *Ops* is the funding for the libraries' hourly student workers. The *Expense* column covers the day-to-day operating costs, including supplies, travel, costs for the libraries' software licenses, staff development, and other direct costs. The funds allocated for the collections are found in the *Special* column. The $17,793 in the *Library Admin* row is a transfer into the libraries' collection development budget for approved new academic programs.

Table 3.1
Line-Item Budget (University of West Florida Libraries)

Description	Rate	Total Salary	OPS	Expense	Special	Total
Univ Libraries Admin						
Univ Libraries Admin				6,470.00		6,470.00
Univ Libraries Reserve			19,608.00			19,608.00
Library Admin	1,443,854.00	2,016,522.00	161,073.00	275,699.00	17,793.00	2,471,087.00
FWB-Library Ctr	106,238.00	138,786.00	25,800.00	5,135.00		169,721.00
Library-Regular Books					1,184,148.00	1,184,148.00
Library Textbook Project					200,000.00	200,000.00
Univ Libraries Admin Total	**1,550,092.00**	**2,155,308.00**	**206,481.00**	**287,304.00**	**1,401,941.00**	**4,051,034.00**

Table 3.2, which is not the entire line-item budget for this library, shows a more detailed and select line-item budget, which uses rows (line items) only. While there are no titled categories, such as those shown in table 3.1, the rows are loosely arranged in groups. The first four rows are direct salaries and the next six rows are benefits. *Advertising*, grouped near benefits, may cover funds allocated for advertising job vacancies. The library's collection development budget appears in the lines before *Utilities (Electricity, Fuel, Water, Sewer)* with its funds allocation of $32,120.

Table 3.2
Selected Detailed Line-Item Budget

LIBRARY	BUDGET
LIBRARY DIRECTOR	99,008
FULL-TIME PAYROLL	300,477
PART-TIME PAYROLL	274,328
SALARY ADJUSTMENTS	5,244
NEW HRS ADULT SERV (Wage/FICA/Medi/Health)	10,116

FICA/MEDICARE	51,547
UNEMPLOYMENT INSURANCE	4,000
HEALTH INSURANCE	134,237
OTHER EMPLOYEE BENEFITS	44,651
PAYROLL ADMIN FEES	3,900
ADVERTISING	100
TRAINING & CONFERENCES	4,000
WORKER'S COMPENSATION	2,600
BOOKS/PRINTED MATERIALS	52,000
NON-BOOK RESOURCES	15,000
ELECTRONIC RESOURCES (E-Books/Media)	16,500
MATERIALS REPAIR & DIGITIZATION	2,200
PROGRAMS	1,000
UTILITIES (Electricity, Fuel, Water, Sewer)	32,120
TELEPHONE	2,500
GENERAL MAINTENANCE	19,000
CLEANING	19,500
GROUNDS MAINTENANCE	14,500
BUILDING INSURANCE	5,000
MACHINE MAINTENANCE	2,500
BANK CHARGES	650
MILEAGE	300
SUPPLIES	16,500

Formula Budgets

Formula budgets are based on criteria that are used in a formula to determine allocations. Parts of a budget may be allocated by one or more formulas; an entire budget is rarely formula-based. Formula budgets are applied at various governance and hierarchical levels in higher education. For example, parts of a budget allocated from the state level to an institution may be based, in whole or in part, on a formula, such as dollars allocated by student credit hours taken. An institution may use a formula to allocate a portion of its central funds to its organizational units as well. An example is salary funds for office administrative staff in the university's colleges based on the number of full-time faculty; units with more faculty receive a larger allocation.

Formulas may be applied within an organization. A library may allocate some of its collection development funds to academic programs based on a formula. Indiana University Northwest (IUNW) library, for example, developed an internal formula for collections (see figure 3.1). The formula governing this allocation is as follows: for any given department, let h be the number of credit hours generated by the department, c be the number of courses taught by that department (weighted so that 100-level courses count as half and 500/600-level courses count as one and a half), p be the average periodical cost of that department, and b be that department's average library budget over the past seven years. Then, for example (with summations taken across all departments), a department's library budget for the academic year 2006–2007 was determined by the formula shown in figure 3.1.[2]

Figure 3.1
Collection Development Formula (Indiana University Northwest)

$$\left(.1 * \frac{h}{\sum h} + .15 * \frac{c}{\sum c} + .1 * \frac{p \cdot h}{\sum p \cdot h} + .15 * \frac{p \cdot c}{\sum p \cdot c} + .5 * \frac{b}{\sum b}\right) \$200,650$$

Formula-based budgets have been criticized because they assume no changes occur in the missions of an institution, college, or organization or in their current context. For instance, a formula could remain static for years while the mission or the context for the formula, such as the objectives and their supportive activities, has changed. One example is a change in student FTE enrolled in an academic department, where the formula remains the same as enrollment or the context changes. This criticism is fair if the criteria applied in a formula are infrequently reviewed, which may occur when parts of the formula are written into state statute.[3] Changes in missions and context, however, can be accommodated by reviewing and adjusting the criteria used in the formula or the formula itself. For example, table 3.3 depicts a formula-based monographs allocation budget for an academic college in a university. The library uses academic department data to calculate the annual monographs allocation; the calculation relies on a formula that weights student head counts, circulation transactions, the average book costs in the annual *Library and Book Trade Almanac*, and the number of faculty. Annual updates to the data used in the formula reflect the most recent completed academic year; the weights assigned can also be adjusted as needed to maintain the relevancy of the formula.

Program Budgets

Program budgets manage financial resources by aligning allocated funding with the programs and services that best support an institution's and organization's stated goals and objectives. Additionally, program budgets facilitate the calculation of costs for programs and services during and after the fiscal year ends. Program budgets can be established by library department, cost center, or function. Examples include reference, cataloging, collection development and acquisitions, collection management, and library administration.

Table 3.3
Monographs Formula Budget

Monographs Budget / College of Arts, Social Sciences and Humanities	Call Number Ranges	Weighted Head Count Acad. Year	% of Total Weighted Head Count	$ of % Total Weighted Head Count	Circulation 3 yr Average with e-book	% of Total Circ	$ of Total Circ	Average Book Cost (current Bowker)	% of Total Bowker	$ of Total Bowker	Number of Faculty	% of Fac	$ of Total Fac	Monographs Allocation
Anthropology & Archaeology	CC, GN-GT, HM-HT	461.20	2.16%	$272.34	3767.83	7.7%	$1,620.63	$82.79	3.5%	$144.90	8	2.4%	$99.85	$2,137.73
Art	N, NA, NB-NE, NK, NX	419	1.96%	$247.42	1699.00	3.5%	$730.78	$66.00	2.8%	$115.52	9	2.7%	$112.33	$1,206.05
Communication Arts	P87-P96, PN4699-PN5650, PN1990-1999, PN4001-4355	860.2	4.03%	$507.95	580.67	1.2%	$249.76	$91.52	3.8%	$160.18	14	4.2%	$174.74	$1,092.64
English & World Languages	P, PB-PM, PA, PN, PQ, PR-PS, PT	307.2	1.44%	$181.40	5837.00	12.0%	$2,510.63	$76.81	3.2%	$134.44	19	5.6%	$237.15	$3,063.62
Government	J	485.20	2.27%	$286.51	2548.67	5.2%	$1,096.24	$79.17	3.3%	$138.57	10	3.0%	$124.81	$1,646.14
History	C (minus CC), D, E, F	332.4	1.56%	$196.28	7630.67	15.6%	$3,282.13	$70.59	2.9%	$123.55	8	2.4%	$99.85	$3,701.82
Music	M	113.00	0.53%	$66.73	652.33	1.3%	$280.58	$65.32	2.7%	$114.33	7	2.1%	$87.37	$549.00
Philosophy	B-BD, BH-BX	54	0.25%	$31.89	2670.00	5.5%	$1,148.43	$74.60	3.1%	$130.57	5	1.5%	$62.41	$1,373.29
Theatre	MT 955-956, GT	140	0.66%	$82.67	103.00	0.2%	$44.30	$79.14	3.3%	$138.51	6	1.8%	$74.89	$340.38

Formula weights = 30% for head counts; 50% for circulation; 10% for average book costs, and 10% for faculty.

Programs are aligned with the measurable objectives from the strategic plan and can be budgeted. For example, a library's objective is to "provide information services to support users." Interlibrary loan (ILL) is a service within this objective. The operating budget can be programmed (allocated) for ILL personnel, annual contractual services provided through a bibliographic utility, and supplies. Expected outputs can be estimated based on data from past years, such as the number of resource items borrowed from (or loaned to) other libraries. Specific costs to borrow and lend items through ILL can be calculated after the fiscal year ends and, in turn, those costs serve as a financial input for the next fiscal year.

Because costs can be calculated after the fiscal year ends, program budgets provide data that can inform a decision such as the expansion in the size and scope of an existing service. Further, the program budgeting process generates financial and expected output data for managers when they consider the introduction of a new service or function. (Chapter 5 discusses program budgeting in more detail.)

Box 3.1 is an example of a selected set of academic library objectives aligned with an annual recurring budget request. For the objective about the recruitment and retention of faculty and staff and filling vacancies, the benchmarks serve as action steps that support the objective. The library then requests annual recurring funds to address the action steps.

Box 3.1
Example of a Budget Request Aligned to Objectives

Objective 2.0 Recruit and Retain Excellent and Diverse Faculty and Staff

2.1 Benchmark: Fill vacant library faculty positions, including fringe benefits.
2.2 Benchmark: Address salary compression issues for library faculty. (Compression is having small differences in pay regardless of experience, skills, level, or seniority. This often happens when the starting salaries for new employees in a job classification are too close to the salaries of existing workers.)
2.3 Benchmark: Address salary compression issues for library staff.
2.4 Benchmark: Increase hourly wages for student assistants to ensure they are paid $0.25 per hour above hourly minimum wage.

Request	Recurring	Non-recurring
Recurring operating funds to fill three vacant library faculty positions, with fringe benefits	$420,000	
Faculty salary compression	$100,000	
Staff salary compression	$ 70,000	
Student assistant raises	$25,000	

Modified Program Budgets

Program budgets, which document costs, serve as an effective system for aligning financial resources because they allocate funds by aligning programs and services with the objectives stated in the strategic plan. Organizations, however, may not see a need to apply program budgets for the entire funding allocation. Modified program budgets are a mixture of line-item and program budgets. The budget is structured generally by program with *header descriptors* or one-sentence narratives. For example, the line-item budget category *library resources* provides additional programmatic details (e.g., funds allocated to specific undergraduate and graduate academic programs).

Performance Budgets

Performance-based budgets are imposed as an accountability mandate from the state level or from other governance authorities such as an institution's board of trustees. Funding allocated through performance budgets is intended to reward, or punish, the activity levels that are attained. Several states, such as Florida, use performance funding to allocate part of an annual appropriation to public higher education institutions. Prior to the introduction of performance budgets, allocations were based on quantitative formulas such as enrollment. Performance funding allocated from the state focuses on achieving desired levels of aggregated institutional outcomes (e.g., retention rates from fall to fall, four- or six-year graduation rates, and salaries of graduates, which replace past quantitative metrics).

Timing is a budget planning constraint of performance funding. Because performance funds are allocated based on past performance, outcomes from a previous fiscal year need to be compiled and verified before funds are allocated for an upcoming fiscal year. As an example, for a July-to-June fiscal year, the performance metrics used in the performance-funding model are compiled at the end of June and the beginning of July 2018 (fiscal year July 1, 2017–June 30, 2018). It may take several months to gather, verify, and submit the data; for this example, the institution's report is submitted in December 2018. This process occurs during implementation of fiscal year 2019. The hierarchical governance and funding authorities review the submitted reports and make decisions in March 2019 about the level of outcomes attained and the performance funding to be awarded (fiscal year 2019 is still underway). The performance funding is allocated to the institution at the beginning of the next fiscal year on July 1, 2019, which is the beginning of fiscal year 2020. Remember, the performance funding is based on the performance outcomes from fiscal year 2018. Furthermore, this example's schedule is based on an ideal process. If there are delays in the data compilation process or questions about data integrity, the state legislature is delayed in approving the budget, or the performance funding appropriation is reduced during the legislative budgeting process, the funds may not be available on July 1 or may not cover the funding level expected by the institution. Fiscal-year budget planning at the institutional level, therefore, can be adversely affected by performance budgets. Negative impacts of performance-based funding allocations on institutions likely affect the recurring funds allocated to its library.

Resource-Centered Budgets

Responsibility Centered Management (RCM) is a decentralized budget model in which revenue-generating organizational units are financially responsible for planning and budgeting. These units make decisions about allocating the revenue realized for support services. Many universities have adopted versions of RCM. An RCM budget model may be based on an institution's implementation, and the model uses lump sum, line-item, formula, program, and zero-based budget (discussed in the next section) processes.

There are two basic types of organizational units under RCM: revenue centers and service centers. Revenue centers, sometimes referred to as responsibility centers, generate income. Incentives are created and barriers removed to allow each revenue center (e.g., a college, school, or department) to increase income (e.g., determination of tuition fees). Other revenue-generating units include auxiliary services, which support the academic and overall mission of the institution and which are not typically responsible for generating revenue. Examples of service centers include administration and institutional support groups, student support groups, libraries, and facilities maintenance.

The first step in applying the Resource-Centered Budgeting (RCB) and RCM is to calculate all the revenue generated by the revenue or service center. The income is often a lump sum, and the center decides how to expend the funds. The next step is the identification of each service center's indirect and direct costs; this process could be applied to extend the calculation to all of the institution's centers, thereby providing an institutional perspective. Indirect expenses, or overhead costs (e.g., insurance and utilities), are charged to the revenue centers based on a designated allocation methodology; most often, this is done as a formula and includes the revenue center's measurable level of activity (e.g., student, faculty, staff full-time equivalents [FTEs], by head counts, or by facility square feet). Direct expenses are allocated directly to the revenue centers based on the costs incurred by service centers.

Turning to the library, those expenses categorized as either indirect or direct costs differ from institution to institution. Indirect expenses are services and functions shared by all revenue centers, including technology services (the integrated library system), library administration, and special collections and archives. Direct library expenses are charged to the revenue centers as costs for supporting their income-generating activities. The library's direct expenses include staff, collections, and library functions (e.g., information services, access services, technical services, acquisitions, and ILL).

The library's direct costs charged back to the revenue centers depend on a formula that addresses the number of student and faculty FTEs, or head counts. For example, if a revenue center has 10 percent of the university's student FTE, the revenue center is charged for 10 percent of the library as a support center's costs. Revenue centers question the benefits they receive from service centers, such as the library, seek to reduce support center costs, and want to retain more of the revenue for their own use.

Zero-Based Budgets

A zero-based budget starts from a zero-funding base and requires organizations to review, justify, and evaluate each of their services, programs, and activities based on the need for each service, program, and activity and its related costs. The process is detailed and structured to determine the meaningful prioritization of services and programs as an outcome of interactive financial discussions among library managers.

To develop a zero-based budget, each service, program, and function is examined to determine if it should be done at all or eliminated. If it remains, the expected level of outputs is identified and the resources needed, together with their costs, are calculated as inputs. Decisions about the programs, services, and functions are ranked in priority order: "We do this first, and this second." The process continues to add programs, services, and functions until the sum of their costs reach the funding cutoff point. Any service, program, and function beyond this funding level is eliminated.

Creating a zero-based budget is not likely to be an annual, library-wide process unless there is a reason to reduce funding levels due to an external cause. Even without a formal requirement from the institution to undertake the process, exercising a zero-based budget every two or three years assists middle managers in identifying and discussing priorities.

Conclusion

Libraries are increasingly asked to demonstrate value, and it is incumbent on them to develop their data-gathering and analytic capacity to provide specific metrics (e.g., how many students from specific colleges or schools use the collections, online resources, and other library services). Program budgeting enables library managers to organize programs to improve their ability to capture data about inputs and outputs. Calculating specific costs using strategic finance processes lets the library document its expenses. Further, libraries can use zero-based budgeting to prioritize services offered and to improve the justification for the services offered.

Exercises

1. In addition to allocating collection funds, discuss another part of a budget that may have its allocation based on a formula.
2. The library has been directed to submit a zero-based budget that can be implemented at the beginning the next fiscal year. What service or program would you expect to first implement? Second? Third? Also, what is the justification for this set of priorities?
3. Line-item budgets are the most common budgets in libraries. Minimally, what lines should be allocated?

(Answers to these questions can be found in the appendix at the back of the book. We encourage different library managers to work together, perhaps with staff members, to answer each question and to discuss the results.)

Notes

1. A chargeback occurs when one unit in the university provides a good or service to another unit and seeks to recover the cost of the good or service. For example, chargebacks include reimbursement for the library to respond to an inquiry from another organizational department (e.g., the department of economic development) to find something (some information item such as a report), and the library finds it using a fee-based database and charges the organizational department for the costs charged to the library for the use of the database. Other examples of chargebacks include the use of supplies for a 3-D print and copyright fees paid by the library.
2. Indiana University Northwest Library, "IUNW Library Budget," 2, accessed March 27, 2017, http://www.iun.edu/~nwacadem/facorg/meeting08/LibraryBudgetDiscussion.pdf.
3. For example, the formula criterion is "cost of the degree to the institution," when it should be "cost of degree to the student" because the institution does not pay for the entire degree; the student bears a cost.

Bibliography

Indiana University Northwest Library. "IUNW Library Budget." Accessed March 27, 2017. http://www.iun.edu/~nwacadem/facorg/meeting08/LibraryBudgetDiscussion.pdf.

Chapter 4

Budgeting

As library managers begin the budgeting process, they should address different stakeholder perspectives and encourage planning and budgeting from the bottom upward within the library's hierarchy; those closest to the services and functions have unduplicated experiences that should inform the budget. Managers should also base the budgeting process on the library's long-term and short-term plans, both of which are aligned with other plans in the institution. Finally, they should review the library-related data that have been gathered; they should be knowledgeable about all sources of internal and external funding opportunities, as the sources and opportunities are likely to shift from year to year; and the budgeting process should be as transparent as possible.

Before continuing, it is beneficial to define budgeting as the functions and processes that support the library's mission in terms of services and programs. Managers determine what they need to provide a service. For example, a long-term objective might be to "provide the academic community with information services." What do they need to fund this objective? First, they must think in terms of the physical and virtual information resources that will be required. Second, they must settle on the personnel, professional and other, needed to acquire the resources, how they intend to pay for both the personnel and the resources, and how to make the resources available to users. As a part of this determination, they settle on matters related to the physical shelving of items and establishing links to virtual resources. Staffing also includes having individuals who can assist users in finding the information resources they need. Assistance also relates to the organization of information resources for user-friendly access and availability, creating and maintaining guides to help users become aware of the resources, and supporting navigation to the resources via signage in the physical stacks or from webpages designed for library-provided or personal technologies (e.g., the user's smartphone).[1] Staff ensure the availability of information resources by opening the library facility and managing the library's space for use.[2] To increase the user efficiency and the effectiveness of use, library personnel may provide instruction services to individuals or groups, face to face or through virtual means such as videos or online chat sessions.

Sources of Funds

Funding for library services, programs, and functions occurs through budget allocations. Most of an academic library's funding originates from the hierarchical organizational unit that oversees the library, such as a division (e.g., academic affairs) or the institution. Funding support for the library relates to the overall amount of funding set at the institutional level, which in turn depends on funding sources that may include allocations from federal or state governments, tuition and fees, grants and sponsored research, and endowments or other individual or group giving.

Internal sources of library funds include interorganization transfers, such as chargebacks to academic departments for their use of the library's 3-D printing services. Libraries may also receive a specific percentage of grants or sponsored research funding from an organizational grantee (e.g., an academic college or department) to support grant activities (e.g., collection development or access to specific information resources). Libraries may also have access to the fines collected from overdue charges and to funds accrued from memberships for library use by external users.

External funding sources are increasingly important because of constraints on institutional sources. Library personnel may submit applications and receive grant funding for library projects through government sources, private foundations, or other philanthropic organizations. A group of friends or associates of the library may provide financial assistance to support specific projects and programs, to expand existing services, or to introduce new ones. Additionally, the library might keep the proceeds from the sale of used books and surplus equipment.

Libraries increasingly seek budgetary support through fund-raising initiatives for special projects and capital needs. The library may benefit from endowments and other types of investments given directly to the library or to the institution. The organization may seek help from the institutional advancement offices to participate in planned giving or estate planning with donors interested in the institution and the library.

Academic libraries are increasingly adopting entrepreneurship as a way to increase revenue. They might provide fee-based consulting services to start-up and established businesses, digitize information content to replace print versions for a fee, provide technology such as 3-D printers, and rent out space for community events such as lectures.

When seeking external funding, academic libraries may follow some best practices. First, they may collaborate with others on and off campus to seek funds to support library services and programs. Managers might get to know personnel at funding agencies and seek help from the institutional fund-raising and sponsored research offices in developing relationships and in competing for grants. As they do these things, they should make sure that the funding requested is program-based and supports the library's mission and its long-range goals and objectives. They should never request more funds than they can manage. For instance, if they ask for one million dollars but the library has inadequate internal support structures to manage that amount of funding, the planned project may be doomed. Managers should maintain complete records of allocations, expenditures, and what was done with the monies in case there is an audit. Additionally, they should publicize the funds the library received and the good or value accomplished with that funding. Failure to do what the library stated it would do or mismanagement of funds received will likely eliminate opportunities for future funding.

Types of Costs

Past expenditures and costs inform the budgeting process. *Expenditures* and *costs* are often used synonymously because both are outflows of funds, but they differ in application. An expenditure, a payment or disbursement of funds, represents the amount of funds spent. It is a number, but it does not provide any feedback about how the library benefits from spending the funds. As an example, assume the library expended $100,000 in staff salaries. Costs provide feedback of a benefit; with such data, managers can determine what happened with the funds spent. The $100,000 of staff expenditures enabled the library to be open for fifty hours a week for fifty-two weeks; therefore, a cost for opening the library for 2,600 hours last fiscal year was $100,000.[3] Knowing the library's expenditures does not always lead to understanding costs, but understanding costs includes knowing about expenditures.

There are varying types of costs associated with budgets and the budgeting process.

Direct and Indirect Costs

Direct costs are incurred to benefit a program. Examples of a direct cost are the salary of a person assigned completely to the reference department and the cost of staff training and development attributed to individual library personnel and their department.

Indirect costs are incurred for the common benefit of at least two programs. An example is the salary of the library director. The costs for this position are shared by every department in the library. As an alternative, costs may not be equally shared among the departments; the library director could keep track of the time spent performing varying functions over the fiscal year and make an allocation to each department based on the ratio of time spent. Other indirect costs include

- general supplies, such as paper and staples, which are shared by many library functions and departments
- shipping and postage
- telephones
- organizational memberships
- license renewals that do not directly support the collections or technologies (e.g., a survey instrument)
- marketing and outreach projects

There are also indirect costs related to bibliographic utilities; costs may support collection development and ILL.

Fixed and Variable Costs

Fixed costs, such as salaries, remain constant even though volume or activity levels increase or decrease. Variable costs fluctuate depending on activity levels. Printing supplies are an example of a variable cost because they increase or decrease based on the number of pages printed.

Overhead Costs

Overhead costs are usually administered centrally by the institution and then assigned to its organizational units based on a formula (e.g., square feet). Examples include insurance, utilities and facilities, and grounds maintenance. As illustrated in chapter 3, in the section on line-item budgets, some libraries allocate funds in their budget for these costs. The decision to include or exclude overhead costs for organizational units is frequently made at the institutional level.

In-Kind Costs

Other organizational units on campus (e.g., the university's foundation) support in-kind costs on behalf of the library; such actual costs are known but incurred by another organizational unit. An example is printed maps of the institution available in the library with the expense paid by the institution's foundation. Another example is volunteers working in the library for which no wage or benefits expenditures are incurred (supplied by an external vocational organization that sends its workers to serve as volunteers as they receive job training). A library, however, should still calculate the benefit received from the volunteers as part of the costs of providing library services.

Capital Costs

The costs of acquiring assets that have a *useful* life that exceeds one year are referred to as capital costs. The institution's governing authority determines the cost level necessary to be labeled as a capital cost. Financial or policy auditors could also recommend the cost level. An example of a capital cost is the funds to upgrade or replace the integrated library system. The annual maintenance costs imposed by the vendor are categorized as direct costs when they are charged to the library, or as an overhead cost if they are charged to the university's information technology department.

Controllable and Non-controllable Costs

Controllable costs are those assigned to a specific manager responsible to implement a service, program, or function. A manager may be empowered to control the costs for staffing a public desk by determining the level of staffing to be deployed (e.g., using two less-expensive part-time library assistants or one full-time, permanent professional librarian who receives fringe benefits as well as a fixed salary). In a non-controllable cost situation, a manager higher in the library hierarchy determines the staffing levels and types of staff for public service desks, thereby removing the direct line manager from being able to make the staffing decisions and affecting the service costs.

A Note about Costs

Library budget allocations vary among institutions. The allocations may not include overhead costs for electricity; heating, ventilation, and air conditioning (HVAC); uniformed security; or cleaning. Institutions may also centralize personnel expenditures, including salaries and fringe benefits, and the funds for student assistants. Library managers may need to seek expenditure data from other organizational units to calculate costs.

Where Do We Get Information for Budgeting?

There are several sources of information for middle managers to use during the budgeting process. A primary source is current and past expenditures data. Table 4.1 is an example of a completed fiscal year's table of budget categories and activities with their associated expenditures for recurring (day-to-day) funds. The table provides columns for "Budgeted," "Expended," and the variances of the amounts budgeted and expended. The expenditures are aligned with the institution's budget categories, and the line items provide sufficient detail for the library financial managers to differentiate line items within the budget categories.

This table provides input data for the next fiscal year's budgeting process. Reviewing similar expenditures tables from previous fiscal years provides historical expenditures data that can be analyzed and displayed as trend graphs. For example, a review of tables from past years shows whether technology expenditures increased, decreased, or remained about the same over the past three to five fiscal years.

Table 4.1
Example of Past Year Expenditures

Library Recurring Operations	Budgeted	Expended	Variance	Variance
Services/Utilities				
External Printing	$500.00	$213.41	**$286.59**	57.32%
Central Copying Charges	$1,500.00	$759.25	**$740.75**	49.38%
Postage	$1,400.00	$378.11	**$1,021.89**	72.99%
Freight	$200.00	$68.81	**$131.19**	65.60%
Nautilus Card Fees	$200.00	$180.00	**$20.00**	10.00%
Tolls & Toll-Free Services	$34.38	$34.38	**$–**	0.00%
Telephone Charges	$300.00	$238.40	**$61.60**	20.53%
Telephone Equipment Installation	$19.20	$38.40	**$(19.20)**	
Telephone Equipment & Line Charges	$12,000.00	$11,092.40	**$907.60**	7.56%
Hand Tools	$200.00	$–	**$200.00**	100.00%
Parts & Fittings	$30.00	$26.97	**$3.03**	10.10%
Gasoline	$100.00	$27.89	**$72.11**	72.11%
Automotive Supplies	$370.19	$370.19	**$–**	0.00%
Repairs & Maintenance, Work Orders	$500.00	$96.25	**$403.75**	80.75%
Office Supplies (70301)		$8,652.61		
Information Technology Supplies (70351)		$5,968.04		
Computer Software (70352)				
General Operating Supplies (70353)		$13,888.11		
Total Planned for 70301, 70351, 70352, & 70353	$30,000.00	$28,508.76	**$1,491.24**	4.97%
Subtotal—Services and Utilities	**$47,353.77**	**$42,033.22**	**$5,320.55**	**11.24%**
Software and License, Renewed				
OCLC-Monthly ILL Costs	$11,200.00	$10,208.42	**$991.58**	8.85%
License—OCLC ILLIAD License & Hosting	$10,858.68	$10,858.68	**$–**	0.00%
License—LibGuides (Online Research Guides)	$1,558.00	$1,558.00	**$–**	0.00%
License—LibAnswers (Online FAQ for Distance & Online learners)	$2,128.00	$2,128.00	**$–**	0.00%

Library Recurring Operations	Budgeted	Expended	Variance	Variance
License—LibAnalytics (Usage tracking for reference & circ transactions)	$1,059.00	$1,059.00	$–	0.00%
License—Counting Opinions (User Assessment) (includes ACRLMetrics)	$6,435.00	$6,435.00	$–	0.00%
License—AdobeCS6 (Creative Cloud CS6 Master Collection)	$8,870.40	$8,870.40	$–	0.00%
License—Bowker Book Analysis System (Collection Assessment Tool)	$3,325.00	$3,325.00	$–	0.00%
License—Copyright Clearance Center	$1,201.32	$1,201.32	$–	0.00%
License—Usage Reporting System	$2,580.00	$2,580.00	$–	0.00%
License—Institutional Repository	$6,475.00	$6,475.00	$–	0.00%
License—CSUL PDA (revised 11/12/15)	$3,578.06	$3,578.06	$–	0.00%
License—QuestBase Premium Gold-renewal	$199.95	$199.95	$–	0.00%
Computer Protection Plan—Apple	$79.00	$79.00	$–	0.00%
License—SmartBoard Software (AVI-SPL; 14 Annual Licenses)	$756.00	$756.00	$–	0.00%
Subtotal—Licenses	**$60,303.41**	$59,311.83	**$991.58**	1.64%
Communication Supplies				
Twillio—SMS Notification Service	$20.00	$20.00	$–	0.00%
Google One-time Charge for AskLibrarian Chat Transfer	$3.00	$3.00		
Subtotal—Communication Supplies	$23.00	$23.00	$–	0.00%
Publications				
PSL -Textbooks (Collections)	$2,166.93	$2,166.93	$–	0.00%
Faculty Publications (Collections)	$5,000.00	$479.58	**$4,520.42**	
Textbooks for Skylab (Staff training)	$274.46	$274.46	$–	0.00%
Subtotal—Publications	**$7,441.39**	$2,920.97	**$4,520.42**	60.75%
Memberships				
Center for Research Libraries (SUS-FLVC Database Access Support)	$3,088.00	$3,088.00	$–	0.00%
CSUL—HathiTrust Membership	$5,178.00	$5,178.00	$–	0.00%
SUS Newspaper LLMC Digital	$5,000.00	$5,000.00	$–	0.00%
NFAIS—Florida Consortium of State Universities	$163.64	$163.64	$–	0.00%
ArchiveSpace (Archive Online Catalog)—Membership	$3,000.00	$3,000.00	$–	0.00%
Lyrasis Membership	$1,395.00	$1,395.00	$–	0.00%
Panhandle Library Access Network (Staff Development)	$1,000.00	$1,000.00	$–	0.00%
Networked Digital Library of Theses & Dissertations	$150.00	$150.00	$–	0.00%
Subtotal—Memberships	**$18,974.64**	$18,974.64	$–	0.00%

Library Recurring Operations	Budgeted	Expended	Variance	Variance
Software Licenses				
Webserver Plugin	$50.00	$50.00	$–	0.00%
License—Statista	$3,240.00	$3,240.00	$–	0.00%
License—LibWizard	$999.00	$999.00		
Subtotal—Software License	**$4,289.00**	$4,289.00	$–	0.00%
Other Contractual Services				
Notary Public Underwriters, INC	$105.43	$105.43	$–	0.00%
A Advanced Superior Phone & Data	$680.00	$680.00	$–	0.00%
SUS Shared Storage Facility (Gainesville)	$25,328.00	$25,328.00	$–	0.00%
Subtotal—Equipment Maintenance Contracts	**$26,113.43**	$26,113.43	$–	0.00%
Equipment Maintenance Contracts				
3M Maintenance Contract	$3,980.00	$3,980.00	$–	0.00%
Book Scanner, Archives	$1,952.00	$1,952.00	$–	0.00%
Book Scanner, Skylab	$1,683.00	$1,683.00	$–	0.00%
Freedom Scientific—Software Updates Maintenance Renewal	$200.00	$200.00	$–	0.00%
Smartboard Maintenance	$2,116.00	$641.50	**$1,474.50**	69.68%
Subtotal—Equipment Maintenance Contracts	**$9,931.00**	$8,456.50	**$1,474.50**	14.85%
Travel and Professional/Staff Development				
Travel and Development (Regional/State/National); Faculty & Staff	$10,000.00	$8,969.73	**$1,030.27**	10.30%
Development (Faculty & Staff; Registrations, etc.	$3,000.00	$905.00	**$2,095.00**	69.83%
Subtotal—Travel and Professional/Staff Development	**$13,000.00**	$9,874.73	**$3,125.27**	24.04%
Technology				
Staff Scanner		$806.87	**$(806.87)**	
Misc Equipment		$2,113.41	**$(2,113.41)**	
12 HD Webcams for Reference Staff & Others		$407.28	**$(407.28)**	
Wacom for Skylab		$3,094.90	**$(3,094.90)**	
Airbook for Ghosting Macs in Skylab		$1,620.00	**$(1,620.00)**	
Mac Mini—Skylab		$1,407.00	**$(1,407.00)**	
Cintiq and Stand—Skylab		$3,094.90	**$(3,094.90)**	
Replacement Cameras for Classroom		$1,591.10	**$(1,591.10)**	
4th Floor Security Cameras	$14,845.00	$14,845.00	$–	0.00%
Security Cameras -Spare pool	$2,750.00	$2,400.00	**$350.00**	12.73%
Replacement Scanners for Public Areas	$156.00	$155.18	**$0.82**	0.53%
Replacement Hard Drives	$2,700.00	$2,649.90	**$50.10**	1.86%
Replacement Computers for Circulation Area	$16,500.00	$16,085.85	**$414.15**	2.51%
Subtotal—Technology	**$50,345.00**	$50,271.39	**$73.61**	0.15%

Library Recurring Operations	Budgeted	Expended	Variance	Variance
Other				
Marketing and Outreach Library Committee	$1,000.00	$850.00	**$150.00**	15.00%
Hiring (Employment Ads & Job Opp. = Advertising)	$2,000.00	$615.00	**$1,385.00**	69.25%
Unemployment Compensation Benefits	$500.00	$400.93	**$99.07**	19.81%
Renovations—Circulation Desk (70356)	$20,000.00	$20,000.00	**$–**	0.00%
Subtotal—Miscellaneous	**$23,500.00**	$21,865.93	**$1,634.07**	6.95%
TOTALS	261,274.64	$244,134.64	$17,140.00	6.56%

Another source of information is the objectives included in the long-term or strategic plan. The annual short-term budgeting plan should be aligned with the objectives in the long-term plan so that progress in meeting the stated objectives can be determined. For example, an objective in the strategic plan might be to "Develop and manage relevant intellectual content, balanced across appropriate information formats, to support teaching, research, and service regardless of geographic location." As a short-term action to support this objective, the library purchases 50 percent of its monographs as e-book titles during the fiscal year because this format is accessible from anywhere faculty and students are physically located. This decision informs the budget.

Existing or expected licenses and subscription agreements are a source of budgeting information. Costs associated with licenses and agreements are contained in the previous fiscal year's expenditures data. Licensing and subscription agreements, however, are "not forever"; there are usually cost increases when the license or agreement is renewed. Knowing about any cost increases factors into preparing next fiscal year's budget. Budget information also comes from non-information content contracts such as for equipment maintenance, licensing agreements for software (e.g., productivity or graphics), and applications used by the library staff in their roles of providing services.

Library vendors provide useful sources of budgeting information. *Library Journal* publishes an annual report each April on the financial landscape of libraries, including numerous tables containing specific financial data on periodical prices. One of the tables, for example, provides the expected average cost increase of the journal titles in an aggregated full-text database, which in turn informs the library of the expected cost increases for full-text e-journal databases. This report, a must-read publication, can be found by using a web search engine to locate the "library journal periodicals price survey."

EBSCO, another library information vendor, annually releases two reports, both of which can be found through a web search. The first is a narrative report, usually released in early fall, that announces the expected serial publishers' price increases for the upcoming calendar year for academic and academic/medical libraries. The second report provides a chart on the history of the most recent five years of journal price increases.

Cost information from professional associations and organizations also provides valuable budget data. For example, *The Library and Book Trade Almanac* (Medford, NJ: Information Today) annually presents narrative, analysis, and tables from the publishing industry, among other things, on the costs for books and serials. Such information is useful when budgeting for new acquisitions as well as estimating the value of an existing collection by subject area.

Commitments made to support new academic programs are a source for budgeting information. Beginning a new academic degree requires additional library collections, and it may also require staff, technology, and physical space. A note of caution is that the library may not be asked about resource needs as the institution plans for (and implements) a new or expanded program or changes an existing program's focus. For example, introducing a new undergraduate degree in mechanical engineering requires the acquisition and upkeep of monographs and serials in the collection. It may also require a library liaison to the engineering department and additional technology placed in the library such as computer-aided design (CAD) workstations and related software.

New applications are continuously emerging to help library managers estimate costs in the budgeting process. For instance, the Digitization Cost Calculator, http://dashboard.diglib.org, a project undertaken by the working group on Cost Assessment, Assessment Interest Group of the Digital Library Federation, collects and makes freely available data on the time it takes to perform various tasks involved in the digitization process to help with budgeting.[4]

Data Used for Budgeting

In addition to sources of information for budgeting, library managers should gather basic data to use in the budgeting process. Demand for library services and programs might be discovered through a review of user requests and comments and staff observations. Demand for services may also be anticipated through a multiplicity of factors, including the number of students and their classification (undergraduate or graduate students), the number of faculty in academic units, and the number and type of academic programs and degrees offered at the undergraduate and graduate levels, with separate consideration of doctoral programs.

For illustrative purposes, the data in table 4.2 shows that the largest head count at the undergraduate level represents seniors, and the second-largest head count is for juniors. These upper division students have different course-required information needs than do lower division students (freshmen and sophomores) because they are enrolled in courses in their majors and focus more on preparing papers and engaging in projects that require specific topic-oriented information. The table shows that there are nearly ten times as many students enrolled in a master's program than a doctoral program. Master's students have different information needs than do doctoral students. It may be that books and serials acquired to support the master's programs may also be used and valued by upper division undergraduates and their faculty.

Table 4.2
Student Head Count by Class Level

Class Level	Head Count	% of Total
Freshman	1,690	13.19
Sophomore	1,393	10.88
Junior	2,575	20.10
Senior	4,129	32.24
Undergraduate Unclassified	415	3.24
Master	2,008	15.68
Specialist	18	0.14
Doctorate	251	1.96
Graduate Unclassified	329	2.57
TOTAL	12,808	100.00

Table 4.3, which provides student academic demographic data by department, covers five academic programs in a college of business. Head count is aligned with the student's level or classification and by academic program. The accounting and finance program has both undergraduate and graduate students. As in the previous table, there are more upper division students and master's students. This finding influences the type of information resources and services that the library provides. The hospitality, management, and marketing programs do not have graduate programs, but a master's degree in business administration has more than 100 students. The management program has a significantly higher enrollment than do hospitality and marketing; this fact influences the library's collection development.

Table 4.3
College of Business Students, 2014 and 2015*

		Fall 2014	Fall 2015
Column Three	Column Four	**Head Count**	**Head Count**
Accounting & Finance	Freshman	49	59
	Sophomore	48	44
	Junior	136	128
	Senior	213	193
	Master	55	43
	Total	501	467

		Fall 2014	Fall 2015
Column Three	Column Four	**Head Count**	**Head Count**
Hospitality, Rec & Resort Mgmnt	Freshman		24
	Sophomore		32
	Junior		65
	Senior		78
	Total		**199**
Management & MIS	Freshman	88	124
	Sophomore	95	74
	Junior	124	161
	Senior	174	199
	Total	**481**	**558**
Marketing & Economics	Freshman	36	34
	Sophomore	39	40
	Junior	83	72
	Senior	92	106
	Total	250	252
MBA Office	Master	114	134
	Total	114	134

*This chart was created through a publicly viewable interactive fact book. Source: University of West Florida, "Enrollment by Level/Classification," Enrollment, ASPIRE: UWF's Interactive Fact Book, accessed September 8, 2017, https://tableau.uwf.edu/views/IR-FB-Enrollment_0/LevelClassification?%3Aembed=y&%3AshowShareOptions=true&%3Adisplay_count=no&%3AshowVizHome=no.

A library prepares and submits its budget based on the categories that the institution uses. A practical approach for library managers when preparing a budget is to organize the data and process aligned to the infrastructure (staff, collections, technologies, and facilities). Support costs such supplies can be aligned with the related part of the infrastructure or with a centralized part of the budget.

Staff and Staffing

Staff salaries and wages are a major component of a library's budget. Salary and fringe benefits are usually determined at the institutional level and then allocated as line items to all the units. Associated resource needs to support the library personnel's job duties include access to technology for increased productivity, supplies, and professional and staff training and development, which may require funding for travel and registration for workshops and conferences.

A primary source of data about staff is a salary schedule from the human resources or payroll department, which includes each position. Library middle managers, however, may not have access to this document.[5] Staff costs are usually classified by position or function (e.g., Assistant Professor (librarian with faculty status), Library Technician I, Fiscal Specialist III, or Computer Server Administrator. There are full-time and part-time staff. Another classification is permanent and temporary staff; temporary staff positions may be project-based or not expected to work throughout the entire fiscal year. A position may also be classified as twelve-month; faculty members may have nine-month appointments. There are exempt and nonexempt staff. Exempt are usually salaried staff or faculty and are not subject to compensation for overtime; nonexempt staff are either salaried or paid an hourly wage and are compensated for overtime through labor laws and regulations.

The most commonly used staff salary cost formula is

number of hours scheduled to work *times* hourly wage

times number of days per pay period

times number of pay periods in the fiscal year

Fringe benefits may be funded through the library; if they are not, they are likely funded centrally (the institution). Fringe benefits are applied if the position meets a minimal threshold, such as thirty hours per week, as established by institutional policy or through labor laws. Fringe benefits

- are calculated for each position and managed by the payroll or personnel office
- are based on the benefits accepted and used by each employee (e.g., coverage by a health care plan) or used (a tuition reduction program or waiver, which is a taxable benefit). This category also covers holidays or other compensated work time provided for the position.

Many academic libraries employ student assistants to supplement library services. There are numerous salary schedules for undergraduates, including federal work-study and those with financial aid and scholarships. If student assistants are funded through the library's operations budget, their salaries and wages frequently appear as a separate line from staff and faculty salaries. Graduate student workers are often addressed differently as they are paid a higher hourly wage than are undergraduates, and the institution may limit the number of hours they can work each week to ensure that they are focused on their graduate work.

Most students have a variable work schedule, which is set by the time of the academic year. For example, student assistants may work fewer or more hours during intersessions depending on their availability. The most commonly used student assistant salary cost formula is

number of hours per week *times* labor cost per hour

times the number of weeks during the specific period such as
the fall semester

The institution or academic departments may apply maximum hourly limits for the work availability of student assistants. These assistants are usually not eligible for benefits unless the number of hours worked a week equals or exceeds the limit imposed by the institution or by labor laws.

A library may develop an internal staffing plan as a management tool to inform its budgeting needs for personnel. The plan, which is organized by the objectives specified in the strategic plan, describes the job duties to implement the objective. Box 4.1, an example of a staffing plan, lists the strategic responsibilities and staffing needs organized by library function and aligned with the library's long-term objectives. As the function's responsibilities change, the staffing plan is updated.

Box 4.1
Example of a Staffing Plan for the Circulation Department Aligned to Strategic Plan

---

Function: Circulation

Reports to: Dean of Libraries

Library Objective 1.0 (Collections), 2.0 (Services), 4.0 (Facility), 6.0 (Administration), and 7.0 (Demonstrate the Libraries' Value to Stakeholders)

Supports University Strategic Directions 1.2, 1.3, and 4.1

Supports Academic Strategic Master Plan Priorities 4.1, 4.2, 5.2, 6.1, 6.2, 8.2

Strategic Responsibilities:
- Open and close the Pace Library (academic year = 112 hours/week over a seven-day period).
- Manage the collection: shelve and reshelve, shelf-read stacks.
- Manage the library's reserves collections, including Textbooks on Reserve.
- Check out and check back in materials borrowed by stakeholders.
- Check out and check back in equipment borrowed by stakeholders.
- Place textbooks and other course materials on reserve.
- Ensure the security of the Pace Library when closing at end of business day.
- Monitor and report facility operation issues to Administration.
- Compile data on a variety of transactions, e.g., entrance/exit, user transactions.
- Maintain item database and transactions.
- Maintain user database and transactions.
- Bill stakeholders for overdue, lost, or damaged materials and equipment.
- Supervise the 7 to 9 FTE student workers upon whom this function depends to help provide services and manage the collection.
- Answer "reference" type questions when Reference Desk not staffed.
- Serve the community at large in addition to the institution's community.
- Provide troubleshooting for access issues for off-campus users; serve as point of contact for anyone encountering issues accessing library resources or services.

Staffing Needs:
- – Head of Circulation to overall manage the function's personnel, policies, and services and provide direct services at the Circulation Desk.
- – Circulation Supervisor to directly manage the personnel and student workers supporting the many day-to-day operations of the function and provide direct services at the Circulation Desk.
- – Desk Student Supervisor to supervise students during late evening hours and provide direct services at the Circulation Desk.
- – Evening Supervisor to manage the function and the library at closing, to supervise student assistants, support weeding and collection maintenance, and to provide direct services at the Circulation Desk.
- – Equipment Coordinator to maintain the quantitative and qualitative variety of equipment loaned, provide direct services at the Circulation Desk, and assist in the Technologies function as needed.
- – Circulation Accounts Specialist to maintain an accurate system of those billed for overdue, damaged, or lost materials and equipment, seek to recover the fines and costs owed, support the libraries' program for marketing and outreach, and provide direct services at the Circulation Desk.
- – Reserves Coordinator to manage the materials added by faculty to course reserve, ensure the materials in course reserves are there appropriately, and provide direct services at the Circulation Desk.
- – Intercampus Loan Coordinator to provide direct services at the Circulation Desk, manage the movement of library materials to and from the Professional Studies Library and the Emerald Coast Campus Library, undertake basic cataloging for paperback and Kindle titles, manage the delivery of books requested by distance learners, and change item status of bibliographic records when item is lost or in binding for repair.
- – Stacks Manager to ensure that the stacks are arranged so that users may find what they need, that the contents of the shelf are in the correct order of placement, that in-hand materials (e.g., books, bound serial volumes) and all areas of the stacks are not "crowded out" but that materials are properly spaced on the shelves in a unit or range to facilitate retrieval, and provide direct services at the Circulation Desk.
- – Textbook Program Manager to manage the reserve program for processing and shelving the faculty-required textbooks for all undergraduate courses for two-hour in-library loan from the Circulation Desk. The staff person works closely with the fiscal specialist for collections in the Administration Office and with Cataloging Services.

Ongoing Observation:
- – The staffing for this function needs continuous review because of the need for student assistants to assist full-time staff
- + because of the increase in hours open from 81 in FY2011 to 112 in FY2015.
- + to assist in extending hours open, including 24/5, for the last three/two weeks of each academic session.

As managers examine budgeting data for staff salaries, they might review comparative data available from various sources. Library consortium members may share annual salary data arranged by function (e.g., reference), job title (e.g., stacks manager), and classification (e.g., library faculty). Some libraries occasionally survey their institutional peers for detailed salary information. Libraries in a public higher education institutions are sometimes able to review specific salary data of the other libraries in their state system.

There are at least three sources of fee-based comparative salary data. The ALA-Allied Professional Association Library Salary Database, a project of the ALA-APA and the ALA Office for Research and Statistics, includes data on both librarian and non-MLS salaries in public and academic libraries. The Salary Survey of the Association of Research Libraries (ARL) lists salaries for more than 12,000 professional positions in ARL member libraries. The survey also tracks minority representation in these libraries in the United States and reports separate data for health sciences and law libraries. One of the most respected salary surveyors is the College and University Professional Association for Human Resources (CUPA-HR, http://www.cupahr.org/index.aspx), which compiles the *Professionals in Higher Education Salary Report* (http://www.cupahr.org/surveys/phe) and the *Staff in Higher Education Salary Report* (https://www.cupahr.org/surveys/publications/staff/). Free reports from the CUPA-HR website provide median salary data by function title and by Carnegie Classification of Institutions of Higher Education, while fee-based reports include additional detail (e.g., salary data grouped into four national geographic areas), which offers more relevant comparative data for an institution (see table 4.4).

Table 4.4

Example of a CUPA-HR Salary Table

	All Institutions	Research Universities **	Other Doctoral**	Master's	Baccalaureate	Associate's
[301010] Head-Campus Printing Services	59,416	81,539	63,672	54,777	50,758	53,347
[301020] Head-Campus Mail Services	47,614	57,858	53,266	45,369	42,719	53,717
[315020] Head-Camp Landscape/Grnds Keep	62,448	78,920	69,305	58,973	58,451	57,872
[315040] Head-Camp Constr	94,300	110,740	102,931	82,713	88,258	87,158
[315050] Head-Camp Skilled Trades	73,706	85,773	75,596	72,600	65,652	68,106
[315060] Head-Camp-Custodial Servs	58,780	71,473	64,309	57,247	51,223	60,598
[320010] Executive Asst to Sys or Inst CEO	69,733	88,900	74,544	68,860	62,797	60,763

	All Institutions	Research Universities **	Other Doctoral**	Master's	Baccalaureate	Associate's
[325000] Admin Speclist/Coord	49,190	53,916	51,064	47,881	45,943	50,749
[400110] Study Abroad Advisor	44,715	44,151	45,406	43,628	47,279	*
[400120] Acad Supt Ctr Coord	49,226	53,604	52,550	47,745	46,883	51,409
[400130] Head-Camp Learning Resources Ctr	64,993	84,150	64,056	63,100	60,203	61,356
[400135] Head-Camp Teaching Ctr	86,994	100,000	98,427	78,911	84,398	65,775
[400140] Credential Speclist	48,665	51,981	51,103	47,774	39,140	54,815
[400150] Acad Evaluator	41,376	43,413	46,889	40,560	38,012	43,517
[400160] Head-Foreign Std Servs	59,515	71,570	67,254	61,275	49,800	54,055
[400170] Head-Athl Acad Affrs	72,619	86,683	67,948	60,840	66,871	*
[401010] Head-Std Acad Counseling	62,883	80,726	59,930	59,674	61,943	62,916
[401130] Acad Advisor/Counselor	43,546	45,074	42,913	42,363	42,693	44,664
[402010] Librarian-Head Acquisitions	63,930	70,716	67,263	64,775	50,583	47,340
[402020] Librarian-Head Tech Servs	67,537	92,642	71,276	64,422	59,720	59,254
[402030] Librarian-Head Pub Servs	63,443	88,287	63,443	61,589	58,358	58,445
[402040] Librarian-Head Cataloging	63,208	73,547	69,056	58,583	61,171	65,616
[402050] Librarian-Head Collection Devel	69,428	78,100	78,991	62,681	64,200	*
[402060] Librarian-Head Spec Col and Archives	63,910	84,250	66,147	59,567	59,846	55,557
[402065] Librarian-Sys/Digital Resources	62,002	71,843	63,610	56,910	60,180	65,384
[402170] Librarian-Head Ref and Instr (II)	61,672	71,879	66,400	61,329	59,765	54,062
[402180] Librarian-Ref and Instr (Ref Level I)	51,814	56,131	57,198	50,779	49,819	49,492
[402190] Librarian-Cataloger/Metadata (Lev II)	55,566	62,204	56,829	53,077	53,096	51,201
[402200] Librarian-Cataloger (Level I)	46,350	51,677	48,586	45,835	41,838	48,599
[402210] Librarian-Electronic Resources/ Serials	56,121	60,984	59,756	53,829	55,642	70,922

	All Institutions	Research Universities **	Other Doctoral**	Master's	Baccalaureate	Associate's
[402260] Librarian-Head Branch Library	80,964	89,458	77,099	73,460	82,931	60,811
[402265] Librarian-Head Access Servs	68,000	73,428	77,779	60,048	66,853	*
[402267] Librarian-Access Servs	50,688	61,044	54,163	48,704	42,529	52,464
[402270] Librarian-Spec Coll/Archives	57,570	61,776	55,864	47,616	56,531	*
[403050] Head-Camp Museum	103,290	124,384	93,348	80,136	90,167	*
[403100] Archive/Museum/Gallery Curator	54,301	59,809	50,000	50,084	54,167	51,423
[404110] Continuing Ed Speclist	55,671	56,078	57,263	53,718	51,446	58,655
[404120] Continuing Ed Conf/Workshop Coord	49,930	50,599	49,689	46,852	44,245	53,075
[406050] Instrl Techngy-Faculty Supt Mgr	66,316	79,302	69,913	65,433	60,000	58,827
[406100] Web Content Developer	54,232	57,267	58,230	51,996	50,743	54,169

Note. The data in this table reflect positions that were reported by 100 or more institutions. To see data for all positions, consult the complete tables in the 2016 Professionals in Higher Education Salary Survey Report. Source: CUPA-HR, "Unweighted Median Salary by Carnegie Classification—All Institutions," Professionals in Higher Education Salary Survey: Select Data, 2017, http://www.cupahr.org/wp-content/uploads/2017/07/PHE16-Selected-Data.pdf

*4 cases or fewer

**Research Universities are doctorate-granting institutions that Carnegie has classified as having either high or very high research activity.

The American Association of University Professors (AAUP) publishes the *Annual Report on the Economic Status of the Profession* in the March–April issue of *Academe*,[6] which includes a Faculty Compensation Survey report. An online results portal allows users to conduct analyses with variables related to full-time faculty salaries and benefits.[7] Users may view national results or create peer groups to analyze and export data using one or more variables. Once a peer group has been selected, a user may review descriptive statistics in bar graphs or tables.[8] While library faculty are not specifically listed in the survey, the report's informative detail may provide useful salary data for budgeting library faculty members by academic rank.

Collections

Collections comprise the second major category of an academic library's budget. A library receives one or more allocations for maintaining and developing the collections; these include funds for one-time acquisition of monographs and backfiles, to continue existing licenses and subscriptions for databases and serials, and, if lucky, to add new resources. Some libraries are allocated line-item funds (e.g., from the provost or institution) to support specific information formats (e.g., print, e-books and e-serials, microforms, maps, streaming video, audio, and photographs).

A library determines how it will allocate its collection development funds, especially if they are a single line item in the annual budget. There are many needs for allocating collection funds; these include maintaining existing serial subscriptions and licenses, adding e- and print monographs, purchasing requested backfiles, responding to the increasing requests for streaming video, and providing patron-driven acquisition (PDA) and demand-driven acquisition (DDA) of purchases based on triggers or evidence-based acquisition (EBA). EBAs use a deposit account and make purchases based on an analysis of use statistics.

Collections are shifting from print to e- everything and to access at any time from anywhere if users have an Internet connection. Academic libraries are also shifting from print serial titles to e-journal titles in aggregated databases and increasingly to publisher-based portals. The acquisition of print monographs is now shifting to access for e-books and to meeting user demand in real time through DDAs and EBAs. Collection development increasingly occurs through library consortia and other partnerships, which increase the economies of scale; a result is the increasing importance of collections that are shared with other libraries. Local print collections are moving to automated retrieval storage attached to or near the library or to remote facilities. While past expenditures are still a mainstay for budget data, a library may be unable to rely on past expenditures data as a predictive budget measure.

Allocation Formulas

The allocation of collection funds to support curriculum and research needs should not be based on happenstance, favoritism, or some other subjective method. Instead, the distribution should be based on an allocation formula. If the library allocates funds among subject areas, managers may want to use data about academic department, such as:

- academic programs offered
- student FTEs or head counts
- faculty FTEs or head counts
- circulation or other usage indicators (e.g., the number of downloads).

Table 4.5
Monograph Allocation Formula

Departments	Call # Range	Weighted Head Count (30% of Weight)	% of Total Weighted Head Count	$ of % Total Weighted Head Count	Circulation 3 yr Average (50% of Weight)	% of Total Circ	$ of Total Circ	Average Cost (Bowker)	% of Total Bowker (10% of Weight)	$ of Total Bowker	# of Faculty (10% of Weight)	% of Fac	$ of Total Fac	This Year's Allocation
Anthropology & Archaeology	CC, GN-GT, HM-HT	516.4	2.4%	$488.31	1,192.00	6.2%	$2,077.00	$84.95	3.9%	$257.52	8	2.5%	169.56	$2,993.22
Art	N, NA, NB-NE, NK, NX	452.0	2.1%	$418.95	983.33	5.2%	$1,713.40	$62.00	2.8%	$187.95	8	2.5%	169.56	2,489.86
Communication Arts	P87-P96, PN4699-PN5650, PN1990-1999, PN4001-4355	828.6	3.9%	$778.05	274.67	1.4%	$478.60	$65.00	3.0%	$197.04	14	4.5%	$296.73	$1,750.42
English & World Languages	P, PB-PN, PA, PN, PQ, PR-PS, PT	338.4	1.6%	$319.20	3,631.33	19.0%	$6,327.41	$89.67	4.1%	$271.83	16	5.1%	$339.12	$7,257.56
Government	J	474.4	2.2%	$438.90	427.67	2.2%	$745.19	$69.93	3.2%	$211.99	6	1.9%	$127.17	$1,523.25
History	C (minus CC), D, E, F	372.6	1.8%	$359.10	4,501.33	23.6%	$7,843.34	$68.10	3.1%	$206.44	9	2.9%	$190.76	$8,599.63
Music	M	136.0	0.6%	$119.70	484.33	2.5%	$843.92	$68.10	3.1%	$206.44	7	2.2%	$148.37	$1,318.42
Philosophy	B-BD, BH-BX	49.0	0.2%	$39.90	1,384.00	7.3%	$2,411.55	$76.70	3.5%	$232.51	5	1.6%	$105.98	$2,789.93
Theatre	MT 955-956, GT	145.0	0.7%	$139.65	94.00	0.5%	$163.79	$70.75	3.2%	$214.47	6	1.9%	$127.17	$645.08

Table 4.5 is an example of a formula-based allocation for monographs for an arts, humanities, and social sciences college. The budget allocation formula for monographs that this library uses is based on the student head count in the academic department, circulation transactions by students and faculty correlated to Library of Congress (LC) call number range for the most current three years, and the number of full-time faculty assigned to the academic departments. Weights are also applied to the formula: student head counts are 30 percent, circulation usage is 50 percent, and the average cost of a book and faculty head counts are each 10 percent. The weights are internal decisions and reviewed annually to ensure they are still relevant.[9] Libraries may vary weights based on their local situation and may also decide to vary weights between the institution's different colleges.

Past collection expenditures also provide useful budgeting data. Table 4.6 is an example of expenditures data for a past fiscal year. These expenditures result from applying a formula such as the one described above. The expenditures, arranged by academic department, provide details for one-time costs such as books, backfiles, and audiovisual items and for ongoing expenditures supporting serial titles and databases.

Consortia

Another source of budget data is the past expenditures made through a consortium. The library may apply a portion of its collection development funds, along with other libraries, in a PDA, DDA, or EBA for which the e-resources (e.g., monographs or streaming videos) acquired through the joint project are chosen by the libraries' institutional users and then become available for all participating libraries. There may be a long-standing practice of extending an individual library's purchasing power through partnerships, with the resultant benefit of realizing economies of scale.

Additional Collections Expenditures

Funds allocated for library collections may need to support the acquisition of information content and its associated processing. These expenditures for collection support vary from institution to institution. For example, the expenditures for cataloging records may be expected to be funded through the collection development budget. Shipping and service fees for the information materials acquired may also be an expenditure from the collections allocation. Annual fees for the library's membership in the Center for Research Libraries[10] or the HathiTrust[11] and membership fees for other consortial memberships may be collections expenditures. The expenditure for off-site collection storage may be assigned to the collections.

Table 4.6

Past Year Collection Expenditures for Select Academic Departments

Departments	Total of information resources, one-time costs					Total of information resources, ongoing costs									Total Expenditures
	Print	Electronic			Audio-Visual One-time Expend	Print		Electronic					Print + Online		
	Total Books Expend	Total E-books Expend	Total E-serials Backfiles Expend	Total E-Literature and other collections Expend		Total Serials Expend	Total Microforms Expend	Total E-journals (single titles) expend	Total E-books Expend	Total Aggregate Databases Expend	Total Indexes/Abstracts Expend	Total Annual Access Fees, Service Fees, & Shipping Fees	Total Serials Expend		
Biology	$1,943.73					$2,071.00		$27,916.30							$31,931.03
Chemistry	$853.60							$54,568.00		$6,870.00					$62,291.60
Computer Science	$2,131.16	$225.93				$1,168.50		$1,415.00							$4,940.59
Electrical & Computer Engineering	$1,237.94									$31,018.00					$32,255.94
Earth & Environmental Studies	$950.32	$32.99				$103.99		$6,866.00					$528.87		$8,482.17
Mathematics & Statistics	$1,663.69					$379.70		$6,280.00		$1,030.00					$9,353.39
Physics	$624.46							$15,865.00		$2,900.00					$19,389.46
MULTIDISCIPLINARY															
Databases—Science Genl										$93,465.96					$93,465.96
Other Serials—Science-Lib Interdisc									$700.00						$700.00
TOTAL	$9,404.90	$258.92	$-	$-	$-	$3,723.19	$-	$112,910.30	$700.00	$135,283.96	$-	$-	$528.87		$262,810.14

Expenditures for supplies directly related to the collection, a variable cost, are based on the information content's format and the need specified. For example, the library may require the covers and spine of paperbound print materials to be laminated to extend their usability and life span. If expenditures for processing supplies are part of the collection allocation, a library may need to place an extraordinarily large supply order toward the end of the fiscal year to ensure that there are adequate supplies to carry the library into the first four to six weeks of the fiscal year until the new budget is allocated and supplies ordered.

Every So Often...

Non-annual occurrences also influence budgeting for collections. For example, an academic program may be planning for a program accreditation. The library may need to strengthen its collection in specific subject areas to comply with the accreditor's guidelines and standards. The cost data for serials and books from information vendors enable the library to develop the necessary budget data. Academic departments may undertake program reviews on a scheduled basis (five to seven years). A finding of an academic department in its self-study document for accreditation or re-accreditation or by the visiting review team may mention the necessity of addressing insufficient library collections. Colleges and schools may also plan to add new academic programs or degrees in the near term, which may have an impact on the library's collection.

Other Sources of Data for Collections

Another source of data for budgeting collections is ILL transactions. Internal analysis of trends from ILL borrowing requests may show the need to purchase specific titles or to develop the collection in specific subject areas. If a new academic program is being planned and the library will be asked to develop a supporting collection, the library may access online the holdings catalogs of libraries with known strong collections to compile a list of information resources and consult subject bibliographies found in library research guides.

Technologies

Budgeting for technologies is more inclusive than just providing public and staff computer workstations. Library-installed technology includes microform reader and printers, interactive whiteboards, landline telephones, photocopiers, printers, teleconferencing equipment, servers, electronic gate counters, theft security systems, and security cameras. The library may also lend a myriad of technologies, including laptops, tablets, graphing calculators, headphones, digital video and still cameras, and portable storage devices such as flash drives. Technologies are not limited to just equipment and hardware. They also include productivity software, web-based applications, and physical and virtual networks supporting wired and wireless communications. The library may also be responsible for the day-to-day management of its integrated library system.

Several factors must be considered when budgeting library technologies. These include the acquisition or purchase, installation, maintenance, security, backups, upgrades, repairs, and replacement of the needed technologies. The acquisition and installation of technologies are often not recurring expenditures, and they may be capital costs depending on the institution's policy concerning acquisition costs. Purchasing and installing technologies may be the easiest to plan, especially if there is a library or institutional hardware and software purchasing process (e.g., state government–approved vendor contracts or being members of a consortium that has negotiated agreements with vendors).

A commonplace tool to facilitate planning and budgeting is a comprehensive inventory of technologies in the library. An equipment asset inventory includes a description of the equipment, purchase date, cost, serial number, physical installation (e.g., a room number or identifiable public area), and primary purpose. A best practice is to have separate inventories for equipment installed for public use, for staff use, and for loan to users. Because of the differences in the information concerning software and applications, a separate inventory helps with budgeting. Such information should include a description of the software and version installed, cost, license number, number of simultaneous users permitted, length of the license (e.g., annual or perpetual), renewal date, specifically where it is installed (e.g., specific staff member workstation and public workstations), and primary purpose. The inventory can be used to answer questions such as "How many public workstations are installed?" and "When were the interactive whiteboards purchased?"

These inventories can be sorted in a variety of ways to help with budget planning, including replacements and upgrades. For example, sorted and analyzed data from the inventory may indicate that the workstations in the instruction room will be four years old during the next fiscal year and should be considered for replacement or that the two-year license for the web-based application used to create and maintain online academic subject research guides will need to be renewed for forty simultaneous users next fiscal year.

An expenditure that a library should be able to plan and budget is equipment maintenance. Although the length of maintenance contracts may be longer than a year, the expenditures are usually stated in annual terms, which can be budgeted as fixed costs. Equipment repairs, which may be needed when the work is no longer covered by maintenance contracts, are a variable, and often unpredictable, cost. Library budget managers may anticipate the need for unexpected repairs by including a line item when developing their working budget.

Replacing broken equipment is an ongoing activity. Keeping a year-to-year list of replacements (e.g., replaced twenty keyboards and ten mice in the public workstation area during the previous fiscal year) and their costs helps a library to develop a predictive replacement schedule that informs planning and budgeting. Building a spare parts pool reduces downtime and queues and increases customer satisfaction. A library may have a policy that if a workstation cannot be fixed in fifteen minutes, it is replaced. The replacement schedule can also be used to budget for preventative maintenance activities (e.g., replacing projector bulbs before they burn out minutes before a librarian-led instruction session).

Technology-related supplies, although a variable cost, can be budgeted using past expenditures data. Consumables (e.g., paper and printer toner or ink) are recurring costs. Filaments used for 3-D printing may be the newest consumable supply appearing in library operating budgets.

Another factor when budgeting considers the expansion of technology-based services identified from the objectives and action steps in the library's strategic plan. A best practice is to plan thoroughly and to budget for expansion by considering the action steps and resources needed to implement the expansion project. For example, to add one computer workstation in a public area may require

- installation of additional electrical sockets
- installation of additional Ethernet network cabling, which may in turn require installing a new network switch
- a table and a chair
- software licenses
- a life-cycle plan to sustain the workstation by recognizing the expenditures to maintain it, providing access to upgrades to keep the workstation and applications current, and providing for repairs and for the eventual replacement of the workstation

Planning and budgeting for technology supports the long-term and short-term library plans. Developing an internal technology plan aids in managing this component of a library's infrastructure. The comprehensive inventory provides details about the current technologies available as inputs; the existing long-term plan describes the intended outcomes, such as increasing the number of mobile devices available to be loaned to students and faculty.[12] The technology plan, which may parallel the structure of the library's long-term plan, states measurable objectives and action steps, which can be budgeted. One section of the plan may cite the library's "Principles of Applying Automation to Information Resources and Services," which applies to the management of information technology and which states, in part:

- Adherence to intellectual property laws, contracts, and licenses will not be compromised.
- The technology applied should employ standards and protocols common in local, regional, national, and international environments.
- The technology deployed must increase a student's productivity, contribute to student learning, or both. An example is a SMART Board, a peer group collaboration tool that contributes to individual and group learning as well as to the group's productivity.

- The priority for acquiring automated information technologies for use by library staff should be based on the improvement of service to students and faculty. (The more directly the technology would benefit the user, the higher the priority.)
- The benefit from application of automated information technologies must at least equal the costs of application.
- The financial basis of the continuing operation of any applied automated information technologies should depend on general operating funds rather than income from grants, endowments, or gifts.

An important section of a technology plan identifies how the plan's directions would be evaluated (see box 4.2).

Box 4.2
The Evaluation Section of a Library's Technology Plan

Evaluation

The University Libraries are utilizing existing statistical measures, and seeking new ones, to evaluate their success in supporting information and learning needs by applying automated information technologies. These measures are collected and reviewed within the Libraries' statistical-based management information system.

Input measures include, but are not limited to
- number of workstations
  + public desktops
  + laptops
  + tablets (e.g., iPads)
  + e-reader devices (e.g., Kindles)
  + scanners
  + microform reader/printers
- initial and recurring costs concerning the acquisition and maintenance of technologies
- staff levels available to support the technology needs
- number of licensed databases made available for access
- number of articles in these licensed databases available for viewing or downloading
- number of online tutorials available
- availability of equipment to use in the library or to borrow
- number of public seats
  + at equipment
  + not at equipment
- number of user-available electrical outlets near public seats
- number of user-available network jacks near public seats

Output measures include, but are not limited to
- number of times the desktop workstations are used
- number of laptops loaned
- number of tablets loaned– number of e-reader devices loaned
- number of proxy server logins
- number of community guest logins
- number of sessions conducted on licensed databases
- number of pages from licensed databases downloaded or viewed
- number of full-text articles requested or downloaded
- number of searches conducted
- number of results per search (if available)
- number of online tutorials used
- number of tutorials created or maintained
- number of repairs to technologies made
- mean time to repair
- number of digital projects completed
- number of pages printed
- queue time for a user to wait for a computer (e.g., n + 1 queue)
- number of upgrades installed
- total expenditures for technologies
- number of digital products available for remote access

Outcomes
- students rate online tutorial as educational
- hardware and software is current (true or false)
- user satisfaction with technologies
- percentage uptime of technologies deployed
  + availability, in hours, of technologies deployed
- upgrades installed resulted in improved performance (true or false)
- user can access collections from all user locations
- students choose the Libraries' web interface as their starting point
  + users characterize the Libraries' interface as intuitive
  + users judge the Libraries' interface as a reason for their success
- length of time spent in the library
- amount of time user logged in

Metrics
- ratio of public computer workstations/student FTE and head count
- clock time of proxy server login (e.g., availability of resources when Libraries are closed)
- average number of search results per search
- cost per student FTE to acquire and maintain equipment each academic or fiscal year
- cost per student FTE to acquire access to licensed databases
- ratio of seats at equipment to those not at equipment

Facilities

The facility as an infrastructure component provides the physical spaces for the library's staff to provide services, programs, and functions and to support users in their educational, research, and personal pursuits.[13] The space houses the physical collections in a variety of formats along with library staff to support the availability of collections through acquisition, processing, and organizing information and knowledge resources. The facilities also contain space for staff to loan items to those needing them, to assist stakeholders in getting answers to their reference questions and receiving assistance for other needs they express, and to manage library functions (acquisitions, cataloging, ILL, and library administration). Other campus services, temporarily or permanently, may use library space to support students and faculty, such as through subject tutors, research assistants, and an information technology help desk. Space may also include instruction and seminar rooms and lecture halls, single and group study rooms, and individual walled and doored carrels providing office space for graduate teaching or postdoctoral assistants. The public use spaces complement the academic-focused spaces with a variety of seats and tables for studying, collaborating, and socializing and programming areas such as a Poetry Center, Great Good Place, and a café. The only microwave ovens available for commuter students may be housed in the public use spaces. These spaces also contain bathrooms and water fountains, vending machines, and photocopiers.

Space may also include an archive or the institution's records function and may contain special collections of unique materials or a research center for area history. As a space, the library tries to be all things to all people, or at least to provide as many services as it physically and financially can.

The facility needs to be open for many of its services and functions to be useful. For instance, the space needs actions taken by the staff to provide, at least, minimal service and assistance (e.g., ensure the lights are on and books and equipment may be borrowed or returned). Once the library, or part of it, is open, users will want to use the available technologies to support their productivity whether educationally, research, or personally based. The technology requires physical space, electricity, network jacks, electrical outlets, chairs, and maybe a table unless the person is using a mobile device. Other users, not having an immediate need for library technology, will want chairs and tables in a variety of furniture types (e.g., task and lounge chairs, single seat and group tables) in a variety of areas (e.g., quiet study areas or close to windows). They will eventually want a bathroom and something to eat or drink if they have not backpacked food and drink with them. Further, the facility spaces will need to be cleaned, including the removal of trash, the cleaning of floors and table tops, and the keeping of bathrooms usable.

Several facility expenditures relate to overhead costs. These may include cleaning the staff and user spaces and replacing burned-out lightbulbs. Maintenance and upkeep to the building and its spaces (e.g., maintaining elevators, repairing minor water leaks, and grounds upkeep) may also be overhead costs. Expenditures for utilities (e.g., electricity and water, and insurance for loss or damage) are likely overhead costs. Many institutions include such costs in their central budget, while others disaggregate costs to the units, oftentimes based on the facility's square footage.

Capital costs are often planned and budgeted a fiscal year or two before the items covered are implemented. These costs usually involve one-time facility projects or major repairs. Expenditures for the renovation of public or staff areas, done infrequently, are typically classified as capital costs. Purchasing new furniture, such as chairs and tables, could be a capital expenditure, as would the installation of a new internal camera security system or the improvement external lighting around and nearby the library.

The sources of data to use for planning and budgeting for facilities come from the central facility department, which uses software to compile and store information about spaces. A library may be asked to provide input data into the centralized space inventory program. The inventory also includes the location and physical sizes (in square feet) of desks, lounge and other chairs, file cabinets for staff, tables, one- to four-seat carrels, and other items in the user and staff spaces. It will also contain information about the interior and exterior utilities (e.g., electrical, natural gas, air handlers, voice and data networks, ventilation and air conditioning, water, sewage and drainage pipes). This information may be transferred onto a large-format floor map, similar to a blueprint, and may be available or accessible to library personnel. These detailed floor plans can oftentimes be reduced in size and provided to the library in electronic form to use as a source of detailed information (e.g., room number) when the library needs to contact facilities to report building problems. A library might use these floor plans to identify the locations of recurring water leaks.

As a best practice, the library should develop its own inventory of facility information, organized by physical area. For example, if the library does not have access to the institutional facilities database, it may want to include the location (room number) and square feet of staff offices and areas. The furnishings for each staff area would also be included. The largest part of the inventory would be data about the public areas and would include detailed information describing seating, tables (e.g., size and if mobile), equipment (may include information from the technology inventory), and other items such as mobile whiteboards. Inclusion of dates of purchase and costs are informative if they are known. With this information, the library can state that it has X number of totals seats, with Y number of seats at equipment and Z number of seats at four-person tables. Managers can also track furniture as users move it throughout the library; such movement may indicate that the furniture's expected location is not as useful as where it repeatedly ends up.

As already noted, keeping the library open requires staff. Equipment and software are available to capture entrances and exits at the library's public doors.

These data can be captured on an hourly basis and summarized in monthly and annual reports. Table 4.7, an example of a summary of monthly entrance gate counts from daily reports by hour during a fiscal year, provides details by month (e.g., the three busiest days of the month, three busiest hours of the day, and slowest hours of the day). Such data inform staffing. For example, the library is busiest from 10:00 a.m. to 3:00 p.m. on Mondays, Tuesdays, and Wednesdays. The data can also be used to trigger observations of whether there are enough seats during the busiest times. If more seats or tables are needed to meet user needs, or if a different type of seat or table (e.g., mobile tables that can be moved together to accommodate large study groups or for group projects) is needed, a measurable objective can be developed and budgeted.

Conclusion

Library facilities are undergoing a transformation. This process began as technologies were developed and installed, as libraries shifted from print to electronic content, and as access shifted from physical formats, such as CDs, to network-delivered resources. Additionally, libraries have shifted their focus from providing space for collections to maximizing the effectiveness of their space for users, such as by increasing the number of collaborative study areas and providing space for user support services, including tutoring and technology support.

A final best practice to mention is the development of an internal checklist for the budgeting process, which starts with the broad infrastructure categories and then provides additional details in each category. For example, for the staff and staffing budget category, managers should include each person's name, official title, working title, salary (if not hourly), and fringe benefits for anyone paid through the library's budget. They could group the staff by assigned library departments or by last name. For hourly staff, the wage formula presented in this chapter applies.

A checklist for collections includes both one-time and recurring expenses. One-time expenditures refer to an estimate of the dollar amount to be expended, for example, for monographs and backfiles. Recurring expenses include estimates based on the past expenditures and estimates for cost increases expected from the information vendors as reported by vendors or organizations or contained in contracts and agreements. There should also be a list of databases to be supported. Some libraries include cataloging costs and shipping costs as part of the collections expenditures; other libraries may budget and expend these costs as part of administration.

Depending on the library's past practices, other collection expenditures include cataloging costs and shipping and handling costs. Technologies appear in the checklist among items in the list detailing the equipment expected to be replaced as well as the need for licenses to support applications and software. The facilities

Table 4.7
Monthly Entrance Data from Daily Reports by Hour

	July	August	September	October	November	December	January	February	March	April	May	June
Total number of entrances for the month	14,683	24,333	70,031	70,739	54,472	30,381	42,216	52,349	45,360	58,417	8,822	12,032
Number of days open during month	26	26	29	31	26	19	27	29	28	29	24	26
Average number of entrances/days open	565	936	2,415	2,282	2,095	1,599	1,564	1,805	1,620	2,014	368	463
Three busiest days during the month	Tu 7/17; 842	M 8/31; 3,062	W 9/23; 3,867	Tu 10/13; 3,661	Tu 11/3; 3,321	W 12/2; 3,815	W 1/27; 2,682	Tu 2/9; 2,983	Tu 3.8; 2,797	Tu 4/12; 3,622	Tu 5/24; 570	Tu 6/21; 925
	Tu 7/21; 773	Th 8/27; 2,736	Tu 9/22; 3,849	Tu 10/6; 3,620	M 11/16; 3,298	M 12/7; 3,785	M 1/25; 2,631	Tu 2/; 2,788	M 3/7; 2,777	W 4/20; 3,404	Tu 5/17; 532	Tu 6/28; 749
	W 7/08; 762	W 8/26; 2,715	M 9/21; 3,769	M 10/12; 3,571	W 11/4; 3,206	Tu 12/2; 3,599	Tu 1/26; 2,625	M 2/1; 2,704	Tu 3/22; 2,700	Tu 4/26; 3,332	Tu 5/31; 526	M 6/20; 600
Three busiest hours during the month	11 a-noon; 1,758	noon-1p; 2,892	noon-1p; 7,764	noon-1p; 7,366	noon-1p; 5,723	noon-1p; 3,072	noon-1p; 5,262	noon-1p; 5,991	noon-1p; 4,925	noon-1p; 5,642	11-noon; 1,028	10-11a; 1,439
	1-2p; 1,709	11a-noon; 2,604	10-11 a; 6,688	10-11a; 6,503	10-11a; 5,194	1-2p; 2,528	2-3p; 4,304	2-3p; 5,260	2-3p; 4,604	2-3p; 5,168	1-2p; 971	1-2p; 1,373
	noon-1p; 1,464	10-11a; 2,545	2-3p; 6,284	2-3p; 6,309	2-3p; 4,852	10-11a; 2,478	10-11a; 4,279	10-11a; 5,189	10-11a; 4,387	10-11al; 4,888	10-11a; 526	noon-1p; 1,330
Three slowest hours during the month (outside of 2–7 a.m. during 24/5)	8-9; 218	7-8p; 1,217	11-midnight; 646	11-midnight; 707	7-8p; 464	11-midnight; 441	11-midnight; 222	11-midnight; 508	11-midnight; 394	11-midnight; 836	8-9p; 152	8-9p; 146
	7-8p; 394	8-9a; 1,429	10-11p; 1,212	10-11p; 1,322	6-7p; 828	10-11p; 696	10-11p; 461	10-11p; 887	10-11p; 779	10-11p; 1,346	7-8p; 233	7-8p; 283
	6-7p; 545	4-5; 1,547	9-10p; 1,661	9-10p; 1,957	9-10p; 1,363	9-10p; 1,007	9-10p; 692	9-10p; 1,340	9-10p; 1,141	9-10p; 2,055	6-7; 303	6-7p; 480

section of the checklist lists the furniture to be replaced and new furniture needed for the public and staff areas. Creating, maintaining, and continuously improving the checklist ensures that, during the budgeting process, no budget details are missed or forgotten.

Exercises

1. Why is it important to differentiate between expenditures and costs?
2. Staff and collections expenditures consume most of the funds allocated to the library. Where would a library manager find data about library staff and collections?
3. Do you plan and implement bottom-up or top-down budgeting?

(Answers to these questions can be found in the appendix at the back of the book. We encourage different library managers to work together, perhaps with staff members, to answer each question and to discuss the results.)

Notes

1. In some instances, libraries rearrange their facilities to make it easier for users to locate what they need, provide user-friendly signage that does not contain library jargon, and offer mechanisms for users to contact staff by text messages and other means. By engaging in such activities, libraries recognize that users rely much more on electronic than print sources and have adapted new strategies in which they gather and use information.
2. It is also important to realize that users see the library, such as its information commons, as a social center or a place to relax or study. A long-term objective for a library might be a way to support a welcoming environment.
3. For clarification, a library states that its annual cost to open the library is based solely on staff expenditures; staff are responsible for opening and closing the library. Without staff, the library is not open. Staff expenditures = $100,000. The library was open for fifty hours per week for fifty-two weeks during the fiscal year. Thus, 50 hours per week times 52 weeks equals 2,600 hours. Consequently, while staff expenditures are $100,000, this is an example of determining a cost for a service or activity rather than stating it as just an expenditure.
4. Council on Library and Information Resources, Digital Library Federation, "About the Project," Digitization Cost Calculator, 2017, http://dashboard.diglib.org/about.
5. The reason is that some institutions, particularly private higher education, both nonprofit and profit, shield salary information. A library manager may need to have specific permission to view a salary schedule. That permission may be limited to senior library administrators and those working directly with the library's payroll.
6. Many academic libraries have a subscription to *Academe* through a licensed database.
7. This portal, (American Association of University Professors, "Faculty Compensation Survey," accessed July 26, 2017, https://www.aaup.org/our-work/research/annual-report-economic-status-profession), carries a charge to subscribers.

8. See American Association of University Professors, "Sample Results," Faculty Compensation Survey, accessed July 26, 2017, https://research.aaup.org/sample-results.

9. These weights were chosen to represent the academic department's demographics (students and faculty), the average cost for a book because this formula supports the monographs budget and to recognize the cost differences among academic departments, and circulation transactions because this library wants to acquire books that will be used rather than depending upon an acquisitions procedure of "just in case" collection development. The weights can be adjusted annually if needed. For example, the library may decide to increase the weight on circulation transactions, thereby increasing the importance of usage, which, in turn, would benefit academic programs with demonstrated monographs usage.

10. Founded in 1949, the Center for Research Libraries (CRL) is an international consortium of academic and independent research libraries. It "supports original research and inspired teaching in the humanities, sciences, and social sciences by preserving and making available to scholars a wealth of rare and uncommon primary source materials from all world regions" (Center for Research Libraries, "About CRL," accessed July 26, 2017, http://www.crl.edu/about).

11. The HathiTrust, a partnership of academic and research institutions, offers a digitized collection of titles from libraries around the world. See HathiTrust homepage, accessed July 26, 2017, https://www.hathitrust.org.

12. The outputs would be the number of mobile devices loaned. The outcome, in this case, is the loaning of mobile devices to enable the students and faculty to access information from any seat rather than just the fixed-seat desktop workstations, increasing user satisfaction ("I don't want to sit at a row of computers; I want to sit where I want.") as well as reduce the number of fixed-seat desktop computers the library has to acquire, maintain, and eventually replace because the library has adopted the use of mobile devices in their place.

13. Library technologies for public use likely occupy considerable square feet.

Bibliography

American Association of University Professors. "Faculty Compensation Survey." Accessed July 26, 2017. https://www.aaup.org/our-work/research/annual-report-economic-status-profession.

———. "Sample Results," Faculty Compensation Survey. Accessed July 26, 2017. https://research.aaup.org/sample-results.

Center for Research Libraries. "About CRL." Accessed July 26, 2017. http://www.crl.edu/about.

Council on Library and Information Resources, Digital Library Federation. "About the Project," Digitization Cost Calculator. 2017. http://dashboard.diglib.org/about.

CUPA-HR. "Unweighted Median Salary by Carnegie Classification—All Institutions." Professionals in Higher Education Salary Survey: Select Data, 2017. https://www.cupahr.org/wp-content/uploads/2017/07/PHE16-Selected-Data.pdf.

HathiTrust homepage. Accessed July 26, 2017. https://www.hathitrust.org.

University of West Florida. "Enrollment by Level/Classification." Enrollment, ASPIRE: UWF's Interactive Fact Book. Accessed September 8, 2017. https://tableau.uwf.edu/views/IR-FB-Enrollment_0/LevelClassification?%3Aembed=y&%3AshowShareOptions=true&%3Adisplay_count=no&%3AshowVizHome=no.

Chapter 5

Program Budgeting

Program budgeting is an effective financial management function, which applies long- and short-term planning to programs and services and produces budget data. Such budgeting expands existing services and focuses on planning new ones. In contrast to a line-item budget, a program budget categorizes planned expenses by a program, as an activity, a service, or a function. As a management tool, an internally developed program budget can be as simple as an enhancement of a line-item budget. In an ideal form, it can be complex and identify all library costs, whether or not the charges appear in the library's recurring annual budget.

Program Budgets in General

Stakeholders do not care how much the library is budgeted for its infrastructure. Instead, they want to know how the budgeted resources are allocated to justify and support services, namely:

- What budgeted resources are allocated to each service?
- What percentages of the budget are devoted to specific programs and services (e.g., what percentage of the entire budget is assigned to cataloging)?
- What resources could be reallocated to support or expand an existing service or to start a new one?

Many library managers cannot answer these questions because they are constrained by the type of data that their line-item budgets generate, resulting in thinking of budgets and expenditures in terms of line items rather than programmatically.

The strategic objectives from the long-term plan help to determine what each program is expected to do, while the measurable action steps from the short-term plan are used to budget the program's implementation for the year. As a budgeting process, allocations originally aligned to the infrastructure are reassigned to programs. Library programs may include information services and consulting (reference), library instruction, ILL, circulation and in-house usage, collection development and maintenance, cataloging and processing, outreach programming, and library administration.

Stakeholders want to learn about how much is expended for the provision of each service. End-of-the-fiscal-year expenditures, when assigned to a program, help library managers to calculate how much a program costs to provide and to support. Coupled to service outputs, expenditures are used to calculate unit costs for the program, such as how much it costs to answer a reference question.

Each program in the program budget appears in a separate section with its assigned line-item budget allocations and past expenditures, where known. The budgets and expenditures from each program can also be summed together with other library programs. With summary expenditure data available for each program, it is possible to compare the total cost of each program and to analyze the types of costs and amount of expenditures incurred for each one. Additionally, the sum for program budgets can be compared with the library's original line-item budget, and its line-item expenditures compared with the summary for end-of-fiscal-year expenditures. Library financial managers should examine any differences between the line-item and program budget sums and their related expenditures sums to ensure the sums for allocations and expenditures have been reconciled between these two types of budgets.

Variations in Program Budgeting

Program budgeting aligns the line-item budgeted allocations and expenditures with programs, or it assigns all calculable full costs to the programs, even if the budgeted allocations are not originally assigned to the library. The types of costs that are often omitted in standard library accounting systems are overhead, depreciation, and in-kind contributions.[1] The library includes these costs, when available, to calculate the full costs for each program. For example, overhead costs (e.g., utilities, insurance, and building maintenance) are often compiled at a centralized department, and costs are charged to organizational units on a per square foot cost. The overhead costs assigned to the entire library would be charged to a program as a cost based on the percentage of physical space that the program occupies in the library even though the budget may not have been originally allocated for the overhead expenditure from the hierarchical level that oversees the library.

Depreciation is an accounting method for allocating the cost of a tangible asset over its useful life. As with overhead costs, depreciation is often calculated at the institutional level, and it is more common for depreciation costs to remain centralized rather than allocated to organizational units. Depreciation costs for the library's buildings, equipment, and furnishings will likely be the most difficult costs to find and apply for determining the full cost of each library program.

The library may be able to estimate and assign in-kind costs to programs based on the observable or measurable in-kind contributions to specific programs. For example, the in-kind contributions of labor from volunteers who reshelve books in the stacks can be estimated by summing the number of volunteer hours, multiplying that sum by the minimum wage per hour, and assigning that calculated cost to the circulation department's stack maintenance program.

Another variation relates to the extent to which the library applies program budgeting throughout the organization. The ideal program budget includes the entire library and calculates the full costs (e.g., overhead, depreciation, and in-kind) for each program. Programming the full cost, however, may be difficult because of the lack of cost data available from year to year, or even the timing of when these costs (specifically overhead and depreciation) will be charged to the library because it might be several months after the start, or end, of the fiscal year when those costs are distributed from the central unit to the organizational units. If the library undertakes a program budget process for the entire library all at once, the learning curve may dissuade managers from completing the project. Thus, a best practice is to start with one or two programs so that the process is not overwhelming. Managers can apply the process, learn about and evaluate the programs, and add additional programs as the process becomes familiar and even routine.

Example of Developing a Program Budget

For illustrative purposes, this section demonstrates the process by program budgeting one service. Program planning precedes the development of a program budget. In the planning stage (see chapter 1), goals are stated, specific objectives are established to support the goals, and the activities necessary to carry out the objective are identified. One objective is highlighted here, the activities needed to implement that objective are identified, a cost center for the program is created, the activities are aligned to budget categories from the library's line-item budget and assigned to the cost center, and budget dollar figures are allocated to the cost center's activities.

Program Budgeting and the Library's Strategic Plan

Program budgeting begins with the library's long-term plan, which, in this case, identifies the following mission statement:

> The Libraries' purpose is to provide information-related resources and services to support the University's learning, teaching, research, and community service missions. It intends to inspire the total individual, encouraging personal, social, and intellectual growth and lifelong learning through the acquisition of information and knowledge.

Two goals support the mission, one of which is to "Enhance the user experience: Foster environments through which staff provide resources, services, and programs supporting learning, teaching, and research." The first objective under this goal is for the library to "Develop and manage relevant intellectual content, balanced across appropriate information formats, to support teaching, research, and service regardless of geographic location."

This library develops its collections to meet the needs of the institution's faculty and students. A needs assessment culled from a survey preceding the adoption of the library's strategic plan, however, found that the library currently does not own or license access to every information resource that the faculty and students need. Further, the library's annual budget allocation for collections does not enable it to acquire or access every information resource that the university community needs.

Turning to the second objective under this goal, "Provide assistance to users seeking information, and for using the library and its resources, services, and programs," one intention is to assist users seeking needed information. The library accomplishes this objective, in part, by providing tools to help them find resources (e.g., the online catalog, librarian-created and -updated research guides, one-on-one and group instruction on the use of the library and its resources, and a web-based discovery application). As aforementioned, the library cannot afford to purchase every information resources needed to become locally self-sufficient. To obtain the resources that it does not have and cannot develop, the library borrows information content through interlibrary loan (ILL) from other libraries. Thus, the library created a sub-objective and two activities specifically for ILL services:

> Objective 2.2: provide interlibrary loan and document delivery services to members of the University community.
>
> – Activities
>   + 2.2.1: borrow needed resources from other libraries
>   + 2.2.2: lend resources needed by other libraries

The library applies program budgeting to plan and budget for ILL services as a distinct program within its internal budget.

Program Budgeting and the Budget

The program budgeting process and the resultant document identifies the source of funds, notes what resources are needed to conduct the activity, assigns resources to program-based budget categories, describes measures of success, and provides metrics of effectiveness and of sustainability. ILL is a critical service for supporting the information needs of the library's stakeholders. The library realizes that it is unable to afford every information resource required to meet user needs from its collections. The need for ILL services, therefore, is continuous. Consequently, the only source of funds programmed for ILL services originates from the annual operating or recurring budget allocation. This program cannot depend on one-time funding.

The resources needed to provide ILL services are not difficult to identify. The following groups of resources become the budget categories with details within the program budget document:

- **Personnel.** Most of the programmed budget for ILL may be assigned to personnel. Details should include a row for each person working on ILL services by job title, describing what the job involves, and that person's annual salary. Fringe benefits are likely earned if the job position is full-time and should be included on the row. If a full-time staff person splits time in another program (e.g., 25 percent of one's time is in the reference program), this individual's salary and fringe benefits must be calculated as a ratio based on the amount of time spent in ILL. There may also be part-time personnel assigned to ILL, including student assistants. Again, there would be a row for each job responsibility, and if it is a "general" job description shared by two or more staff or assistants, the number of personnel is indicated along with the hours per week and the hourly wage. As a best practice, assign one row to each person working in ILL even if more than one person occupies one job title. For example, two staff members may have the job title of Interlibrary Loan Technician. Assigning a row for each person, even though they share a job title, provides an easy way to visualize the entire staffing needed and utilized for the service.
- **Equipment.** ILL services make intensive use of technology. Workstations are used to process and fill requests. Printers, as well as flatbed scanners with automatic document feeders, are used. Libraries with high volume of lending information content through ILL may have access to book scanning equipment. Budget may be allocated for replacement equipment as necessary, and the program may fund its own spare parts pool for broken equipment, such as mice.
- **Software.** ILL is a software-intensive activity. Productivity software includes spreadsheets and word processing, along with image management software, to accommodate document and other image formats received from other libraries. An annual license may be required to support the software used in this program.

- **Contractual services.** The program budget recognizes the contractual services used in this program. Institution-supplied services, which are annually budgeted through the library, may include telecommunications support for telephones and fax machines. Other contractual services may include equipment maintenance for the program's workstations and scanning equipment. Licenses and subscriptions such as ILLiad/Tipasa[2] and service charges from OCLC are also included as contractual services support for ILL services.
- **Supplies and materials.** ILL consumes supplies throughout the year. Paper is used for printing, and mailing envelopes and book pouches are used for shipping physical items between libraries and to the end users.
- **Shipping and postage.** ILL may be responsible for mailing physical information items to those users physically remote from the campus. If a pick-up and drop-off courier service for area libraries is not available, the library may have to pay the costs to ship materials to other libraries.
- **Staff training and development.** Staff should have opportunities for their development throughout the fiscal year. Costs may include registration fees for conferences and workshops and associated travel.
- **Marketing and public relations.** Budget may be allocated to ILL to advertise its services on campus. This may include advertisement space in the student newspaper or posters or signage to increase awareness of various services offered.
- **Copyright.** Depending on the library's current practices, copyright fees may be assigned to ILL, when necessary, to support downloading articles or other information content. This cost can be difficult to budget due to the annual variable volume of material requested for copyright compliance. Analysis of past expenditures, however, provides a good estimate.

Other costs that may be included in ILL's program budget include

- **Indirect.** A share of the library's administrative costs based on a formula may be applied to the program. For example, if the indirect costs formula is based on the number of staff full-time equivalents in a program, a share of administrative costs may be based on the ratio of staff assigned to ILL to those working in the entire library.
- **Overhead.** A share of the centralized utilities and insurance costs for the library may be charged to the ILL program as a percentage of the physical square footage occupied.
- **Depreciation.** ILL is often a discrete physical space within the library that has furniture (desks and chairs, file cabinets, wall-mounted shelving, sorting tables, and book carts). The institution may apply an annual depreciation schedule on these furnishings, which could be applied to the program.

Program Budgeting and Metrics

Outputs and outcomes are important metrics for determining any program's effectiveness and efficiency, and such metrics are important for ILL, which is an ongoing, year-to-year service.

- Relevance metrics of success for ILL, which are usually quantitative, include the percentage of how many interlibrary loans were requested and successfully filled; this yields a fill/unfilled ratio. Another metric is the average processing time to yield a fill. Filling an ILL request for a faculty member may take several attempts.

- Effectiveness metrics for ILL include customer-stated satisfaction with the service, the number of repeat users of the service, and acknowledgement from authors in publications citing the ILL for its assistance in obtaining the necessary resources to support their scholarly endeavors. Another metric is that the cost per successful ILL request is less than the cost for the library to purchase the information resource. This metric requires the library to calculate the cost to fill an information request through ILL. (Chapter 8 discusses the calculation of this cost.)

- Sustainability metrics try to demonstrate that ILL, a mission-critical service, is worth doing every year. One metric is that borrowing an item through ILL remains cost-effective compared to purchasing the requested information resource. A second metric is that the data from the library's requests to borrow items are used for collection development decision making. ILL requests can point to collection weaknesses that should be addressed. For example, if there is an unusually large volume of borrowing requests for information content in a specific topic area, such as consumer behavior, the library should review this area of the library's collection and consider strengthening it.

Program Budgeting Template

Table 5.1, an example of a simple program budget template for the ILL program, is divided into four sections: PERSONNEL SALARIES and WAGES, NON-PERSONNEL, OTHER COSTS, and EXPECTED MEASURES of SUCCESS. Additional rows for detail are added to each section as needed. Personnel, in the first section, includes full-time, part-time, and student assistants. Full-time staff are budgeted for the entire fiscal year. If staff members split their time with another library department or program, however, only the percentage of time working in the ILL is budgeted when using this template. A more detailed template could indicate the percentage of time for each person assigned to the program in a column; for this template, it could be included as narrative in the personnel column under Responsibilities. The shaded parts of the table, such as fringe benefits for part-time personnel and student assistants, are not expected to be filled out. The budgeted costs for each person are calculated in the last column on the right.

The non-personnel costs are those expected during the fiscal year to support the personnel and the program. Some of the rows may not be used by all ILL programs or for each fiscal year. For example, not every ILL program purchases equipment each year or allocates budget annually for marketing its services. Contractual services would likely have rows detailing telecommunications costs and charges or fees for ILL services, including those from a bibliographic utility, if applicable. Supplies could add rows for printer paper and mailing envelopes.

Table 5.1

Program Budget Template

Objective 2.2: Provide interlibrary loan and documents delivery services to members of the University community.

Program: Interlibrary Loan Services
 – Activities
  + 2.2.1—borrow needed resources from other libraries
  + 2.2.2—lend resources needed by other libraries
Source of funding: annual recurring operating budget

PERSONNEL SALARIES and WAGES	Job Title	Responsibilities	Fiscal Year Salary	Hours per Week	Wage per Hour	Fringe Benefits	Total per Person Budgeted
Full-Time	Person 1		$			$	$
	Person 2		$			$	$
Part-Time	Person 1			$	$		$
	Person 2			$	$		$
Student Assistants	Person 1			$	$		$
	Person 2			$	$		$
NON-PERSONNEL	Vendor	Description					Budgeted
Equipment							$
Software							$
Contractual Services							$
Supplies and Materials							$
Shipping and Postage							$

Staff Training and Development						$
Marketing and PR						$
Copyright						$
OTHER COSTS		Description				Cost Assigned
Indirect						$
Overhead						$
Depreciation						$
TOTAL BUDGETED						$
EXPECTED MEASURES of SUCCESS	**Number of Item Requests Expected to Be Borrowed from Other Libraries**		**Number of Items Requests Expected to Be Lent to Other Libraries**			
Books	1,200		3,000			
Articles	3,200		10,000			
TOTALS	4,400		13,000			
Net Lender or Borrower?			Expected to Be Net Lender			

The section on OTHER COSTS may not appear in many program budgets. If the information is available, it should be included so that the library can determine the full costs of the program. The row labeled TOTAL BUDGETED is the sum of the budgets from the previously mentioned three sections. This sum is the expected expenditures for the service: the cost for the ILL program.

The last section on the template displays an example of metrics of success. For this program, the number of expected borrowed and lent items is the most important. This template does not differentiate between expected filled and unfilled requests. Processing requests to lend materials that are not fulfilled for a variety of reasons (e.g., the resource is in circulation or is lost) still places a workload burden on library personnel; they must look for the item requested and report back to the requestor that it is unfilled.

Table 5.2 is an example of an output metric of success for ILL from the previous fiscal year. Any such metrics are included in the library's ILL budget for the previous fiscal year. Once the outputs are compiled after the fiscal year ends, they are used with data about the program's expenditures to create cost data for the program. (Chapter 8 more thoroughly discusses the creation of cost data from expenditures and outputs.)

Table 5.2
ILL Measures of Success from Previous Fiscal Year

Borrowing Items from Other Libraries			
	Filled	Unfilled	Fill Ratio (%)
Book requests	1,431	422	77.2
Article request	3,447	250	93.2
Document delivery (through commercial services)	0	0	
Totals	4,878	672	
Lending Items to Other Libraries			
Book requests	1,794	2,763	39.4*
Article requests	4,756	9,600	33.1*
Totals	6,550	12,363	

*Note: These percentages do not represent a summed percentage. A summed fill rate would be the percentage of 6,550 filled and 12,363 unfilled. So, the overall fill rate is only 34.6% and the unfilled rate is 65.4%.

Success can be viewed from different perspectives. When borrowing items from other libraries, the fill ratio is higher for articles than it is for books. Second, based on the metrics of success in the program budget, the number of requests to borrow items, a total of 5,550 (see table 5.2),[3] may be above or below the library's expectations. Further, the library may have planned to request fewer items through the ILL program than the output at the end of the fiscal year. Third, after comparing the number of requests to borrow from other libraries to the number of filled requests lent to other libraries, this library is a net lender, meaning that it borrowed fewer items (4,878) than it loaned (6,550).[4]

Effectiveness and sustainability metrics are qualitative and not well-suited to presentation in a table. Both program metrics may appear in narrative form in the library's annual report. These metrics may be used as decision-making inputs for the next fiscal year's budget cycle as outcomes of an evaluative analysis. For example, library managers may decide that a subject area of the collection must be strengthened if they intend to reduce the number of requests to borrow items in that specific subject area from other libraries. This decision directly affects the funds allocated in the collections program. This decision specifically to build the collection, however, may not be considered when budgeting ILL even though the expectation is to reduce the number of requests to borrow information items from other libraries. The library may wait to review the borrowing request data related to this collection area until the end of the fiscal year to determine if there was a measurable impact on the ILL program from strengthening this subject area of the collection.

Conclusion

Program budgeting as a process helps to organize the library's budget allocations into programs that more directly support the library's goals, objectives, and activities in the long-term plan than does a line-item budget. The program often, but not always, budgets parts of the infrastructure. Allocating funds aligned to a program budget places the emphasis on what is to be accomplished rather than on the infrastructure inputs necessary to support a library's services and functions. In this format, there is accountability in terms of fiscal responsibility and in the extent to which program objectives are achieved. Politically, the move to this type of accountability yields aligned and measurable outputs of the dollars allocated for library services. This process can help the library explain to its stakeholders what it does and how much is budgeted for each program.

The program budgeting process can also be used to plan and budget for the expansion of existing programs and services or to add new ones. To do this, managers refer to the objectives and supportive activities in the long- and short-term plans. They apply the template in the process described in this chapter to determine the needed funds aligned with the appropriate budget categories for the expanded or new program, and then identify relevant metrics for success, effectiveness, and sustainability.

Annual objectives and their related activities are subject to continuous review so that managers can make adjustments to programs as they address changing conditions. This information derived from the short-term plans informs the long-term planning by applying the systems model (see figure 2.1). However, a limitation to program budgeting recognizes that, while it organizes budget allocations into programs and is used to develop cost information and data (see later chapters), it does not directly answer questions relating to the quality of service.

Exercises

1. Create a program budget outline for librarian-led library instruction. In doing so, complete the following steps:
    - Use a library's existing mission statement.
    - Create a library goal that would include library instruction.
    - Create a library objective for that goal.

- Create at least one activity to support the objective.
- Identify the budget categories for the program's budget and the detail necessary to allocate budgeted funds.
- List one measure each for its success, effectiveness, and sustainability.

Explain how this program may be used by the library to inform the long-term plan. What can the library do with this information?

2. Create a program budget outline for developing the collections. To do this, use a library's existing mission statement from this chapter's first question and then
   - Create a library goal that would include collection development.
   - Create a library objective for that goal.
   - Create at least one activity to support the objective.
   - Identify the budget categories for the program's budget and the detail necessary to allocate budgeted funds.
   - List one metric for success, one for effectiveness, and one for sustainability.

   Explain how this program may be used by the library to inform the long-term plan.

3. Explain how the program budget for the ILL program highlighted in this chapter can be improved.

(Answers to these questions can be found in the appendix at the back of the book. We encourage different library managers to work together, perhaps with staff members, to answer each question and to discuss the results.)

Notes

1. An in-kind contribution is a gift of services or goods that the library would have had to purchase if it had not been donated. An example is volunteers donating their time to the library.
2. ILLiad/Tipasa is resource-sharing management software from OCLC that automates routine ILL functions.
3. This number is the sum of filled borrows (4,878) and unfilled borrows (672).
4. From table 5.2, this is the total number of filled items lent.

Chapter 6

Managing a Budget during the Fiscal Year

An important financial function is the management of the library's budget during the fiscal year. By monitoring budget expenditures throughout the twelve-month period, managers ensure that funds are expended for their intended purpose, in the correct amounts (not overexpending the allocation), and can reconcile errors (e.g., transposed numbers or expenditures assigned to the wrong budget category). Financial managers may encounter conflicting roles and responsibilities during the fiscal year when they consider both the library's overall and long-term directions and the details of implementing the short-term budget.

Financial managers partner with business officers and others with direct financial management responsibilities to become familiar with the expenditures and reporting processes, including the mechanics of comparing the library's budget allocations with the expenditures and how budget categories and expenditures may affect each other (e.g., limitations and restrictions for transferring allocated funds between categories). While library financial managers master the details of the expenditures process, they must avoid micromanaging the personnel involved with the financial procedures. Further, as the chapter discusses, although the library plans for the long term, managers with financial responsibilities monitor internal control tools concerning the short-term fiscal year expenditures and reporting processes.

Control: A Technical Term and Function

Financial control is the technical processes involving budgetary control, expenditures review and analysis, and reconciliation. To further accountability and transparency, library managers with financial responsibilities increasingly spend time on systematic budget review, analyzing and evaluating expenditures to justify what has been expended and why, and applying this information as feedback to the planning and preparation for the next budget cycle.

To determine how efficiently they are using library resources, financial managers measure how many units of inputs (e.g., staff hours) are being used to produce a unit of output (e.g., the number of circulation transactions). Organizational controls are important in reviewing the quality of services so that the library can make continuous improvements to quality. This process helps managers to keep the organization more responsive to library users by maintaining a control system to evaluate how well customer-contact employees perform their jobs.

An effective control system is flexible and enables managers to respond as necessary to unexpected events, to provide accurate information, and to do so in a timely manner. Managers apply the system in four steps:

1. Review the standards of performance, goals, or targets against which the performance is to be evaluated. Standards of performance measure efficiency, quality, and responsiveness, and they are contained in organizational goals or in detailed job descriptions or expectations. Both managers and employees should create and agree on performance standards.

2. Measure actual performance by counting outputs and observing employee accomplishments.

3. Compare and analyze actual performance against the chosen standards of performance. For example, a library has spent 90 percent of its non-personnel budget (e.g., supplies) at the end of the third quarter of fiscal year. Expending this percentage of the non-personnel budget with three months left to go may be alarming to many, as they ask, "Will the library run out of funds before the end of the fiscal year?"[1] To avoid that concern and having to deal with this question, managers should plan at the beginning of the fiscal year that all of the non-personnel funds will be expended before the end of the fiscal year, ensuring that orders placed will be received in time to be expensed in the fiscal year they were ordered.

4. Evaluate the result of the comparison in meeting the objective and fulfilling the standard, and initiate corrective action if the standard is not being met.[2] The evaluation step returns managers to the first step in

planning in the system model (see figure 2.1). Two factors to consider in evaluation are the inputs which are the amount of resources involved, and the outputs which are the quantities of service.

Control functions provide financial managers with guidance and structure for implementing and monitoring the budget throughout the fiscal year. In an academic library, the three most commonly used financial management control functions are tools, policies, and processes for monitoring budget expenditures.

Control Tools

Academic library financial managers likely use one or two of four common control tools: a single-entry accounting system, a dual or double-entry accounting system, program evaluation and review technique (PERT), or operations research (OR). The library, however, may not be empowered to choose the tool; the decision as to which one will be implemented may be made at the institutional level and passed down to the organizational unit.

A single-entry accounting system is based on cash flow into and out of the library's accounts. The transactions involve deposits into the account while checks or charges remove money from the account. Each transaction is assigned one account number: one for the income and the same one for the expenses paid. This accounting method, sometimes referred to as the "cash basis" method, resembles personal bookkeeping.

A double-entry accounting system is most commonly used in higher education institutions. Finances are categorized as revenue, liabilities, and expenses. The easiest explanation of a liability is a purchase order that has been sent to a vendor, but the items ordered have yet to arrive or be paid for, therefore incurring a liability or a promise to pay. There is an equation for this accounting system:

$$\text{balance} = \text{income} - (\text{expended} + \text{expected})$$

Each transaction made is assigned to a chart of account numbers for each side of the equation. Using two account numbers provides the system with its name: dual entry. The important characteristics of the process are that all financial transactions are entered into a journal and then periodically posted to the general ledger; a summary of transactions is commonly made available for review through the BSR (budget status report). Financial managers monitor the BSR to ensure accounting entries are made to the correct categories (e.g., equipment is not charged to collections) and that the numbers entered are accurate (e.g., not transposed, which can happen when dealing with hundreds of entries). A commonly applied variation of the dual-entry accounting system is the "modified accrual" basis because this methodology recognizes liabilities as expenses when the liability is incurred (e.g., when the order is placed).

Two other tools are also used, although less often than dual-entry accounting. PERT, also known as CPM (critical path method), is a method of planning and scheduling work that is used primarily for one-time events (e.g., renovation projects). The critical element is the time it is expected to take to do something; a manager makes decisions on which activities to undertake based on the time frames estimated and the ability to do necessary activities sequentially or simultaneously. A simple example would be the activities related to renovating a public use area. The library may paint the walls in the area before installing the floor covering, and install furniture only after the floor covering is installed. A new ceiling may be installed at the same time the walls are being painted. A Gantt chart, a type of bar chart, helps to visualize the activities for a project using PERT or CPM. Using specialized software, managers can create PERT charts, or they can use a spreadsheet to generate a PERT chart manually. Figure 6.1 is an example of a PERT chart.

Figure 6.1
A PERT Chart

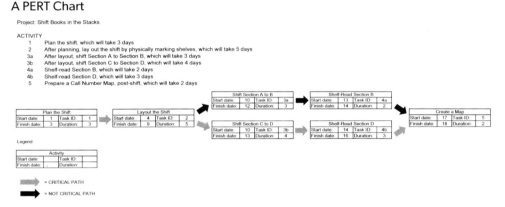

Operations research (OR), also known as systems analysis (SA), applies scientific methods to study the functions of an organization to develop better methods of planning and controlling changes in an organization. Its purpose is to assist decision makers in choosing preferred future choices of action by systematically identifying and examining the alternatives that are available to managers and predicting the outcomes for such actions. The emphasis is on math and statistics rather than management judgment.

Personnel are critical in managing and implementing library budgets and expenditures. Although it sounds awkward, there are a couple of positive control tools for managing personnel arising from both management and leadership theories. First, managers can empower staff with the authority to make decisions, be responsible for their outcomes, improve quality, and cut costs. This delegation increases a manager's ability to get things done and staff involvement and commitment.

Additionally, managers can motivate staff members. Numerous motivation theories and practices might be relevant. Briefly, motivating staff helps to define work goals that are clear, challenging, and attainable and to create supportive work environments that reinforce performance and are personal; managers should adopt a management style that accommodates individual approaches to workers based on a system of individual-related inducements rather than across-the-board inducements. Managers can also provide an organizational environment that releases the capacity for work through training and career development. A key to the development of such an environment is a managerial commitment to participatory management, in which employees are involved in sharing information, making decisions, solving problems, planning projects, and evaluating the results.

In brief, a manager:

- develops personnel by serving as a mentor, coach, and teacher;
- honestly appraises a person's talent and ability;
- recognizes good performance;
- involves personnel in developing and managing the budget;
- makes a difference in the lives of the personnel;
- holds personnel and himself or herself accountable;
- hires well, and retains those who are good.

Policies Influencing Financial Management

There are several policies that financial managers will likely encounter while managing a budget during the fiscal year. First, the library needs formal procurement policies and procedures. Oftentimes, these policies and procedures are delegated downward from the institution's central procurement office. Procurement policies outline when and how to conduct competitive bidding and mandate the formal process to track and oversee contract compliance. Performance is measured in terms of institutionally stated standards. For example, replacing a library's integrated library system is a large acquisition, which is likely required to be bid for by two or more industry competitors. A standard in the contract states that the system should not experience loss of availability (downtime) measured in hours of more than 1 percent annually. Failing to meet this standard would result in the library not having to pay a stated percentage of the vendor's annual maintenance charge.

Another policy is risk management, which integrates recognizing risk, assessing risk, and developing strategies to manage risk. The objective is to reduce different risks in a preselected domain to the level accepted by the institution. A risk management review process may identify numerous types of threats caused by the environment, technology, humans, organizations, and politics. Traditional risk management is focused on risks stemming from physical or legal causes (e.g., natural disasters or fires, accidents, death, and lawsuits). Personnel from the institution's risk management office may visit the library to ensure it is reducing exposure to risk. Library financial managers may be required to expend funds to remedy one or more risks found. A simple example is that the library may need to install additional electric power outlets to reduce the number of power strips used in the facility that may pose a fire or hazard risk (e.g., tripping over electric extension cords or strips).

Institutional risk managers might ask the library to place a value on its collections in the event of partial or total loss. Table 6.1 is an example of a simple valuation report of the print collection for risk management.[3] The total number of print volumes is calculated by counting the number of volumes in the collections at the end of the previous fiscal year, recording the number of additions and withdrawals from the collections, and subtracting a .5 percent expected annual theft loss from the collection.[4] The number of print collection volumes are summed for the three libraries, and the valuation is calculated by multiplying the summed number of volumes by the average value per volume as reported in the *Library and Book Trade Annual*. Thus, as shown in the table, a value of $73.34 per volume totals $52,566,812.

Table 6.1
Print Collection Valuation Report for Risk Management

(Per your request, here are the statistics for holdings as of June 30, 2016, for the John C. Pace Library, the Emerald Coast Campus Library, and the Professional Studies Library, University of West Florida.)

John C. Pace Library	
Size of basic collection as of June 30, 2015	684,194
Additions to the collection in 2015–2016	3,145
Withdrawn volumes in 2015–2016	11,353
Estimated losses in 2015–2016 (.5% of basic collection)	3,437
Net additions in 2015–2016	−11,645
Size of basic collection as of June 30, 2016	672,549

Emerald Coast Campus Library	
Size of basic collection as of June 30, 2015	33,064
Additions to the collection in 2015–2016	170
Withdrawn volumes in 2015–2016	0
Estimated losses in 2015–2016 (.5% of basic collection)	166
Net additions in 2015–2016	4
Size of basic collection as of June 30, 2016	33,068

Professional Studies Library	
Size of basic collection as of June 30, 2015	11,129
Additions to the collection in 2015–2016	339
Withdrawn volumes in 2015–2016	273
Estimated losses in 2015–2016 (.5% of basic collection)	57
Net additions in 2015–2016	9
Size of basic collection as of June 30, 2016	11,138

Totals	
John C. Pace Library	672,549
Emerald Coast Campus Library	33,068
Curriculum Materials Library	11,138
Total volumes	716,755

Value at $73.34 per volume*   **$52,566,812**

*The source for this amount is table 5, "U.S. College Books: Average Prices and Price Indexes 1989, 2012–2014," compiled by Frederick Lynden, in *Library and Book Trade Almanac*, ed. Dave Bogart, 60th ed. (Medford, NJ: Information Today, 2015), 431.

Procedures concerning when to lease versus purchase are another example of a financial management policy. Most often associated with equipment, these policies consider the life cycle of a program or technology, including the investigation of the purchase and its acquisition, negotiation of price and contract terms, installation, staff training to use it, maintenance over time, evaluation of its efficiency and effectiveness, and its eventual upgrade, migration to another system or vendor, replacement with a different technology, or abandonment as being no longer needed. Libraries may have an option to lease or purchase based on a financial analysis of the life cycle. For example, a major factor in the decision may be the acquisition cost; the library may be unable to afford the cost to purchase and, instead, may have to lease.

Some libraries have financial policies for outsourcing or otherwise contracting for services. Although many institutions centralize services (e.g., cleaning the facilities and providing police security), some libraries are responsible for arranging and financially supporting these services. Financial managers may decide to outsource these and other services to a third party. Libraries outsourcing a function to a company, for example, may avoid the direct costs for personnel fringe benefits.

A long-time library financial policy and practice is to maintain membership in library consortia, which provide mechanisms to share costs of automated technologies (integrated library systems), to purchase supplies from a vendor at a discount, and to lease or otherwise subscribe to information content, such as through databases. An objective of many of these consortial partnerships is for their members to realize cost savings through economies of scale.

Monitoring Budget Expenditures

A primary responsibility for financial managers is to monitor the expenditures of the budget allocations during the fiscal year. Such monitoring is not difficult, and it becomes much easier with experience. Much of this work is completed through the library's business office, which as an administrative unit may include accountants, human resource managers, and procurement specialists.

The monitoring process involves five steps. The first one is to keep accurate records of the funds allocated, when and why funds have been encumbered (e.g., in September, encumbered funds are needed to pay for database licenses), when the invoices arrive and are due to be paid, when each invoice is paid, and the ongoing balance of funds available by budget categories and subcategories.

In the second step, managers need to reconcile library expenditures with those recorded in institution or division financial reports through tools such as budget status reports (BSRs). They are looking for errors (e.g., expenses charged to the wrong budget category or subcategory or transposed numbers). They should make corrections at least monthly because an error carried forward from month to month deeper into the fiscal year becomes much harder to find and fix as more expense transactions occur and as the fiscal year's closing processes begin.

During the third step, managers track expenditures to the library's expected spending plan by calculating the percentage of expenditures of the budget based on the progression of the fiscal year and by comparing the percentage of expenditures to the budget line by line to ensure expenditures are on track. To this end, table 6.2 is a portion of a weekly internal expenditures report for services and utilities. This library's fiscal year runs from July 1 until June 30. The report is dated mid-April, which means the fiscal year ends in approximately ten weeks, or, as stated in percentages, less than 20 percent of the year remains. Financial managers reviewing this table would conclude that there is more than adequate funding remaining for subcategories such as for External Printing, Postage, and Gasoline. Expenditures are right on schedule for Telephone Charges, and all of the budget for Hiring and Parts and Fittings (minor facility-related repairs) has been expended. Based on this report, the library has 33.4 percent of this budget category available for expenditure for the remaining 20 percent of the fiscal year.

Table 6.2

Expenditure Percentages during the Fiscal Year

As of mid-April		Budget	Expended	Variance Remaining	% Variance Remaining
Account Codes	**Services/ Utilities**				
70251	External Printing	$500.00	$107.04	**$392.96**	78.5
70255	Central Copying Charges	$1,000.00	$425.89	**$574.11**	57.4
70010	Postage	$1,000.00	$151.11	**$848.89**	84.9
70011/70012	Freight/ Shipping	$150.00	$82.85	**$67.15**	44.8
70052	Hiring (Employment Ads & Job Opp)	$470.00	$470.00	**$–**	0.0
70203	Telephone Charges	$350.00	$289.40	**$60.60**	17.3
70204	Telephone Equipment Installation	$125.00	$76.80	**$48.20**	38.6
70205	Telephone Equipment & Line Charges	$11,500.00	$8,462.50	**$3,037.50**	26.4
70459	Parts & Fittings	$197.23	$197.23	**$–**	0.0
70501	Gasoline	$75.00	$16.55	**$58.45**	77.9
70760	Nautilus Card Fees	$180.00	$135.00	**$45.00**	25.0
70901	Repairs & Maintenance, Work Orders	$250.00	$148.05	**$101.95**	40.8
Subtotal—Services & Utilities		**$15,797.23**	**$10,562.42**	**$5,271.60**	**33.4**

In the fourth step, managers become aware of the budget and expenditure time schedules and procedures established higher up in the hierarchy. The institution sets deadlines to have the necessary expenditures information completed for reporting to its stakeholders and for auditing and other compliance purposes. Noncompliance with deadlines is a sure way to fall afoul of key institutional financial officers.

In the last step, the library financial managers recognize that they may not have all twelve months of the fiscal year to expend the funds allocated. For example, the collections budget will be closed the day the fiscal year ends. Those information resources ordered but not yet received or invoiced as of the last day of the fiscal year may not be expensed against the fiscal year in which it was ordered. For example, if the library has $30,000 in outstanding book orders at the end of the fiscal year, that liability may be forwarded to the next fiscal year and the unexpended funds returned to the institution. The result is that the library will begin the next fiscal year with a $30,000 liability to be paid. Library financial managers may, therefore, plan to expend all of the allocated funds for collection development in the first ten months of a fiscal year to avoid having outstanding liabilities when the fiscal year ends.

Conclusion

Best practices facilitate the functions for managing a budget during the fiscal year. First, managers should assign personnel specifically to business office functions (e.g., accounting or bookkeeping). Second, many, if not all, of the business office personnel need not have a master's degree in library and information science, but they should have experience in accounting or bookkeeping functions. Creating and managing spreadsheets, for example, is a necessity. Third, the library business office personnel need to be knowledgeable about financial processes and functions. They must also be personable with their colleagues in the institution's business offices because inevitably the library's business office will work with its central offices' counterparts during the fiscal year.

Fourth, and most importantly, library managers must create a separation of accountability in the library's business functions, avoiding the "all eggs in one basket" practice. Business office responsibilities need to be shared among two or more staff so that more than one person produces purchase orders, approves invoices, and reconciles budget status reports. Having a business operation staffed by a single person who is responsible for these financial functions increases the library's risk; it may result in negative audit findings, or it could result in financial fraud.

Exercises

1. How often should the library reconcile its expenditures with the institution's budget status reports, and why?
2. List at least one financial managerial practice concerning the business office that should be avoided.
3. Briefly explain the benefits of "economies of scale" to a library.

(Answers to these questions can be found in the appendix at the back of the book. We encourage different library managers to work together, perhaps with staff members, to answer each question and to discuss the results.)

Notes

1. They key point to remember is that the library planned at the beginning of the fiscal year that all orders would be placed by the end of the third quarter (end of April) to ensure they would be received in time to be processed and expensed in that fiscal year.
2. Returning to the previous bullet, if the library has expended less than 90 percent of its non-personnel budget by the end of the third quarter (standard = 90 percent; the evaluation is a comparison of meeting that ratio to the actual ratio at the end of the third quarter), the library needs to act (place more or fewer orders, depending on the situation).
3. They might also ask for additional valuation reports for special collections, physical media, and microforms.
4. Risk managers set this percentage, which may perhaps serve as a guideline for print library collections.

Bibliography

Lynden, Frederick, compiler. "U.S. College Books: Average Prices and Price Indexes 1989, 2012–2014," table 5. In *Library and Book Trade Almanac*, 60th ed. Edited by Dave Bogart, 431. Medford, NJ: Information Today, 2015.

Chapter 7

Reports and Reporting

Personnel in the library's business office review reports generated at the institutional level to monitor expenditures, and they may reformat these reports to inform library managers about the expenditures of the funds allocated for services. Library managers review these as well as other reports (e.g., those based on studies that measure throughputs and outputs); such reports inform the next year's planning. Simultaneously, the institution reviews financial reports to monitor library spending and may occasionally report aggregate expenditures to its governing body as the fiscal year progresses.

Financial reporting serves as a communications tool for internal and external purposes. After the fiscal year ends, the library reports financial data to various external stakeholders, most often to demonstrate its accountability and transparency. Annually, managers respond to surveys from professional organizations, associations, and consortia and requests from commercial entities repackaging information for consumers (e.g., college guidebooks from Peterson's Publishing). Libraries also report financial data through their institution to the Integrated Postsecondary Education Data System (IPEDS), as required by the federal government. Additionally, libraries may provide:
- reports required by regional accrediting organizations;
- financial data to support academic program reviews.

Internal Reporting

As chapter 6 discussed, much of the expenditures process is conducted through the library's business office operations, an administrative unit, with accountants or bookkeepers and personnel specialists. It is critical for the library to monitor expenses and to reconcile internal library reports at least monthly with those made available from the institution as a function of the expenditures process, usually referred to as budget status reports (BSRs).

Table 7.1 is an example of a section of a BSR from the institution's budget office, which the library's business office would review. The table, which displays the general budget category of non-personnel expenditures, lists the account code (five-digit number such as 70353) and the title of the sub-budget categories such as General Operating Supplies. The numbers in the Current Period column are the same as the Year-to-Date column because this report is inclusive of the fiscal year to date.

Table 7.1
Example of a Budget Status Report

	Current Budget	Current Period	Year-to-Date	Encumbrance
7000 Expenditures Current Operating				
70010 Postage	$0.00	$151.11	$151.11	$0.00
70011 Freight	$0.00	$29.27	$29.27	$0.00
70012 Shipping	$0.00	$53.58	$53.58	$0.00
70052 Employment Ads & Job Opp	$0.00	$470.00	$470.00	$0.00
70154 Information Technology Services	$0.00	$61,885.48	$61,885.48	$0.00
70165 Other Contractual Services	$0.00	$22,295.00	$22,295.00	$0.00
70202 Tolls & Toll-Free	$0.00	$13.21	$13.21	$0.00
70203 State Suncom	$0.00	$289.40	$289.40	$0.00
70204 Telephone Equip Installation	$0.00	$76.80	$76.80	$0.00
70205 Dept Telephone Equip & Line Charge	$0.00	$8,462.50	$8,462.50	$0.00
70251 External Printing	$0.00	$128.67	$128.67	$0.00
70255 Central Copy Charges	$0.00	$462.89	$462.89	$0.00
70301 Office Supplies	$0.00	$2,129.73	$2,129.73	$0.00
70351 Information Technology Supplies	$0.00	$7,436.77	$7,436.77	$0.00
70353 General Operating Supplies	$0.00	$11,289.34	$11,289.34	$0.00
70355 Communication Supplies	$0.00	$20.00	$20.00	$0.00
70356 Equipment—Expense	$0.00	$10,261.95	$10,261.95	$000
70358 Furniture—Expense	$0.00	$5,375.06	$5,375.06	$0.00
70459 Parts & Fittings	$0.00	$197.23	$197.23	$0.00
70501 Gasoline	$0.00	$16.55	$16.55	$0.00
70551 Educational Supplies	$0.00	$5,820.83	$5,820.83	$0.00
70751 Subscriptions	$0.00	$14,135.47	$14,135.47	$0.00
70752 Dues & Memberships	$0.00	$12,337.64	$12,337.64	$0.00

While table 7.1 is a summary by budget sub-category, the next table (7.2) shows the details for account code 70353, General Operating Supplies, from the previous table. This report lists the expenditures by transaction date in ascending order and the vendor. The Doc. No. is a link to the invoice in electronic form. Library business office personnel ensure that the expenditure charges to this sub-category reconcile with the transactions records and that each of these expenditures belongs in this budget sub-category.

Table 7.2
Example of Detail from a Budget Status Report for General Operating Supplies

INDEX: 6292 (Library Admin) Account Code: 70353		CURRENT PERIOD TRANSACTIONS				
Transaction Date	Transaction Desc	Doc. No.	Doc. Ref. No.	Encumb. No.	Tran. Type	Transaction Amount
08-15-2016	Kent Adhesive Products Co.	S0370339			IPNI	$800.43
08-25-2016	Amazon.com Inc.	S0371235			IPNI	$13.04
08-25-2016	Amazon.com Inc.	S0371237			IPNI	$38.18
08-25-2016	Library Store Inc.	S0371239			IPNI	$426.83
09-06-2016	Amazon.com Inc.	S0379473			IPNI	$29.35
09-13-2016	Kent Adhesive Products Co.	S0380809			IPNI	$400.22
09-13-2016	Gaylord Bros Inc.	S0380838			IPNI	$43.68
09-21-2016	Library Store Inc.	S0381997			IPNC	($363.93)
09-28-2016	DEMCO Inc.	S0382886			IPNI	$38.61
09-28-2016	DEMCO Inc.	S0382888			IPNI	$174.02
09-28-2016	DEMCO Inc.	S0383136			IPNI	$163.99
10-24-2016	Information Mgmnt Services LLC	S0386833			IPNI	$54.18
11-04-2016	Amazon.com Inc	S0388654			IPNI	$295.00
11-17-2016	DEMCO Inc.	S0390101			IPNI	$623.53
11-21-2016	DEMCO Inc.	S0390291			IPNI	$1,338.01
11-29-2016	Amazon.com Inc.	S0391370			IPNI	$20.99
12-06-2016	DEMCO Inc.	S0392027			IPNI	$29.96
01-13-2017	DEMCO Inc.	I0194181			INNI	S5,007.87
01-18-2017	Kent Adhesive Products Co.	S0394893			IPNI	$1,584.06
02-08-2017	Library Store Inc	S0405527			IPNI	$78.48
03-06-2017	Info Tag Inc.	S0408875			IPNI	$77.00
03-13-2017	Gaylord Bros Inc.	S0409739			IPNI	$6428
03-29-2017	Staples	S0412651			IPNI	$87.78
04-17-2017	Staples	S0415149			IPNI	S58.52
04-19-2017	Gaylord Bros Inc.	S0415356			IPNI	$131.56
04-28-2017	Gaylord Bros Inc.	S0416703			IPNI	S73.70
					Total:	$11,289.34

The library's business office likely uses the financial data from these institutional reports to prepare a summary report for the library's financial managers. Table 7.3 is an example of a summary expenditures table that the business office provides to library management on a weekly, biweekly, or monthly schedule. The financial managers review the *variances*[1] of the planned expenditures of allocated funds (the Budget column) to actual expenditures (Expended column) to determine how well the library is aligned to the time of the fiscal year (e.g., midway through, last quarter, and last month). If the progress for expenditures is not on schedule, the library managers make adjustments by directing the business office to slow down or speed up the release of new purchase orders.

Table 7.3
Expenditure Summary for Managers

Account Code		Budget	Expended	Encumber	Variance	% Variance
	Services/Utilities					
70251	External Printing	$500.00	$128.67		**$371.33**	74.3
70255	Central Copying Charges	$1,000.00	$462.89		**$537.11**	75.7
70010	Postage	$1,000.00	$151.11		**$848.89**	84.8
70011/ 70012	Freight/Shipping	$150.00	$82.85		**$67.15**	44.8
70052	Hiring (Employment Ads & Job Opp)	$470.00	$470.00		**$–**	0.0
70202	Tolls & Toll-Free Services	$50.00	$13.21		**$36.79**	73.6
70203	Telephone Charges (State Suncom)	$350.00	$289.40		**$60.60**	17.3
70204	Telephone Equipment Installation	$125.00	$76.80		**$48.20**	38.6
70205	Telephone Equipment & Line Charges	$11,500.00	$8,462.50		**$3,037.50**	26.4
70458	Hand Tools	$15.00	$7.99		**$7.01**	46.7
70459	Parts & Fittings	$197.23	$197.23		**$–**	0.0
70501	Gasoline	$75.00	$16.55		**$58.45**	77.9
70760	Nautilus Card Fees	$180.00	$135.00		**$45.00**	25.0
70901	Repairs & Maintenance, Work Orders	$250.00	$148.05		**$101.95**	5.0
	Subtotal— Services & Utilities	**$15,862.23**	**$10,642.25**	**$–**	**$5,219.98**	**32.9**

Account Code		Budget	Expended	Encumber	Variance	% Variance
	General Operating & Office Supplies					
70301	**Office Supplies**		$2,129.73	$214.26		
70351	**Information Technology Supplies**		$1,274.47	$33.40		
	IT Supplies—**Toner**		$6,162.30			
70353	**General Operating Supplies**		$6,628.35	$360.33		
	General Operating—**Binding Supplies**		$4,587.29	$471.74		
	Total Planned for 70301, 70351, & 70353	$25,000.00				
	Subtotal— Supplies	**$25,000.00**	**$20,782.14**	**$1,079.73**	**$3,138.13**	12.5

The library also reports internal efficiency output metrics that are useful as inputs for the next fiscal year's budgeting and expenditures plan. A common efficiency study reports on the workflow and time needed to complete a routine activity. As an example, a library might conduct a time-and-motion study to learn how long it takes student assistants to reshelve a cart full of books. The study might report that student assistants shelved 6,616 books from January 21 to May 13, that the total time consumed shelving these books was 5,211 minutes, and, consequently, that it took about 48 seconds to shelve each book (5,211 minutes/6,616 books).

If each cart averages 70 books to reshelve, the library can expect a student assistant to take 56 minutes to reshelve a cart of books (70 books times 48 seconds per book). This report helps the library to plan for the number of student assistant hours it needs to reshelve books annually and to review the reshelving workflow process to determine if an alternative methodology might reduce the time to shelve a cart of books. The workflow information also informs the library's time-to-reshelve metric. The library may state publicly that all books are reshelved within twelve hours of each book's return. From the results of this report, library managers may decide that to satisfy this objective requires scheduling an additional student assistant every six hours to reshelve books. This decision has an impact on the staffing budget for the next fiscal year.

Another library efficiency report might help to determine optimal staffing based on the busiest times for users to borrow books from the circulation desk during an academic year (e.g., September 8–May 8), the busiest days of the week, and the busiest hours of the day based on entrance counts. For example, in a study a library found

- Circulation checked out 88,107 items during the academic year.
- The busiest day was Monday, September 15, with 940 items checked out.
- The busiest hour was 1:00 to 2:00 p.m. on Monday, September 15, with 125 items checked out.

- The busiest months for library entrances in order were October, September, April, November, February, and March.
- The busiest day of the week was Tuesday, followed by Wednesday and Monday.
- The busiest three hours of the day were noon to 1:00 p.m., 10:00 to 11:00 a.m., and 2:00 to 3:00 p.m.

Applying the report data helps the library to plan in its efforts to maintain and even increase its efficiency. Managers can use the report to budget staff at the circulation desk, where they are most needed from 10:00 a.m. to 3:00 p.m. They may budget for an extra student assistant during those hours on Tuesdays. Because September is a busy month for circulation use and the first month for training new student assistants, library managers will want to plan and budget to staff the desk with its most experienced student assistants in September to ensure high-quality customer service. It is likely that the most experienced library student assistants receive a higher hourly wage than do new student assistants.

At the end of the fiscal year, library managers review the fund allocations (the budget) line by line within the broader budget categories against the actual expenditures to learn where variances between the budgeted amounts and expenditures occurred. Further analysis of the variances should reveal what caused them and if a change in the expenditures process is warranted. A completed and thoroughly reviewed expenditures plan becomes an input into the next fiscal year's budget-expenditure plan.

The library reports its expenditures to various institutional stakeholders, including senior administrators, faculty, and students. These reports support the library's need for oversight and accountability and often cite operational data as they identify allocations as inputs, expenditures as throughputs, and the related counts of outputs. As an example, a library reports it budgeted $100,000 for monographs, expended that amount, and purchased 1,500 titles. The report may include some details, such as the number of titles acquired by academic program or the amounts separately expended for print and e-books. The intent is to demonstrate the library's efficiency and effectiveness at managing funds allocated to meet stated service objectives. Additionally, the library may report findings to the institution from the circulation desk usage and entrances efficiency studies mentioned earlier in the chapter, pointing out the busiest times of the day and busiest months as an indicator of library use and that the library undertakes these types of studies in order to improve library services.

A library may use a management information system (see chapter 2) to compile and analyze the financial and usage inputs, processes, and outputs data to include in reports. Such systems, which have been around for decades, range in complexity from an internal library-created spreadsheet to a licensed commercial application.[2]

External Reporting

Financial reports intended for external audiences outside of the institution are brief and are used for accountability, public relations, and advocacy. These reports demonstrate the effectiveness of how the support the library receives has been used to provide services. Rather than providing details, they promote the library's accountability by summarizing inputs, outputs, and outcomes, and they may discuss the general progress toward meeting the objectives in the library's long-term plan. Public relations reporting highlights library services and what has occurred over the past year. Such reporting may also tactfully request continued or expanded support: "With support (usually funding or in-kind support from volunteers or donations), we can provide this program or service that we have identified as a critical need of our users." Advocacy reports are intended for specific stakeholders to highlight what has been accomplished through mutually beneficial partnerships. For example, a report might include an output, the expenditure of hours spent by library staff to assist community organizations (e.g., those working with the library on an information literacy program or with downtown associations on assistance to small businesses).

Financial data are used by the library to respond to survey requests from a multiplicity of sources (library consortia, professional associations and organizations, the federal government, and those providing commercial repackages of higher education data). Library consortia may ask for salary and other financial data from its member libraries and then share the data with all member libraries for internal comparisons. The Association of College and Research Libraries (ACRL), for example, conducts an annual survey, which requests financial expenditures information from all academic libraries.

Table 7.4, part of a worksheet from the annual ACRL survey, requests non-personnel expenditures data. The Association of Research Libraries (ARL), by the way, collects similar data from its member libraries. Through the US Department of Education, National Center for Education Statistics, the IPEDS Survey collects financial data annually from higher education institutions, including the Academic Libraries component.

Table 7.5 shows the IPEDS Academic Libraries (AL) component survey questions related to expenses. This survey asks for salaries and wages, fringe benefits, materials/services, and operations and maintenance expenses supporting the library. Several commercial firms, including *US News and World Report*, collect financial data about higher education institutions and repackages them for paid consumer use through guide books and online databases. Library expenditures data collected include general expenses (e.g., supplies and equipment), salaries, fringe benefits, and collection development.

Table 7.4
Part of the Worksheet for the ACRL Annual Survey Form

Expenses (exclude staff)		
	Amount	
Materials/services expenses		
One-time purchase of books, serial backfiles, and other materials	$	
E-books (if available)	$	
Ongoing commitments to subscriptions	$	
E-books (if available)	$	
E-journals (if available)		
All other materials/services cost	$	
Total materials/services expenses	calculated sum of 20, 21 and 22	
Operations and maintenance expenses		
Preservation services	$	
All other operations and maintenance expenses	$	
Total operations and maintenance expenses	calculated sum of 24–25	
Are expenses reported in Canadian dollars?		Yes (radio button)
		No (radio button)
Total Expenses		
Includes salaries and wages from all identifiable sources, includes fringe	calculated sum of lines 06 (column 2), 09, 23 and 26	
Includes salaries and wages from all identifiable sources, excludes fringe	calculated sum of lines 06 (column 2), 23 and 26	

Table 7.5
IPEDS Academic Libraries Survey for Expenses, 2016–2017

Expenses

Section II: For degree-granting institutions with library expenses >= $100,000 Library expenses should be reported for the most recent 12-month period that corresponds to your institution's fiscal year that ends before October 1, 2016.		
		Prior Year Amount
⑦Indicate the number of branch and independent libraries (exclude the main or central library).		
⑦Expenses	**Amount**	
Total salaries and wages for the library staff		
Are staff fringe benefits paid out of the library budget?		
○ No		
○ Yes	Total Fringe benefits	
Materials/services expenses		
One-time purchases of books, serial backfiles, and other materials		
Ongoing commitments to subscriptions		
All other materials/service cost		
Total materials/services expenses		
Operations and maintenance expenses		
Preservation services		
All other operations and maintenance expenses		
Total operations and maintenance expenses		
Total Expenses		
Total Expenses (minus Fringe Benefits)		

Libraries provide financial data (e.g., staff and collections expenditures) for academic programs or departments undergoing scheduled program reviews. Additionally, many accrediting organizations, both program and regional, require financial data from the library demonstrating its compliance with minimum guidelines such as collection development and maintenance and its having adequate numbers of qualified staff working in the library. Table 7.6 is an example of information requested from a library for inclusion in a department's self-study document for application or renewal of a program accreditation from the National Association of Schools of Music. One of the seven questions (G.4) requests financial data about the library's music-related collections for three fiscal years.

Table 7.6
National Association of Schools of Music, Library and Learning Resources

---

G. Library and Learning Resources
1. A description of music library holdings and learning resources, including electronic access, as published by the institution.
2. Information concerning student and faculty access (a) to the institution's library in terms of hours of operation, catalogs and indexes; and (b) to the holdings of other institutions through various means.
3. If the music unit relies substantially on libraries or learning resources beyond the institution for information access, collections, or facilities, information concerning (a) accessibility; (b) collections in relationship to major areas of study, curricular offerings and levels; (c) agreements regarding student/faculty use of these facilities; and (d) student use of these facilities.
4. Expenditures for music acquisitions as documented by the institution— ideally, a break-down with expenditures (a) the year before last, (b) last year, and (c) budgeted for this year in the following categories: books, collected editions, periodicals, videotapes, scores, recordings, microfilm/ microfiche, electronic access, and other holdings (specify). Also, a total for each year.
5. Number of staff dedicated to the music collection and the qualifications for each position.
6. Policies and procedures for acquisitions, preservation, and replacement, including music faculty involvement.
7. Plans for library equipment acquisitions and maintenance.

Source: National Association of Schools of Music, Procedures for the Self-Study Document: Format A (Reston, VA: National Association of Schools of Music, 2016), 27. See https://nasm. arts-accredit.org/accreditation/procedures-for-comprehensive-reviews/procedures-for-self- study.

The Annual Report

The annual report may be the most common and visible document the library creates for both internal and external audiences. Every library is encouraged, as a best practice, to compile such a report and to make it publicly available through the library's website. The value of this report is that it describes what happened during the past fiscal year, including expenditures, and it may illustrate the progress the library has made, or not made. Table 7.7, an example of an expenditures table from an annual report, includes five fiscal years of expenditures for salaries, collections, and other operating expenses. It also reports the number of full-time equivalent (FTE) students, provides calculations for library expenditures per FTE student, and how much is expended per FTE student on the major budget categories for salaries, collections, and other operating costs (e.g., supplies and equipment).

Table 7.7

Example of Expenditures from Annual Report

	FY2012	FY2013	FY2014	FY2015	FY2016
TOTAL EXPENDED FROM ALL FUNDS	**$3,339,937**	**$3,440,556**	**$3,688,782**	**$3,668,699**	**$3,800,913**
Total of Salaries, Wages, and Fringe	$1,920,807	$2,011,221	$2,134,740	$2,148,871	$2,244,735
Total Library Operation (non-personnel)	$1,419,130	$1,429,336	$1,554,042	$1,519,828	$1,556,178
Collections	$1,004,639	$1,079,914	$1,132,714	$1,177,967	$1,218,793
Other Operating	$414,491	$349,421	$421,329	$341,861	$337,385
	FY2012	**FY2013**	**FY2014**	**FY2015**	**FY2016**
Full-time Equivalent (FTE) students	9,973	10,240	10,137	10,150	10,176
	FY2012	**FY2013**	**FY2014**	**FY2015**	**FY2016**
Library Expenditures per FTE Student	$334.90	$335.99	$363.89	$361.45	$373.52

Major Library Expenditures Categories Expressed in Dollars Expended per FTE Student

	FY2012	FY2013	FY2014	FY2015	FY2016
Expended per FTE student					
Salaries	$192.60	$196.41	$210.59	$211.71	$220.59
Collections	$100.74	$105.46	$111.74	$116.06	$119.77
Other operating	$41.56	$34.12	$41.56	$33.68	$33.16

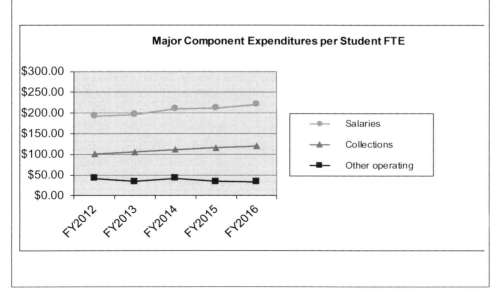

By reviewing annual reports from the past decade, a reader, for example, may learn how the library evolved through changes in its organizational structure (organizational charts), services and programs offered and discontinued, and financial and descriptive inputs and outputs. As the library changes, especially in its administration and organizational culture, the focus or value placed on the document changes, exhibited through the differences in the reports' structure, content, and quality from year to year. Library managers may occasionally use the annual report to voice dissent with institutional policies and resource allocation.[3]

Audits

Audits are powerful tools that are used to improve financial operations and to prevent and detect various types of fraud. There are three general types of audit reports. The most common are financial audits, which review the accounting, recording, and reporting of financial transactions, as well as the adequacy of internal controls. Operational audits evaluate if an organization utilizes its resources in the most efficient and effective way to fulfill the department's or institution's mission and objectives. Compliance audits, sometimes referred to as program audits, determine if the organization adhered to applicable rules, regulations, policies, and procedures; if funds were expended on programs as planned and reported; and if the outputs and outcomes reported were, indeed, factual.

Conclusion

Libraries report financial data to show how the funds budgeted were spent. The structure, content, and use of these reports inclusive of financial data vary among academic libraries, and over time as well. Reviewing financial data may illustrate why more or fewer books or serial titles were acquired, or why weekly library hours open increased or decreased. Financial data, when used for public relations, inform non-users and remind users of the services and value they receive (or could receive) from the library (this is discussed more in the next chapter). In all instances, the goals of library financial reporting are to demonstrate

- accountability and transparency by communicating clearly and concisely with internal and external constituencies.
- consistency with the issuance of reports at scheduled times (e.g., monthly, biannually, or annually). In other words, the library does not release a monthly report one year and then change to an annual report the next year.
- consistency and truthfulness with the content of what is reported.

Exercises

1. What types of financial reports does your library create, and for whom?
2. What content does your library present in its annual report? Who are the audiences?
3. How would the library prepare for a compliance audit?

(Answers to these questions can be found in the appendix at the back of the book. We encourage different library managers to work together, perhaps with staff members, to answer each question and to discuss the results.)

Notes

1. In this instance, *variance* means the difference between the number budgeted and the number expended, expressed as a sum (budget minus expended) and as a percentage (percent of budgeted remaining).
2. See Peter Hernon, Robert E. Dugan, and Joseph R. Matthews, *Managing with Data* (Chicago: American Library Association, 2015).
3. Regarding institutional policies, libraries may find that the need for the institution to review, approve, and sign each license agreement presents a burden to the library acquiring needed databases, especially with the number of databases a library acquires and the time it takes for the institution to implement its side of this process. The institution's license review process is the same whether it is for a $500 or a $10,000 database. *Resource allocation* refers to the budget; the library usually thinks it is underbudgeted for collections and staff. Occasionally the library expresses how disgruntled it is about its budget through the annual report. Another popular topic is facility maintenance (library's building issues such as water leaks, ignored requests for repairs, and recurring broken toilets) highlighted in the annual report. The reality is that the institution rarely reads the annual report and, consequently, the library complaints through this means are not so much ignored as they are just not read.

Bibliography

Hernon, Peter, Robert E. Dugan, and Joseph R. Matthews. *Managing with Data: Using ACRLMetrics and PLAmetrics.* Chicago: American Library Association, 2015.

National Association of Schools of Music. *Procedures for the Self-Study Document: Format A.* Reston, VA: National Association of Schools of Music, 2016. https://nasm.arts-accredit.org/accreditation/procedures-for-comprehensive-reviews/procedures-for-self-study.

Chapter 8

Uses of Expenditures Data

An academic library is expected to demonstrate, not just claim, that it is accountable and provides value to its stakeholders. There are at least three ways that libraries use to convey this expectation. The first is by describing quantity. The library explains what happened and what it produced through processes covered in the systems model (see figure 2.1) with the resources applied (inputs, including funding), and the outputs viewed as expenses in aggregate or as individual units. The second way is by demonstrating quality, the degree of excellence attained from application of a process or of an achievement as an output. A library may have produced extensive output, but how good is that output? As a simple example, a library reported to have purchased 10,000 print volumes for $100,000 ($10 per volume). Efficiency is creating an output using a minimal amount of input. For this example, the library achieved efficiency—saving money—by purchasing a lot of output (10,000 volumes) for the funds expended ($100,000). If the volumes acquired were of the same title, or if the volumes were all obsolete science books, or if the reading level of the material was at the third grade, the volumes lack the library's expected mission-related quality. The third way is effectiveness, which involves applying the inputs and the processes as throughputs so that the output achieves an objective in the library's long-term plan.

Effectiveness is also concerned with using feedback from evaluation and assessment processes for continuous quality improvement. Continuing the example, if the volumes purchased did nothing to support the institution's curriculum, then the output lacks quality, which, in turn, renders the expenditure for the volumes ineffective. Given this background, this chapter discusses the use of expenditures data to demonstrate accountability for inputs, throughputs, and outputs, and, as possible, quality and effectiveness.

Evaluation and Assessment Processes

Evaluation and assessment are processes to assist in determining effectiveness and efficiency when an organization tries to demonstrate accountability. Although the terms are frequently used interchangeably, each is a different process leading to different conclusions. Evaluation measures if a program, service, or system did what it was designed to do in an efficient and effective manner. For example, when making personnel evaluations, did the individual do what the job description calls for? Another example is the review conducted and conclusion reached that the integrated library system is doing, or not doing, the functions it was acquired to do.

Evaluation processes are used in financial management because evaluation is best applied to inputs, the amount of resources involved such as funds; throughputs, applied to the inputs to produce the outputs; and outputs, expenditures and quantities of transactions or other activities. Evaluation helps to explain if the library met its objectives from the long- and short-term plans. For example, an objective might be, "The library will strengthen the collection in biomedical sciences for undergraduates based on a finding from an academic program review." Managers examine the data, including the number of resources acquired and their related cost, and if there was an increase, decrease, or no change in the number of book and serial titles from the previous year, they conclude that the objective was or was not met.

Assessment measures the changes in library users from their contact with the library's programs, resources, and services. The assessment process includes statements about what library users will be able to know, think, or be from their contact with the library, such as an increase in known content (could be tested on knowledge), development of skills and abilities (information retrieval and evaluation), and acquisition of attitudes and values (self-sufficient; lifelong learning).

Assessment processes demonstrate the usefulness and value of the library indirectly through financial management. Outcomes would be related to improving the productivity and quality of the education experience for library users. For example, assessment processes may find that the titles acquired improved the collection by applying a collection conspectus tool (used to measure the quality of the collection) or from departmental faculty feedback.

Metrics Used by Academic Libraries

For decades, the metrics that libraries most often used were inputs and outputs. Inputs are the resources used to provide services such as collections, staffing, the physical facility, and installed information technologies. These are often described in financial terms as budgeted resources, such as the book budget is $100,000. Other input metrics include the number of staff, the volume or title count of the various parts of the collection, the physical square footage of the facility, the number of users' seats, and the number of desktop computers or microform readers available.

Output metrics quantify the workload undertaken or completed after applying the resources available. Common outputs mentioned in the literature of library and information science are the number of books circulated, the number of reference questions answered, and the number of hours the library is physically open. Outputs are valuable metrics for decision making, such as for determining the staffing levels needed for the library to be open the number of hours planned. An example of decisions concerning student assistant staffing was discussed in chapter 7, which reported outputs about the library's busiest hours, days of the week, and months of the academic year based on counted entrances and circulation transactions to inform the following fiscal year's staffing budget as input.

Performance metrics or indicators answer routine questions about program performance. For example, the collection turnover rate (a derived ratio, calculated by dividing the library's total annual circulation by total library holdings) is a performance indicator. Such an indicator informs library managers about what is happening (collection turnover rate has increased or decreased over the past five years), but it does not explain the reason for the change. The library may decide to conduct an evaluation study to identify and analyze the possible reasons for the rate change. The reasons for a decreasing collection turnover ratio may vary from finding that the collection needs to be weeded to understanding that a decrease may be the impact of an academic program changing its curriculum focus (e.g., from exercise science to sport management).

While the use of inputs and outputs has fallen out of favor and been replaced by assessment efforts, these metrics are still important to compile and analyze as part of the library's internal decision-making processes, and for other functions such as preparing annual reports and responding to surveys. Additionally, the number of possible inputs and outputs has increased due to the functionality of spreadsheets and the growing availability of third-party applications (e.g., those used by libraries, including Springshare [https://www.springshare.com] and Tableau Software [https://www.tableau.com]).

Institutional outcomes are aggregated statistics, which are frequently used to report to stakeholders and to compare internal year-to-year performance. Outcomes demonstrate institutional effectiveness by informing the planning processes for documenting continuous quality improvement. Additionally, they are used as comparative benchmarking metrics with other institutions. Several institutional outcomes, including graduation rates, retention rates, and the median incomes of recent graduates, receive media attention. User outcomes differ from institutional outcomes in that they reflect changes in users from their contact with the library and its resources, programs, and services (e.g., what do they know, or what can they do, that they did not know or could not do before contact with the library). User outcomes are the focus of current assessment efforts in academic libraries.

Financial Metrics

Financial metrics focus on expenditures and costs. An expenditure is a simple, yet important, output metric for an amount of money spent. A more complicated financial metric is cost, which is the price to do something, and as such, it may require expenditures from more than one budget category. For example, what does it cost to purchase a new print monograph for loan in the general collection? There are eleven expenditures involved:

1. staff time to choose the book
2. staff time to order the book
3. the expenditure for the book
4. the expenditure for shipping and handling of the book
5. staff time to receive the book, check it against the packing list, place it on a book cart, and provide the receipt information to the business office
6. staff time to process the invoice and pay for the book
7. staff time to catalog the book
8. bibliographic utility fee to catalog (copy or original cataloging) the book
9. staff time to process the book so that it can be shelved
10. supplies to process the book so that it can be shelved (prepare it for use, such as stamping the library's name onto the book and affixing the call number label)
11. staff time to shelve the book for availability

The cost for this process is far greater than the expenditure solely for the book. Academic libraries may be interested in determining the costs of library functions. Examples of calculating costs are discussed later in this chapter.

Another type of measure is a derived ratio. Derived ratios could be an input, output, or performance indicator that is divided by another input, output, or performance indicator. A commonly used derived ratio is calculating the number of full-time equivalent (FTE) staff, which divides the number of weekly work hours for a full-time employee (e.g., 40 hours per week) into the actual number worked by each staff person. If the full-time work week is forty hours, and a person works twenty hours, this person is a .5 FTE (20 divided by 40). If the library has three employees and they work forty hours, thirty hours, and twenty hours per week, totaling ninety hours, and the full-time work week is forty hours, the full-time equivalent is 2.25 FTE (90 hours divided by 40 hours).

An example of a derived ratio of a financial performance indicator is the expenditure for collections per FTE student; the library might say, "The library expended $200 per FTE student for collection development in the past fiscal year." There are dozens of derived ratios useful for library financial management.[1]

Expenditures and costs metrics and derived ratios are also used for peer institutional benchmarking and for best practices studies. Benchmark and best practices studies are discussed later in this chapter.

Calculating Unit Costs

Costs and expenditures differ; costs represent the expenditures from two or more budget or sub-budget categories. Calculating unit costs—for example, the cost to borrow a book through interlibrary loan (ILL) or the cost to answer a reference question—helps the library to demonstrate accountability and influences decision making. This section examines developing unit cost data using three examples and how such data are useful.

The question is, "What is the cost of using a database?" Table 8.1 shows the unit cost for a full-text article viewed from a select list of databases. To calculate the unit cost per full-text article viewed, the number of full-text articles viewed is the denominator and the cost for the database is the numerator. Although seemingly simplistic, this cost does provide library managers with useful financial data for collection development. For example, if the use per article exceeds twenty-five dollars, is it worthwhile to continue licensing the database? It may be more cost-efficient to request those articles through ILL. Before canceling a database subscription, however, library managers should ascertain the extent of the loss of content (e.g., Is an archive included with the database that may be lost when canceling?), and they should determine if maintaining the database is necessary to comply with one or more academic program accreditations.

Table 8.1

Cost per Database Use

Database	Full-Text Articles Viewed	Cost of Database Content	Cost/FT Article Viewed
Academic Search Complete	68,476	$34,803.00	$0.51
American Chemical Society Journal Package	6,093	$41,218.00	$6.76
APA PsycArticles	15,123	$14,726.00	$0.97

Database	Full-Text Articles Viewed	Cost of Database Content	Cost/FT Article Viewed
Business Source Complete	32,927	$21,879.00	$0.66
Cambridge University Journals	1,469	$15,832.00	$10.78
CINAHL with Full Text	28,436	$7,757.00	$0.27
Communication & Mass Media Complete	2,569	$5,057.50	$1.97
Communication Source	2,978	$811.00	$0.27
EconLit with Full Text	1,937	$6,571.00	$3.39
IEEE All Society Periodicals	610	$31,018.00	$50.85
JSTOR	35,643	$35,600.00	$1.00
Oxford University Press Journals	12,599	$20,206.66	$1.60
Political Science Complete	4,088	$6,064.00	$1.48
Project Muse	3,230	$16,992.00	$5.26
ProQuest Nursing & Allied Health Source	9,373	$4,060.00	$0.43
ProQuest Psychology Journals	8,328	$3,610.00	$0.43
SAGE	13,339	$63,309.95	$4.75
ScienceDirect	63,001	$90,465.96	$1.44
SPORTDiscus with Full Text	8,749	$7,464.00	$0.85
SpringerLINK Online Libraries	10,721	$50,839.94	$4.74
Wiley Interscience Journals	15,929	$136,332.67	$8.56

Table 8.2, which offers a second example, shows the calculation of the unit costs for borrowing and lending physical items through ILL. Expenditures for staff, fees, postage and freight, supplies, and services directly related to ILL are compiled. Because of the differences between the borrowing and lending processes, costs are separated when possible. Both lending and borrowing processes break out the staff time spent on each of the functions in hours and as a percentage of staff time for the entire fiscal year. Each staff member working in ILL does this breakout by keeping time sheets for each activity performed during an entire fiscal year. The time spent on work activities can also be estimated but would not be as accurate. The cost per activity for staff includes their salary or hourly wage, plus a share of the fringe benefits (as applicable) based on the percentage of labor for the activity.

Table 8.2
Unit Costs for Interlibrary Loan

Borrowing				
	Time Spent in Hours	Who	Percentage of the Job	Cost
Book ordering	213.85	ILL Tech #1	11%	$4,390.03
Book processing	304.33	ILL Tech #2	22%	$1,844.04

	Time Spent in Hours	Who	Percentage of the Job	Cost
Book processing	164.00	ILL Tech #3	21%	$1,245.91
Journal ordering	448.95	ILL Tech #1	22%	$9,216.29
Journal processing	227.92	ILL Tech #1	11%	$4,678.80
Document delivery, off-campus	98.40	ILL Tech #1	5%	$2,020.01
Unfilled	153.00	ILL Tech #1	8%	$3,140.87
Document delivery, on-campus	32.00	ILL Tech #2	2%	$193.90
	32.00	ILL Tech #3	4%	$243.11
In-state unmediated maintenance	90.00	ILL Tech #1	5%	$1,847.57
In-state unmediated processing	142.10	ILL Tech #3	18%	$1,079.54
In-state unmediated processing	76.65	ILL Tech #2	5%	$464.44
Problem requests/ILL management	725.00	ILL Tech #1	36%	$14,883.19
Management/e-mail/problems	200.00	ILL Manager	8%	$6,522.89
Subtotal for Staffing				**$51,770.56**
Other Direct Costs, Borrowing				
ILL charges				$0.00
Copyright fees				$1,201.32
Paid for ILL books lost by users				$324.90
Subtotal for Other Direct Costs				**$1,526.22**
TOTAL, Borrowing				**$53,296.78**
Lending				
Book ordering	455.90	ILL Tech #4	23%	$10,142.44
Book processing	388.67	ILL Tech #2	28%	$2,355.03
	209.33	ILL Tech #3	27%	$1,590.31
Journal ordering	1445.25	ILL Tech #4	72%	$32,152.59
Journal processing	79.27	ILL Tech #2	6%	$480.30
RAPID	472.70	ILL Tech #4	24%	$10,516.19
In-state unmediated processing	292.95	ILL Tech #2	21%	$1,775.06
In-state unmediated processing	157.50	ILL Tech #3	20%	$1,196.53
Management/e-mail/problems	60.00	ILL Tech #4	3%	$1,334.82
Subtotal for Staffing				**$61,543.30**
Other Direct Costs, Lending				
Postage and freight				$4,061.38
Photocopying				$0.00

	Time Spent in Hours	Who	Percentage of the Job	Cost
Subtotal for Other Direct Costs				$4,061.38
TOTAL, Lending				$65,604.68
Other Direct Costs Supporting Both				Cost
Office supplies				$0.00
ILL hosting				$10,858.68
ILL monthly costs				$10,208.42
Courier (5-day stop)				$0.00
TOTAL, Shared Direct Costs				$21,067.10
TOTAL COSTS				$139,968.56
Borrowing	Filled	Unfilled		
Book requests	1,431	422		
Article requests	3,447	250		
Document delivery	0	0		
In-state unmediated	625	348		
Totals	5,503	1,020		
Lending	Filled	Unfilled		
Book requests	1,794	2,763		
Article requests	4,756	9,600		
In-state unmediated	1,287	959		
Totals	7,837	13,322		
Allocation of Shared Direct Costs		Shared Costs		
Borrowing activity, filled and unfilled	6,523	$4,964.26		
Lending activity, filed and unfilled	21,159	$16,102.84		
Total	27,682			
Total Costs				
Borrowing	$58,261.04			
Lending	$81,707.52			

Calculating Transaction Costs				
Formula	cost per filled request = total cost of activity divided by number of filled request plus (.55 times the number of unfilled requests)			
Borrowing				
filled requests, each	$9.61			
unfilled requests (.55 of filled cost)	$5.28			
Lending				
filled requests, each	$5.39			
unfilled requests (.55 of filled cost)	$2.96			

Non-personnel expenditures charged to borrowing include any copyright fees paid by the library and the reimbursement for books borrowed but subsequently not returned to the lending library because the borrowing user lost the item. Direct expenditures charged to the lending function included postage and freight to ship items to users and photocopying items (which was zero). Direct costs shared by the borrowing and lending functions included office supplies and fees to the bibliographic utility for hosting ILL processes and their related transactions. A state agency assumes the expenditure for the statewide courier service used for interlibrary delivery.

In the table, the personnel and direct costs for borrowing totaled $53,296.78; the costs for lending were $65,604.68, and the shared costs totaled $21,067.10. The costs for lending and borrowing physical items through ILL totaled nearly $140,000. The shared costs were split between borrowing and lending by the percentage of the number of total requests for each of the functions: there were 6,523 borrowing requests and 21,159 requests from other libraries to lend items.

Knowing the cost for the entire ILL service is important. From that amount, unit costs can be calculated. There are four unit costs: filled requests for lending and borrowing and unfilled request for both activities. It is important to calculate unit costs for the unfilled as well as filled requests because staff time is expended even if the request to lend or borrowed is unfilled. The library maintains separate records of the unfilled and filled requests for lending and borrowing. It was decided internally that the cost of an unfilled request represented 55 percent of the cost of a filled request because the transaction did not take as long and did not use the supplies needed when filling a request.

The formula for the unit cost of a filled request (lending or borrowing) was the total cost of the function divided by the number of filled requests. Unfilled requests were calculated at 55 percent of a filled request. Thus, the following unit costs are calculated:

- borrowing: a filled request cost $9.61/unfilled request cost $5.28
- lending: a filled request cost $5.39/unfilled request cost $2.96

Knowledge of these unit costs can be applied to collection development decisions. Note that the borrowing cost was $9.61 per filled request. Financially, requesting ILL to borrow any information item with an acquisition expenditure over ten dollars would be cost-beneficial. However, not wanting to burden the interlibrary system by becoming a borrowing pest, this library decided that it will consider borrowing items only when the acquisition cost is thirty dollars or more or the item cannot be purchased.

The spreadsheet used to determine the unit costs can be updated annually if needed, if only to update the staff labor costs. A performance indicator, time to fill (usually measured in days), is not included in the calculation of the unit costs. These unit costs were developed for decision making from a financial perspective only.

A third cost example is determining the unit cost for answering an in-person reference question at the reference desk. Table 8.3, which provides the details for the calculation, includes only the questions received at one public service desk in the main library and excludes transactions from the branch libraries. Directional and virtual questions were excluded from the calculations. The cost calculations are based only on labor and do not include the value of the reference collection because responses to questions do not completely depend on the collection.

Each library faculty and staff member who worked at the reference desk kept track of their time using an internal reporting system.[2] The library breaks down the fiscal year into eight time frames, including summer, fall, and spring academic sessions (when classes are held) and non-academic sessions, during which classes are not held. The number of weeks for each session (e.g., fall semester is sixteen weeks) is indicated in the columns in the table. At the end of the fiscal year, the hours worked on the reference desk for each person are summed. The ratio of time worked on the desk is calculated as a percentage of the total time he or she worked for the entire fiscal year. That percentage of time at the desk is multiplied by the person's total salary expended, including benefits as applicable. The total cost of all labor is summed. This sum is divided by the number of in-person reference questions answered during the fiscal year. The result is the cost per reference transaction, which is $12.75 in the fiscal year.

Learning about the unit cost to answer a reference question has financial implications for staffing. The calculation of the unit cost is replicable year to year, which means that increases and decreases in the unit cost can be placed on a trend chart. Are these costs increasing or decreasing? Second, if library managers conclude that the cost per transaction is too high, staff with cheaper per-hour labor costs could replace the more expensive per-hour librarians at the desk, which will likely reduce the cost per transaction. The quality of the response to the users' questions because of this change in staff, however, is unknown.

Table 8.3

Cost to Answer a Reference Question

Reference Department

Cost to answer a reference question

Fiscal Year July to June — Library Personnel	Hrs/Week Summer Academic Semester	# of Weeks	Hrs/Week Summer Non-academic Semester	# of Weeks	Hrs/Week Fall Academic Semester	# of Weeks	Hrs/Week Fall Non-academic Semester	# of Weeks	Hrs/Week Spring Academic Semester	# of Weeks	Hrs/Week Spring Break	# of Weeks	Hrs/Week Spring Non-academic Semester	# of Weeks	Hrs/Week Summer Academic Semester	# of Weeks	Total Desk Hours	Percentage of Year	Salary/Benefits	Costs
Reference Librarian #1	4	6	4	2	8.5	16	4	2	8.5	16	4	1	4	1	4	8	352	17.60%	$97,751.09	$17,204
Reference Librarian #2	0	6	0	2	10	16	0	2	10	16	0	1	0	1	0	8	320	21.33%	$81,536.07	$17,394
Reference Librarian #3	4	6	4	2	8	16	4	2	8	16	4	1	4	1	4	8	336	16.80%	$83,332.00	$14,000
Reference Librarian #4	4	6	4	2	8.5	16	4	2	8	16	4	1	4	1	4	8	344	17.20%	$85,704.59	$14,741
Reference Librarian #5	4.5	6	4	2	8.5	16	4	2	9	16	4	1	4	1	4.5	8	367	18.35%	$53,554.73	$9,827
Reference Librarian #6	28	6	4	2	23	16	4	2	23	16	4	1	4	1	18	8	1072	53.60%	$66,481.64	$35,634
Reference Staff #1	5	6	4	2	6	16	4	2	6	16	4	1	4	1	4.5	8	282	14.10%	$41,986.52	$5,920
Ref Desk Staff #1	4	6	4	2	4	16	4	2	4	16	4	1	4	1	4	8	208	10.40%	$41,057.07	$4,270
Ref Desk Staff #2	4	6	4	2	4	16	4	2	6	16	4	1	4	1	2	8	224	11.20%	$44,494.16	$4,983
Ref Desk Staff #3	0	6	4	2	4	16	4	2	6	16	4	1	4	1	4	8	216	10.80%	$37,915.17	$4,095
Ref Desk Staff #4	2	6	0	2	4	16	0	2	0	16	0	1	0	1	0	8	76	7.60%	$25,844.04	$1,964
Ref Desk Staff #5	4	6	2	2	4	16	2	2	4	16	2	1	2	1	4	8	196	9.80%	$64,578.96	$6,329
Librarian #1	5	6	2	2	5	16	2	2	5	16	2	1	2	1	5	8	242	12.10%	$82,500.00	$9,983
Part-Time Librarian #1	0	6	0	2	12	16	0	2	12	16	0	1	0	1	10	8	422.5	100.00%	$6,429.40	$6,429
Student Assistant #1	0	6	0	2	14	16	0	2	14	16	0	1	0	1	0	8	448	49.10%	$9,057.98	$4,447
Student Assistant #2	10	6	0	2	5	16	0	2	5	16	0	1	0	1	12	8	253	100.00%	$2,205.98	$2,206
Student Assistant #3	0	6	0	2	5	16	0	2	5	16	0	1	0	1	8	8	185.75	100.00%	$1,631.44	$1,631
Student Assistant #4	0	6	0	2	12	16	0	2	12	16	0	1	0	1	0	8	287	100.00%	$2,813.50	$2,814
Student Assistant #5	12	6	0	2	0	16	0	2	0	16	0	1	0	1	0	8	72	7.30%	$10,035.54	$733
Student Assistant #6	0	6	0	2	0	16	0	2	0	16	0	1	0	1	10	8	78	100.00%	$643.50	$644
Total Cost			$165,248																	
Number of Reference Desk Transactions			12,963																	
Cost per Transaction			$12.75																	

Library Value from a Financial Perspective

As stated earlier, a library is expected to demonstrate, not just claim, that it provides value to its stakeholders. Valuation is increasingly discussed in the literature of library and information science. ACRL's initiative on the value of academic libraries 2010 report, *Value of Academic Libraries: A Comprehensive Research Review and Report*, was a catalyst for a sustained and ongoing effort to demonstrate and document the value of academic and research libraries and their contribution to institutional mission and goals.[3] ACRL's comprehensive website on the valuation project, http://www.acrl.ala.org/value, provides access to reports, examples, and ideas about academic library value that far exceed the scope of this monograph.

There are a couple of means to collect information concerning financial value of academic libraries. Customer satisfaction surveys and user anecdotes may provide information that can be extrapolated to relate to the efficiency and effectiveness of the financial management of the library.[4] Financial metrics, such as those related to expenditures and costs, and derived ratios help to describe the programs and services offered.

It is important to remember that costs and usage are important input and output metrics, but they are not evaluative metrics. Costs and usage neither tell how well a library is doing nor explain the impact of library services and programs on people. Nonetheless, financial metrics can help explain library usage by putting usage in terms of a financial perspective that customers and other stakeholders understand. For example, the library loaned 10,000 books and enabled the download of 10,000 scholarly articles. Because everyone has a financial perspective, it may be more meaningful to tell users the value of usage: "Last year we loaned $150,000 worth of books." There are several approaches for looking at library financial value: money and time, cost-benefit analysis, intellectual capital, return on investment, value of usage, and actual and potential value.

Money and Time

A library saves users' money by acquiring information resources on their behalf. A user may borrow, read, and return a book for another person to use. The price of the book is such that users could buy the book, but they would rather use the library's copy and save their personal funds. This analogy extends to the other items loaned by the library (e.g., laptops and graphing calculators). In academic libraries, students or faculty members may use a library resource that they cannot afford because of the cost (e.g., a set of industry handbooks) or a resource that information vendors do not make directly available to individuals, such as full-text article databases, portals, and datasets. A library may also save users' time. Library personnel can find information faster than users who are unfamiliar with the various information resources available.

Cost-Benefit Analysis

Cost-benefit analysis is not the same as cost-effectiveness. Cost-benefit analysis asks: Which is the best (least expensive, most efficient) way to perform an operation? Cost-effectiveness, on the other hand, asks: Because this is what the service costs, is it worth it?

Cost-benefit analysis (CBA), a systematic approach, determines whether the potential worth or value of a service is greater than or less than the cost of providing the service. For example, it costs $10,000 for alternative A for $12,000 amount of benefit, and it costs $5,000 for alternative B for $7,000 amount of benefit. It is sometimes difficult to apply this method in academic libraries because determining the value of a service is intangible; for example, what is the value of education? Costs, however, are often calculable, and the calculations can be applied when reviewing alternatives to make decisions, as in the example of calculating ILL costs to help the library to decide when it is prudent to purchase an information item or when to borrow it, as discussed earlier in this chapter.

Intellectual Capital

Intellectual capital is the knowledge library personnel have about library operations and the library's relationship with other organizations. Briefly, measures for intellectual capital include staff competencies, the relationships with users, service models (e.g., staffed reference desk or reference by appointment only), and the library's computer and administrative systems (e.g., the integrated library system and its internal management information system for collecting and analyzing data). Replacing personnel due to turnover is an example of an intellectual capital financial cost because of the temporary loss of competencies, organizational culture, and institutional or organizational memory.

Return on Investment

Return on investment (ROI), a performance metric, is used to evaluate the efficiency of an investment or to compare the efficiency of several different investments. From an academic library perspective, it is a financial metric that can be communicated to a variety of stakeholders who hold different perspectives.

A common formula for a library's ROI is

$$\text{ROI} = \frac{\text{summed value of benefits}}{\text{sum of all expenses}}$$

The result of an ROI is expressed as a percentage or a ratio in order to make a statement such as "For each dollar spent on the library, the institution's community receives $____ in benefits from library service."

An example of a ROI study was undertaken by Syracuse University, where faculty and students were surveyed using contingent valuation methodology[5] to measure their willingness to pay in time and money for the services of the academic library. Their travel time and use of the online library were measured to determine the environmental value of the academic library. The economic and environmental value of the Syracuse University library shows an ROI of $4.49 returned to the university for every $1.00 spent each year.[6]

Some academic libraries have calculated an ROI for institutional use based on services provided through the library. Table 8.4 is the spreadsheet used to calculate the ROI from the John C. Pace Library at the University of West Florida. The spreadsheet is updated annually. The library's eight most used services have been identified, and each includes measurable transactions. Central to the spreadsheet is calculating the unit costs and applying a formula to generate a total value for each service. A note field explains the calculation for each service. For example, the library has calculated the average cost per hour to operate the library. That value can be multiplied by the number of annual library entrances to produce a value for the library being open and used. However, since the cost unit is the average cost per hour, the library decided to value only the estimated number of entrances who stayed in the library for at least one hour; it is estimated that 10 percent of those entering the library did so. Consequently, the value for students studying in the library is the sum of the number of entrances times the average cost for the library when open multiplied by 10 percent. Other services costed include borrowing materials from the collection, asking a reference questions (cost calculated as an example earlier in the chapter), a research consultation, an instruction session conducted, borrowing a study carrel (small closed room), and using the databases from off campus. The value assigned to each service was as conservative as possible; the reason is that managers want to understate, rather than overstate, values:

- All books borrowed were considered used and valued at 20 percent of the average cost of a new book.
- E-books were valued at $2.00 each.
- The value of a study carrel was related to the cost of renting office space at $1.00/hour.
- It was estimated that 5 percent of all off-campus database usage saved the student from driving thirty miles round-trip to the library at the current cost of a gallon of gasoline.

Table 8.4
Library Return on Institutional Investment

Services	Number of Occurrences	Value per Occurrence	Value	Notes
Students studying in the Pace Library	485,613	$438.75	$21,306,270	average annual cost per hour to open = $438.75; figure 10% of gate count stayed one hour
Students borrowing				
a book from the general collection	25,641	$14.67	$376,153	we considered the book as used; used books are 20% of the average cost of a new book ($73.34)
a DVD from the Media Collection	2,364	$2.00	$4,728	average cost for each DVD if rented
an e-book from the collection	57,600	$2.00	$115,200	average Kindle e-book is $10; we used 20% of that cost even though the e-books are academic based and thereby costlier
Students borrrowing a laptop	13,727	$300.00	$4,118,100	hardware and installed software
Students asking reference questions	12,963	$12.75	$165,278	cost to answer a reference question during FY2016
Individual research consultations with a reference librarian	1,475	$25.00	$36,875	lasting at least 20 minutes; a southeast library charges $75/hour for library fee-based research services
Library instruction sessions conducted	214	$56.25	$12,038	number of library instruction sessions at Pace; use the cost of a research consultation; average library instruction session = 45 minutes
Students using a day study carrel	8,727	$6.00	$52,362	day carrels are loaned for 6 hours/per use. The average asking rental rate per sq ft/year for office properties in Pensacola as of August 2016 was $12.86. Calculate at $1/hour.
Database use from off campus	436,293	$2.30	$50,174	estimate that 5% of occurrences saved the student from driving 30 miles roundtrip to the library; saved 1 gallon of gas
TOTAL VALUE			**$26,237,178**	
Fiscal year expenditure for Libraries			$3,800,913	
Return on Investment			**$6.90**	**for each dollar invested in the library, it returned $ 6.90 in measured services to students**

The value of each service when summed as a total value becomes the numerator, and the library's actual expenditures for the related fiscal year's services is the denominator. The ROI for this specific fiscal year from the table is $6.90; for each $1.00 invested by the institution into the library, the library returned $6.90 in service to students.

Value of Usage

Value of usage serves as a proxy for helping people understand the library from their financial perspective. An example of a value for usage calculation is the number of articles downloaded (the output is measured by a counter) multiplied by the cost per article (this unit cost can be assigned by the library, assigned by the user, or assumed to be an accepted benchmark such as the average price from a commercial article provider). If 10,000 articles were downloaded, and the assigned price was $15.00 per article, the value of usage is $150,000.

A formula for the value of usage is a variant of the calculation of the production of a commodity:

- Value = Quantity (of the commodity produced) multiplied by the Price Unit (of the commodity) as $V = Q \times P$;
- A variant of production of a commodity recognizes the value of a library benefit (resource or service) as evidenced by its use;
- Value of usage = Measured Output (of a service) multiplied by the Assigned Price (per unit) as $Vu = MO \times AP$.

In 2009, Cornell University conducted a value of usage study. Its brief report stated that if the library did not exist, the university would have had to pay the following amounts last fiscal year to secure services that are comparable to the use that the Cornell community makes of the library for:

- the use of physical volumes: $15,135,782;
- articles accessed online and through interlibrary services: $61,265,783;
- answering questions to build research skills and contribute to Cornell research results: $1,176,615;
- in-depth consultations that contribute to Cornell research results: $126,900;
- Cornell's use of preprints from arXiv.org: $740,250;
- distributing Cornell-created content to the world through eCommons: $12,001,290;
- laptops borrowed: $202,165.

The library concluded that the value of services totaled $90,648,785. Expenditures for that fiscal year were $56,678,222.[7]

Students may have a different financial perspective of the library. A library can create a personal ROI—a Student ROI—giving their perspective on value of usage calculations. Table 8.5 is the worksheet used to create a student value of usage calculation. This worksheet is used to calculate the value for the ten services that students use the most, and the time line is based on an academic year. The services are based on the minimum expected use by an individual student. For example, studying in the library is based on a student spending only one hour in the library during an entire academic year. For a conservative dollar value assigned by the library for the service, the cost for one hour is equal to 25 percent of the average library operating cost per hour. Another cost is calculated based on the student asking one reference question and consulting with two online research guides during the academic year. This library has all the print textbooks for undergraduate courses on reserve, and the value assigned is the savings if the student borrows one reserve textbook.

Other values are assigned to borrowing two books from the general collection, borrowing one book through ILL rather than purchasing it, borrowing one DVD and one laptop, and using a desktop computer once during the academic year. Based on the summed value of services ($458.76), a student using a minimum level of services realizes a savings—a personal ROI—from the value of his or her tuition money allocated to the library per full-time-equivalent student ($373.52).

Table 8.5
Student Value of Usage Worksheet

Service	Factors	Measure Applied	Value Academic Year
Studying, which requires the library to be open	• hours open during year = 4,769 • $2,092,415 expended for all salaries, wages, and benefits • $2,092,415 / 4,769 = $438.75/hour to open • use 25% of that cost to represent cost/hour open	• use the library for 60 minutes during the entire academic year	$109.69
Ask a question at the Reference Desk AND use a research guide	• answered 12,963 questions in FY2016 • students viewed pages from UWF librarian-created research guides (LibGuides) 824,239 times • cost per question or use of a research guide = $12.75	• ask one reference question AND • use two research guides each academic year (same cost as reference question)	$38.25
Use a print textbook on reserve	• expended $41,501.90 for 413 textbooks in FY2016 • average cost = $100.49	• use one print textbook on reserve during the academic year rather than purchasing it	$100.49
Access and download full-text articles for a paper from a subscription database	• Commercial firms may charge in excess of $30.00 an article • let's use $10.00/scholarly article	• access 3 scholarly articles per course for 2 courses during each semester 2 semesters in the academic year total of 12 articles during the academic year	$120.00

Service	Factors	Measure Applied	Value Academic Year
Use the library's proxy server to access and download full-text articles while at home OR while at work	• do not have to come to the library to conduct your research • do not need to pay for gasoline • let's say you live 15 miles from the library and your car gets 30 miles to the gallon • gallon of gas is $2.30/gallon	• save 2 trips to the Pace Library during the academic year	$4.60
Borrow a book from the general collection	• the average cost to purchase an academic book was $73.34 (2015 Library and Book Trade Annual, Table 5) • let's use 20% of that cost to reflect a "used book" (Morris, Sumison & Hawkins, 2002) • therefore, use $14.67	• borrow 2 books during the academic year	$29.34
Borrow a book from another library	• the book you need is elsewhere and we borrow it for you via interlibrary loan • if bought, the book would cost you $50.00 • it costs the library $9.61 to borrow it for you via interlibrary loan	• borrow one book from another library via interlibrary loan (net savings from borrowing rather than you or library buying)	$40.39
Borrow a DVD for a course or entertainment	• rental rates are $2 per film	• borrow one video from the library during the academic year	$2.00
Borrow a laptop computer	• rental rates seen from $79 to $109/day • let's use $9/hour	• borrow a laptop once during the academic year	$9.00
Use a desktop computer to search for information	• rental rates seen from $60 to $70/day • let's use $5/hour	• use a desktop computer once during the academic year	$5.00
TOTAL			**$458.76**
Per student FTE investment this fiscal year: $373.52			

Students may not want to review a worksheet to calculate their personal return on investment. Figure 8.1 is a web-based Value Calculator that the library uses so that students can enter their usage and view their personal value of services provided through the library. The calculator uses the values from the worksheet in table 8.5. Value is calculated for the academic year even if students choose to enter their usage on a weekly, biweekly, monthly, or per semester basis. Incidentally, from May 2015 to May 2017 at the John C. Pace Library, University of West Florida, the calculator was used 1,283 times.

Figure 8.1
Student ROI Calculator

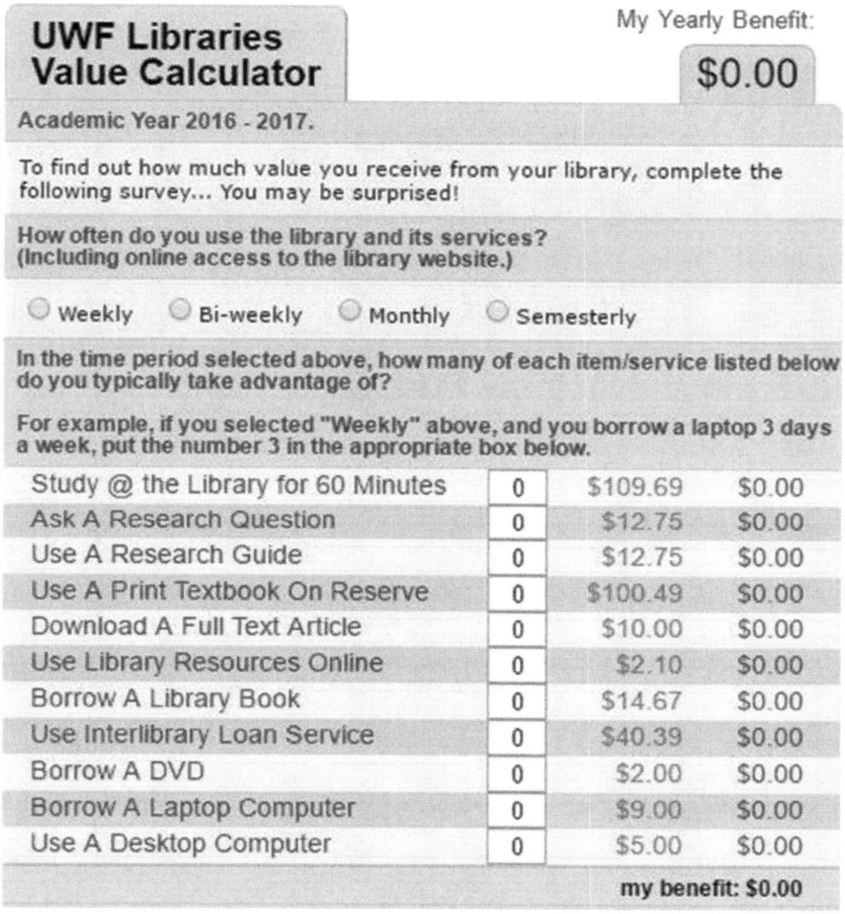
UWF Libraries
Value Calculator
My Yearly Benefit:
$0.00
Academic Year 2016 - 2017.
To find out how much value you receive from your library, complete the following survey... You may be surprised!
How often do you use the library and its services? (Including online access to the library website.)
Weekly
Bi-weekly
Monthly
Semesterly
In the time period selected above, how many of each item/service listed below do you typically take advantage of?
For example, if you selected "Weekly" above, and you borrow a laptop 3 days a week, put the number 3 in the appropriate box below.
Study @ the Library for 60 Minutes 0 $109.69 $0.00
Ask A Research Question 0 $12.75 $0.00
Use A Research Guide 0 $12.75 $0.00
Use A Print Textbook On Reserve 0 $100.49 $0.00
Download A Full Text Article 0 $10.00 $0.00
Use Library Resources Online 0 $2.10 $0.00
Borrow A Library Book 0 $14.67 $0.00
Use Interlibrary Loan Service 0 $40.39 $0.00
Borrow A DVD 0 $2.00 $0.00
Borrow A Laptop Computer 0 $9.00 $0.00
Use A Desktop Computer 0 $5.00 $0.00
my benefit: $0.00

Value of usage does not reflect the library's quality. It can, however, be applied as a proxy for one financial measure of the library's use, and it is an improvement over the aforementioned concepts for saving the user *money* and *time*.

Potential and Actual Value

Potential value refers to the resources that the library has available for use. The sum of the value of the library's infrastructure (staff, collections, facilities, and technologies) represents the potential value. Actual value is measured when the resources are used. The ratio between potential value (Vp) and actual value (Va) is represented as

$$Vp / Va$$

This ratio can be estimated. For example, the sum of the potential value of the library is estimated at $100,000,000, which includes the replacement values of the facility, collections, furnishings, and technologies. The actual value is the sum of the valuation from the earlier example of the institutional ROI, estimated at $26,000,000. The ratio of potential to actual value for the fiscal year is 3.85. If the potential to actual value ratio is calculated annually, the ratios can be graphed and the trend line studied. This ratio may supplement the library's annual institutional ROI as a financial measure.

Financial Metrics for Studies on Benchmarking and Best Practices

There are many uses of expenditures data for internal financial management. Yet library managers sometimes want to compare the library's financial inputs and related outputs with other academic libraries, and at other times they want to improve an internal input, process, or output and to learn how other libraries may do something better. These types of studies are benchmarking and best practices.

Benchmarking

Benchmarking, a tool to review and analyze comparable metrics of other libraries, is a useful technique that provides administrators with indicators of performance. The technique enables librarians to learn from one another by examining why there are differences in performance results among organizations that undertake similar functions.

Performance benchmarking, also known as comparative or metric benchmarking, compiles and compares measures of performance, such as the library's ratio of inputs (e.g., budget) to services provided (outputs), to determine how the library's operation compares with that of other libraries. Library managers also use the benchmark comparisons to illustrate the level to which the local library's resources and activities are supported (e.g., above average, below average, at average) when compared with other libraries.

Most higher education institutions have identified peers (comparable institutions with a similar role, scope, and mission) when they need to make comparisons for institutional and program accreditations and for internal program reviews. Academic libraries are encouraged to use existing institutional peer groups for comparisons. Some academic libraries have also identified peer and aspirant organizations separate from those on their own institution's list to expand the number of libraries for comparison for their benchmarking use. This list may include libraries based on some other factor (e.g., other members in a consortium, in a state university system, in other cooperative relationships, or from a defined geopolitical area).

Sources of benchmarking data with peers include ACRL's annual survey of academic libraries, which offers aggregated data for survey responders and detailed organized data through ACRL*Metrics*, an online subscription service providing access to ACRL and NCES academic library statistics together with a subset of IPEDS data specific to academic libraries. Other comparison tools include IPEDS's Compare Academic Libraries web application, https://nces.ed.gov/surveys/libraries/Compare/Default.aspx?AspxAutoDetectCookieSupport=1; the Association of Research Libraries' (ARL) collection of quantitative and qualitative data; and the data collected from the libraries participating in member, consortial, or other group surveys.

There are numerous library metrics that can be benchmarked with other libraries.[8] Examples of these metrics include:

- total operating expenditures;
- operating expenditures per FTE student and faculty;
- personnel expenditures as a percentage of total operating expenditures;
- collections expenditures as a percentage of total operating expenditures;
- other direct expenditures (operations and maintenance expenses) as a percentage of total operating expenditures;
- total personnel expenditures;
- personnel expenditures per FTE student and faculty;
- personnel expenditures as a percentage by staff type (librarians, other professional staff, all other paid staff, student assistants);
- personnel fringe benefits if paid for through the library;
- total collections expenditures;
- total collections expenditures per FTE student and faculty;
- collection expenditures, one-time purchases of books, serial backfiles, and other materials;
- collection expenditures, ongoing commitments to subscriptions;
- collection expenditures, all other materials or services not reported as one-time or ongoing (e.g., ILL expenses and copyright fees);
- collections expenditures on print materials;
- collections expenditures on audio materials;
- collections expenditures on video materials;
- collections expenditures for electronic resources;
- collections expenditures for microforms;
- collections expenditures for other (e.g., cartographic, photographs);
- total operations and maintenance expenses;

- total operations and maintenance expenses per FTE student and faculty;
- operations and maintenance expenses, preservation services;
- operations and maintenance expenses, all other operations and maintenance expenses;
- cost per hour open.

Table 8.6 is an example of a benchmark review of salary and wages expenditures per FTE student for a fiscal year using ACRL*Metrics*. The library (labeled "home library" in the table) wanted to benchmark staff expenditures per FTE student with its peer institution libraries. Salary and wage expenditures exclude fringe benefits. The table provides total salaries and wages and the total of expenditures by the four categories of personnel: Librarians, Other Professional Staff, All Other Paid Staff, and Student Assistants. Full-time equivalents of students are provided and become the denominator to the total salaries and wages, which is the numerator. One library, Peer library #3, did not submit a total of FTE students. The column on the far left is sorted on the column labeled Total Staff Expenditures per FTE Student from highest to lowest dollar value. The average (mean) and median are also included in the table.[9] The "home library" has a total staff expenditures per FTE student below the average and median for its peer group of libraries. The home library could sort this table in several different ways to review how it ranks with its peers.

Table 8.6
Benchmarking: Salary and Wages Expenditures per Enrolled Student

Salary and Wages Expenditures per FTE Student. Salaries Exclude Fringe Benefits. Sorted on Total Staff Expenditures per FTE Student.	Total Salaries and Wages (Excluding Fringe)	Librarians Salaries and Wages (Excluding Fringe)	Other Professional Staff Salaries and Wages (Excluding Fringe)	All Other Paid Staff Salaries and Wages (Excluding Fringe)	Student Assistants Salaries and Wages (Excluding Fringe)	Total Staff Expenditures per FTE student	Full-Time Equivalents (FTE)
Peer library #8	$2,353,623	$1,270,209	$0	$1,001,929	$81,485	$239.80	9,815
Peer library #2	$2,860,067	$1,450,157	$291,464	$1,098,484	$19,962	$214.04	13,362
Peer library #5	$1,454,147	$629,583	$349,096	$346,631	$128,837	$196.51	7,400
Average	$1,925,644	$953,764	$328,177	$598,601	$118,029	$179.26	10,575
Peer library #6	$2,000,193	$1,118,685	$7,500	$674,739	$199,269	$173.48	11,530
Median	$1,897,947	$946,988	$349,096	$629,677	$119,144	$169.15	10,078
home library	$1,677,178	$786,510	$0	$693,291	$197,377	$164.82	10,176
Peer library #7	$1,602,425	$766,576	$391,389	$325,316	$119,144	$160.56	9,980
Peer library #4	$1,279,055	$634,648	$382,056	$204,873	$57,478	$143.42	8,918
Peer library #1	$1,897,947	$980,524	$277,371	$629,677	$10,375	$141.44	13,419
Peer library #3	$2,206,164	$946,988	$598,366	$412,473	$248,337	$0.00	not provided

Best Practices

A best practices study seeks to discover methods that other libraries deploy to attain successful processes, services, and outcomes. Learning about these successes may help the library improve its own performance by duplicating the beneficial processes from these libraries. For example, a library may seek to find other libraries with similar staffing levels that are open more hours during the average week in an academic semester. The best practices study question is, "With similar staffing levels, how is it that these libraries can provide more open hours than we do?"

A financial measures benchmarking study with peers is one means to look for best practices. Table 8.7 is an example of a benchmarking study using ACRL*Metrics* to examine peer institution libraries and to discover a best practice about collection expenditures.[10] The home library has an objective of expending 50 percent of its allocated resources to develop and strengthen its collections. Currently, this library expends only 32.6 percent of its total on collections. From the study, the library finds that two of its peers satisfy the objective: Peer Libraries #2 and #5. Both libraries have total expenditures exceeding that of the home library. Additionally, Peer Library #2 expended above the average on other operating expenses, whereas Peer Library #5 expends less than average. The home library can compile additional data about Peer Library #5, such as staff FTE, to analyze the differences and seek comparable measures between the two libraries for further study.

Table 8.7

Best Practice: Peer Libraries with Collection Expenditures Exceeding 50 Percent of Total Expenditures

Salaries, Collections, and Other Operating as a Percentage of Total Expenditures (Triad); sorted on Collections	Total expenditures (includes fringe)	Total salaries & wages expenses as percentage of total expenditures	Total collections expenses as percentage of total expenditures	Total other operating expenses as percentage of total expenditures
Peer Library #2	$8,017,237	35.7%	54.4%	9.9%
Peer Library #5	$4,513,340	41.9%	52.4%	5.7%
Peer Library #1	$5,180,066	47.6%	44.3%	8.1%
Average	$4,589,950	53.8%	40.9%	8.0%
Peer Library #4	$3,176,570	48.0%	40.8%	11.3%
Peer Library #7	$3,611,018	58.5%	33.9%	7.6%
Peer Library #8	$5,202,547	60.5%	33.5%	6.0%
Peer Library #6	$3,046,630	65.7%	33.3%	1.0%
home library	$3,800,912	59.1%	32.6%	8.3%
Median	$4,513,340	54.6%	29.9%	7.0%
Peer Library #3	$4,761,227	60.5%	28.3%	11.2%

A best practice study also seeks to identify libraries outside of the peer group meeting specific criteria. Table 8.8, a best practice study using the ACRL*Metrics* database, shows libraries with a total collection expenditures per FTE student equal to the home library or exceeding it by no more than 10 percent. The data collected for this study include total expenditures, total collections expenditures, and the total number of staff FTE. The percentage of collection expenditures of total expenditures is an example of a derived ratio (total collections expenditures divided by total expenditures). The home library's collection expenditure per FTE student is $121.84. The library was not interested in reviewing other libraries spending less per FTE student than it does, but also realized that increasing its expenditures more than 10 percent above this current student FTE expenditure was unlikely in the next fiscal year. Therefore, it limited the study to libraries with a higher collections expenditure per student FTE of 10 percent, which was about $12.00 for a total of $135.00. The study also sought the total number of staff FTEs to review that range. Based on this table, Library #6 had the highest collection expenditure per FTE student. It also had fewer staff FTE than the home library. However, this library expended less of a percentage of its total expenditures on collection than did the home library. Given this finding, the home library would not pursue gathering additional information on Library #6. The most interesting of the libraries is #8, which spends more per FTE student, has a higher percentage expended on collections, and has fewer staff than does the home library.

Table 8.8
Best Practices: Collection Expenditures per FTE Student

Collections: Sorted on Libraries with Library Materials Expenditures per FTE no More than 10% Above Home Library.	Total Expenditures	Total Collections Expenditures	Collections as Percentage of Total Expenditures	Total # of Staff FTEs	Total Collections Expenditures per FTE Student
Library #6	$5,094,360	$1,518,636	29.8%	43.69	$133.00
Library #1	$12,965,440	$4,570,155	35.2%	150.50	$131.56
Library #7	$3,873,407	$1,210,280	31.2%	48.89	$131.10
Library #4	$6,293,423	$2,239,089	35.6%	51.05	$131.06
Library #5	$5,944,580	$2,401,444	40.4%	62.00	$127.93
Average	$6,362,913	$2,234,110	35.1%	67.28	$127.86
Median	$5,519,470	$1,878,863	34.0%	51.18	$127.77
Library #2	$9,788,502	$3,535,647	36.1%	93.65	$127.61
Library #8	$3,629,655	$1,388,126	38.2%	34.06	$127.61
Library #3	$8,627,829	$3,014,398	34.9%	91.59	$124.34
Library #9	$3,611,018	$1,223,470	33.9%	51.30	$122.59
home library	$3,800,912	$1,239,859	32.6%	46.08	$121.84

Conclusion

Most financial data are expressed as inputs (budget allocations) to outputs (expenditures), and a key application of compiling and analyzing library expenditures data is to demonstrate accountability to stakeholders. There are several means for measuring library financial value, including money and time, return on investment, and value of usage. Financial metrics expressed as costs, the price to do something that is not solely a line-item expenditure, inform stakeholders about the resources expended for specific services and functions, such as ILL. Calculating costs is the basis for presenting a simple return on investment from the institution's or the student's perspective and for providing guidance to internal decision making, including staffing and collection development.

Benchmarking studies using financial metrics and data demonstrate the comparative availability and use of library resources, including those of peer institutions. Studies seeking to identify best practices in academic libraries can help the library to improve its internal processes to meet service-oriented, long-term planning objectives.

Exercises

1. How does your library identify, measure, and report its value to stakeholders?
2. How would a library calculate the cost to conduct a librarian-led instruction session?
3. A library wants to compare its operating expenditures with its benchmarking peers. First, which libraries comprise benchmarking peers? Second, how is this determination made? Third, how would the library develop this benchmarking report? Finally, what specific derived ratios would be useful for the benchmark study?

(Answers to these questions can be found in the appendix at the back of the book. We encourage different library managers to work together, perhaps with staff members, to answer each question and to discuss the results.)

Notes

1. For other examples, see Robert E. Dugan, Peter Hernon, and Danuta A. Nitecki, *Viewing Library Metrics from Different Perspectives* (Santa Barbara, CA: Libraries Unlimited, 2009).
2. The internal system is a text-based reporting system in which staff enter the date and their start and end times each time they work at the reference desk.

3. Association of College and Research Libraries, *Value of Academic Libraries*, researched by Megan Oakleaf (Chicago: Association of College and Research Libraries, 2010), http://www.acrl.ala.org/value/?page_id=21.

4. See Peter Hernon, Ellen Altman, and Robert E. Dugan, *Assessing Service Quality*, 3rd ed. (Chicago: American Library Association, 2015); and Peter Hernon and Joseph R. Matthews, *Listening to the Customer* (Santa Barbara, CA: Libraries Unlimited, 2011).

5. This is a method of estimating the value that a person places on a good. People are asked to report their willingness to pay (to obtain a specified service) or their willingness to accept (to give up a service) rather than making inferences from observing behaviors.

6. Bruce Kingma and Kathleen McClure, "Lib-Value: Values, Outcomes, and Return on Investment of Academic Libraries, Phase III: ROI of the Syracuse University Library," *College and Research Libraries* 76, no. 1 (2015): 63–80.

7. Cornell University Library, Assessment and Communication, "Library Value Calculation Experiment 2009," accessed July 26, 2017, https://ac.library.cornell.edu/value.

8. See Dugan, Hernon, and Nitecki, *Viewing Library Metrics from Different Perspectives*, 253–308.

9. The mean is the average, the one in which we add all the numbers and then divide by the number of numbers, whereas the median is the middle value in the list of numbers. In benchmarking, the mean and the median can be quite different numbers.

10. See Peter Hernon, Robert E, Dugan, and Joseph R. Matthews, *Managing with Data* (Chicago: American Library Association, 2015).

Bibliography

Association of College and Research Libraries. *Value of Academic Libraries: A Comprehensive Research Review and Report*. Researched by Megan Oakleaf. Chicago: Association of College and Research Libraries, 2010. http://www.acrl.ala.org/value/?page_id=21.

Cornell University Library, Assessment and Communication. "Library Value Calculation Experiment 2009." Accessed July 26, 2017. https://ac.library.cornell.edu/value.

Dugan, Robert E., Peter Hernon, and Danuta A. Nitecki. *Viewing Library Metrics from Different Perspectives: Inputs, Outputs, and Outcomes*. Santa Barbara, CA: Libraries Unlimited, 2009.

Hernon, Peter, Ellen Altman, and Robert E. Dugan. *Assessing Service Quality*, 3rd ed. Chicago: American Library Association, 2015.

Hernon, Peter, Robert E, Dugan, and Joseph R. Matthews. *Managing with Data: Using ACRLMetrics and PLAmetrics*. Chicago: American Library Association, 2015.

Hernon, Peter, and Joseph R. Matthews. *Listening to the Customer*. Santa Barbara, CA: Libraries Unlimited, 2011.

Kingma, Bruce, and Kathleen McClure. "Lib-Value: Values, Outcomes, and Return on Investment of Academic Libraries, Phase III: ROI of the Syracuse University Library." *College and Research Libraries* 76, no. 1 (2015): 63–80.

Chapter 9

A Smorgasbord

Budget Reduction Strategies, Fraud, and Best Practices

A reality that all academic library managers face is having to cope with budget reductions. Although uncertainty and uneasiness arise whenever budget reductions occur, they will nonetheless eventually happen. Another occurrence, but one that's preventable, is financial fraud. As often as budget reductions are discussed in the news, reports about academic library fraud are nearly invisible. In its conclusion, this chapter summarizes some of the more important best practices covered in previous chapters.

Reductions in Expected or Allocated Budgets

At some point in a library manager's career, that person encounters a budget reduction from one fiscal year to the next, or worse, an approved allocation is reduced (rescinded) after the fiscal year has begun. With adequate notice, maybe three months, a library can alter its planning for the next fiscal year if a budget reduction is announced or expected. It is much more difficult to manage a rescinded budget allocation, especially the further the institution is into the fiscal year when it occurs.

Budget reductions occur for a variety of reasons. Expected enrollment declines are most frequently the cause for the reductions before a fiscal year begins. Another cause is a reduction in allocations from a funding source (e.g., state government) or a dramatic decline in revenue from endowments. A rescission is usually caused by an unanticipated event (e.g., a terrorist attack [e.g., 2001], a recession [e.g., 2007 onward], or fraud that is uncovered and the institution finds itself in a debt crisis). There are some best practices to consider for allocation reductions expected for the next fiscal year or when these reductions occur during a fiscal year.

Libraries should align their budget plans with their strategic plan. When managing a strategic finance planning process (see chapter 1), they should revise their short-term plan (i.e., alter their planned activities to support achieving a stated objective) when they need to reduce allocated budgets. Table 9.1 is an example of an expected budget reduction for a library using a strategic finance plan. The required budget reductions of $88,070 are aligned with the objectives of the strategic plan. The reductions are identified and the impact is noted. This library also developed principles to guide this specific set of budget reductions:

- No layoffs—do not eliminate any occupied staff or faculty positions.
- The primary objective for the libraries relates to the collection.
  - Do not reduce funding for collection development (e.g., books and journals).
  - Continue the second year of the weeding project as planned; stopping the project has a negative impact on the ability of the circulation department to shelve books.
- The loudest and most frequent student criticism is about the number of hours that the library is open.
  - Still increase library hours open on Fridays and Saturdays by five to seven hours per week despite the reduction in budgeted funds for student assistants.

Table 9.1
Reducing a Budget as Aligned to a Strategic Plan's Objectives

TOTAL Reduction Required	$88,070			
Details				
Strategic Plan Objectives	**Reductions**	**Reductions How Much**	**Sum Reduced**	**Impacts**
Objective 1: Collections	Cataloging Services; -18 hours/week; undergrad student	$6,526		will slow down acceptance/ processing of graduate theses and dissertations
	Cataloging Services; -30 hours/week; grad	$6,270		will slow down processing of books
			$12,796	
Objective 2: Providing Public Services	branch library; -4 hours/ week; undergrad student	$1,450		reduce student hours available to staff public desk
	branch library; -10 hours/ week; undergrad student	$3,625		reduce student hours available to staff public desk

Strategic Plan Objectives	Reductions	Reductions How Much	Sum Reduced	Impacts
	ILL; -4 hours/week; undergrad student	$1,450		eliminate delivery of interlibrary loan books to faculty offices
	GovDocs; -10 hours/week; undergrad student	$3,625		eliminate student assistance in Government Documents
	Special Collections; -17 hours/week; Visiting Librarian	$8,682		reduce student hours available to help users in Special Collections
	Media lab; -16 hours/week; graduate student	$8,000		reduce hours available to help students in the media lab
			$26,832	
Objective 3: Information Literacy		$0	$0	
Objective 4: Technology Support	reduce acquisition and repair of computer hardware/software	$2,500		broken/obsolete staff/user computer equipment will not be repaired/replaced
	Reference; -4 hours/week; undergrad student	$1,450		reduce assistance in Reference for users needing help with library technology
	branch library; -10 hours/week; graduate student	$5,000		eliminate all mobile application development at branch library
	reduce salary/benefits for vacant library technology faculty position	$32,377		will reduce the available salary and benefit funding for a vacant faculty position
			$41,327	
Objective 5: Facilities Management		$0	$0	
Objective 6: Administration	Administration; -10 hours/week; graduate student	$1,995		will reduce student assistance support to Administration by 34%
	reduce travel and professional development by 44%	$3,620		will reduce in-state travel; eliminate out-of-state travel to national conference
			$5,615	
Objective 7: Demonstrating Value	reduce 50% of funding for Marketing and Outreach Committee	$1,500	$1,500	will significantly reduce library outreach and public relations to University students and faculty
TOTAL REDUCTIONS			$88,070	

Libraries react differently to budget reductions. A common reaction for them is referred to as the Washington Monument Strategy, which says that, if funding is cut, the organization threatens to reduce, or otherwise halt, a popular or mission-critical program. This strategy received its name as a reaction to federal budget cuts decades ago; federal budget cuts or shutdowns result in a shutdown of popular parks such as the Washington Monument. Libraries frequently use this strategy. Examples include reducing hours or even days open and canceling subscriptions or databases.

During and following the recession that started in December 2007, most libraries experienced budget reductions that threatened core library services. Some of them implemented the Washington Monument Strategy by closing library facilities, reducing hours open, and terminating staffed positions as a "this is what you get for cutting our budgets." Oftentimes, it was the tone of the announcements that greatly differed so much; while sustaining similar and painful cuts, some libraries sounded less confrontational. One more extreme example from a library newsletter written for the institution's faculty:

> Collection Budget Cuts
>
> The Library again had to make subscription cuts to make a flat budget cover yearly price increases. Cuts included:
>
> - IEEE journal package
>
> - Institute of Physics journals package
>
> - Numerous low use paper format journals
>
> - Decrease in funds for purchasing books
>
> Since the budget remains flat, we must cut more later this year.

That was the entire message from this library about budget cuts. Nothing was shared about how the cuts were made, nor were faculty, the intended audience for this newsletter issue, asked for suggestions or feedback about the cuts.[1]

Another reaction is known as "squeaky wheels"—budgeting decisions are heavily influenced by those making the most complaints; eventually the library succumbs and meets the funding demand in the effort to satisfy the person or department so that the library can address other needs. A third reaction is responding to accreditation needs. In order to obtain, or maintain, accreditation status, the library diverts resources from one or more programs as it satisfies the accreditation needs of the program coming up for review.

Will Manley, a public librarian, city administrator, and longtime columnist for *American Libraries*, identified different strategies for libraries when confronted with budget reductions:

- Avoid trashing the institutional leaders.
- Get supporters out for public meetings: be vocal but be respectful (see bullet above).
- Think strategically (ask the institution to restore the cuts when times improve).

- Get institutional leaders into the library so that they can see the activity.[2]

Although these practices pertain to public librarians, they also are applicable to academic libraries. Expanding on Manley's list, academic libraries should

- Know their users' needs and remind all stakeholders that the library provides important and valued services.
- Let users know the library is meeting their needs and how it is doing this by implementing marketing strategies to inform users of services.
- Be prepared with proposals and alternative proposals when reductions are required; basically, do not let others decide what services the library will alter to meet the budget reductions.

It is of interest to review briefly budget reduction strategies implemented by academic libraries as their budgets began to decline in fiscal year 2009 as examples of the information that was communicated to users. In its October 2009 newsletter, the Polk Library at the University of Wisconsin-Oshkosh discussed budget reductions in the collections budget and reaffirmed its approach to provide information content for the community by giving users what they want in the format they want it and by providing content "just in time" rather than "just in case." The managers moved some serial titles from print only to online only; canceled several high-cost-per-use electronic resources, which allowed the addition of new electronic resources requested by users; cut allocations for books and media across academic departments; and reallocated funding by eliminating a book approval plan and targeting collection development and a patron-driven electronic book collection.[3]

Several libraries employed marketing techniques to inform users that the library was meeting their needs during budget reductions. In 2014, the University of North Carolina, Greensboro (UNC-G), presented a webpage that informed the university community about how it was handling budget reductions. In FY2014, cuts were made in the categories of equipment, travel, supplies, and student wages, and four vacant, full-time positions were eliminated. Collection development, however, was spared. During the next fiscal year, 2015, additional cuts were made: equipment, travel, supplies, and student wages, and five more vacant positions eliminated. With little left to cut and with inflationary increases in the costs for maintaining the collections, the library informed the community that reductions to the collection were inevitable. The library spent months on a data-driven analysis of the collections and usage patterns. The managers and the staff developed a draft cancellation plan and actively sought faculty feedback and discussion so that cuts to the collections would have the least possible impact on the university's teaching, research, and community engagement missions.[4]

On a webpage, Appalachian State University's Belk Library and Information Commons noted that any reduction in the university budget brings a consequent reduction in library funding. The library experienced a 36 percent reduction of non-personnel funds in fiscal year 2012, and made these cuts:

- Three library faculty positions in the past three years were eliminated.

- Library hours were cut 18 percent.
- Student assistant hours were cut 20 percent.
- Library public computer funding was cut 80 percent.
- Collections (e-resources, databases, books, and journals) were cut $1 million (−25%).

For the following fiscal year, the library expected inflationary increases in the collections of more than $150,000 and had to accommodate a reduction of $400,000 in library funding. The criteria for the expected reductions included low-use and the most expensive resources, and these were announced to the university community, along with an identification, by title, of the resources subject to elimination. University Librarian Mary Reichel encouraged comments from faculty, staff, and students on these planned reductions.[5]

The library at the University of California, Santa Cruz, mounted a Frequently Asked Questions (FAQ) on its website concerning its budget reductions in fiscal years 2009 and 2010. There were twenty-six questions and answers on a wide range of budget reduction topics, including the time line for the reductions and how it would impact faculty and students.[6]

The Massachusetts Institute of Technology (MIT) Libraries implemented a similar FAQ strategy when informing the institutional community about budget reductions for fiscal years 2010 and 2011. The webpage also presented a rationale from then-Director of Libraries Anne Wolpert about planning for the future of the MIT Libraries, including a major reorganization of the libraries because of the budget reductions.[7]

Another strategy informs users how the library participates in the accomplishment of the institutional mission. In a fall 2010 web-based newsletter, the interim university librarian at the University of California, Irvine, Libraries (UCI) discussed the impact of the reductions to the libraries' base budget of more than $5,000,000 since fiscal year 2008. These reductions included a 22 percent reduction in staff, loss in the number of hours open, and decreased collections expenditures. Positive changes were also identified, including the introduction of patron-driven acquisition models, more library instruction moving to online delivery, redistribution of personnel to areas of highest priorities, and improvements in interlibrary loan. A proposal under consideration was to reallocate library space to house non-library units currently occupying off-campus leased spaces, saving the institution about $1,000,000 in rent.[8]

Informing library users about the impact of budget cuts might convert users into library advocates. In a letter dated January 27, 2014, the executive vice chancellor and provost of the University of California, Berkeley, and the chair of the Academic Senate announced a proposal to restore $8.1 million in funds to the library. The library's budget decreased due to reductions in state funding. Those reductions, coupled with inflationary costs, had a significant impact on both collections development and staffing. Many faculty members felt underserved by the library and appealed to the provost, in 2012, to reverse this trend. The provost and the chair of the Academic Senate appointed a Commission on the Future of the Library to examine the problem and make recommendations. The report, completed in October 2013, concluded that libraries would be even more critical to university teaching and research in the coming years. The commission recommended a permanent increase in the library's annual collection budget, the hiring of additional professional librarians as well as support staff, and other critical investments.[9]

Even another strategy is for the library to set its own priorities when budget reductions are necessary instead of having the institution make service, program, and function cuts to the library. An example of this strategy is displayed in a July 2009 web-based announcement from University Librarian Karen Butter at the University of California, San Francisco, about the fiscal year 2010 budget cuts. Because of the statewide fiscal crisis, the library budget was being reduced by 15 percent. After explaining the library's principles, she announced the specific reductions that would occur in library hours, collections, the elimination of vacant staff positions, and the institution of a hiring freeze. These reductions were made, but the library also forewent the replacement of computer workstations and reduced supply purchases and staff travel to meetings. She welcomed comments and suggestions from the institutional stakeholders.[10]

Some library functions should not be cut during budget reductions, if possible. Staff training should continue, including job-related training and keeping current with procedures and policies (e.g., personnel training about discrimination and harassment). Staff training is different from staff development, which is intended to prepare personnel for different or additional jobs. Second, managers should not defer minor interior and exterior maintenance. Although maintenance is one of the first functions to suffer during budget reduction cycles, deferring maintenance only deepens the problems as time accrues, eventually escalating the minor repairs into major overhauls.

Library Fraud

Academic library financial managers and leaders (see coverage of leadership in the next chapter) are expected to be good stewards of the resources entrusted to them for the benefit of the institution and its stakeholders. Organizational managerial leaders must understand and acknowledge the financial stresses that they experience. Briefly, financial stress is the degree to which the day-to-day operating budgets are under pressure from having too few resources to meet the objectives of the library's long-term plan. Stress is also increased from the pressure to demonstrate or otherwise prove to stakeholders the value the library adds to the education enterprise. This stress is further accentuated because of the attention in the media to topical and timely issues (e.g., student debt, retention, and progress to degree in a timely manner). A third source of stress is the political pressure of balancing internal competing interests and values such as satisfying the ongoing demands from "squeaky wheels" or the occasional but urgent requests from other organizational members and units for special treatment or favors for needed information resources or services as they complete scholarly activities or research projects necessary for promotion or tenure.[11]

Occurrences of financial fraud are occasionally blamed on financial stress. A more likely cause of fraud is behavior in which one or more people, within and outside of the library, take advantage of a lack of controls or procedures in order to take funds or assets for their own personal use. Examples of financial fraud include

- **Lack of controls.** Formal procedures concerning financial management are not followed, or the procedures do not exist. This would include a single person having the responsibility for ordering items or services, receiving the items, approving the invoice submitted, and reconciling the expenditures with the budget status report.
- **Credit card abuse.** The library's credit card is used for personal use or for purchases of services or items that should not be acquired using the credit card.
- **Employee theft.** An employee steals items from the library. This could be as minor as office supplies in small amounts, or as major as the theft of equipment or of physical books or media.
- **Employee benefiting from selling services.** An example is an employee who grants an unauthorized person remote access privileges to subscription or licensed databases in exchange for money or some other asset.
- **Embezzlement.** This is the theft or misappropriation of funds placed in one's trust or belonging to one's employer. The nature of embezzlement can be either small or large. Embezzling funds can be as minor as an employee pocketing a few dollars from a cash transaction, such as fines paid for overdue books. Embezzlement, however, can involve thousands of dollars transferred into personal accounts.
- **Use of library funds for personal items.** Library funds are used to purchase personal items. The employee orders items (e.g., books) or equipment (e.g., a pair of headphones) and diverts them to his or her personal use.
- **Use of shell companies.** An employee or an acquaintance or relative of an employee sets up a company that invoices the library for services that may not be provided at all, or the services provided may be unnecessary. The invoice is placed in a pile with other invoices. Bookkeeping personnel pay the invoice thinking that the services have been rendered. This fraud can go undetected for years if the invoices are for small dollar amounts and submitted on a regular basis.

- **Selling library-owned items.** An employee sells books, media or documents, and artifacts from special collections or archives.
- **Overpayments for goods or services.** The vendor invoices the library for an amount higher than the value of the items or services, the library pays the invoiced amount, and a library employee receives a portion of the payment from the vendor as a kickback.

Although very little is reported about academic library fraud in the news or in the literature of library and information science, it does occur. In addition to the loss of funds or other assets, a result of discovered fraud is the loss of trust of the library from its stakeholders. Prevention and detection should be important to all library managers.

There are some best practices that can be adopted. First, assign responsibility for implementing appropriate controls to prevent and detect fraud and theft and establish the consequences for fraud and theft by employees. Second, segregate finance-related job duties among several employees. This practice makes it easier to find errors and to catch those who perpetuate fraud. Third, avoid handling any cash, if possible. For example, relocate the collection of cash-based fines to another unit in the institution, such as the cashier's office. Fourth, seek help from the institution's audit office to review the library's financial practices and procedures.

A fifth best practice is to review the work of Herbert Snyder, PhD, CFE (certified fraud examiner), who has written a readable and understandable book on library financial matters: *Small Change, Big Problems: Detecting and Preventing Financial Misconduct in Your Library*.[12] While this work is no longer available to purchase in print, it is available as an e-book and, of course, is available through ILL. Snyder, a professor and department chair of the department of accounting, finance, and information systems at North Dakota State University, thoroughly explains financial misconduct, how it occurs, and how to discover and prevent fraud in a library.

As a final best practice, learn from past fraud cases related to libraries. Review these cases when they are reported in the news or appear in the literature. The institution's audit office may also be able to share its experiences with examples of past fraud cases.

Conclusion: Summary of the "Best of" Best Practices

There are a few best practices that all library financial managers should keep in mind:
- Involve and inform as many stakeholders as possible, including library staff, users, and the library's advocates and critics, when planning library services, programs, and functions.

- Create and maintain an internal checklist for the budgeting process so that no financial detail is overlooked.
- Collaborate with others when seeking internal and external funding. The more advocates for the library, the better.
- When implementing a program budgeting process, start with one or two programs so that managers can become familiar with process; evaluate the success of the process before adding other programs or services.
- Do not request more funding than the library can successfully manage. Failure to expend the amount awarded appropriately and for the specific purposes as promised by the library will likely result in a loss of stakeholder confidence in the library.
- Maintain pristine financial records.
- Publicize the value and accomplishments provided by the funds the library receives and uses from all sources.
- Develop and maintain accurate and current inventories of library assets (e.g., furniture and equipment, library spaces). The library already maintains an inventory of information items; other and additional inventories should be easy to undertake when compared to a collections inventory.
- Write and submit an annual report, and make it publicly available for both internal and external audiences through the library's website.
- Assign personnel specifically to business office functions.
- Library business office personnel need to be knowledgeable about financial processes and functions, such as accounting or bookkeeping, and to create and manage spreadsheets.
- Personnel in the library's business office must also be personable with their colleagues in the institution's business offices because, inevitably, they will need to work with their central office's counterparts during the fiscal year.
- Library managers must create a separation of accountability and duties of the library's business functions, avoiding the "all eggs in one basket" practice that can lead to financial misconduct and the loss of trust of the library's stakeholders.

Many of these best practices are grounded in decades of practitioner-based financial management. The adoption and application of best practices, however, vary from library to library and manager to manager. The purpose of these best practices is to improve financial management in libraries, while helping to prepare the organization for financial leadership.

Exercises

1. What may a library do when it learns about a budget reduction from the current year's budget level two months before the next fiscal year begins?

2. The library has sustained a budget rescission three months into the fiscal year. What are two strategies that should be considered for immediate implementation?

3. A financial audit of the past fiscal year's expenditures reveals that the library overexpended its non-personnel budgeted allocation by $100,000. The library dean places the blame on the library's business office; the business office counters that it had reported to the library dean that the budget was being overspent, but nothing was done. What may happen now?

(Answers to these questions can be found in the appendix at the back of the book. We encourage different library managers to work together, perhaps with staff members, to answer each question and to discuss the results.)

Notes

1. Eastern Michigan University Library, "New @ EMU Library: Fall 2010—Faculty Edition," October 2010, http://www.emich.edu/library/users/Faculty-NewAttheLibraryFall2010.pdf (page now discontinued).

2. Will Manley, "Winning the Budget Wars," *American Libraries,* May 6, 2010, https://americanlibrariesmagazine.org/2010/05/06/winning-the-budget-wars.

3. Pat Wilkinson, "Renewed Focus," *Polk Library News* (Polk Library, University of Wisconsin Oshkosh), no. 46 (October 2009): 1.

4. University of North Carolina, Greensboro Library, "Budget Information for 2013/14 and 2014/15," accessed April 19, 2014, http://library.uncg.edu/info/budget (page now discontinued).

5. Appalachian State University, Belk Library and Information Commons, "University Library Budget Reduction Strategies FY 2012/2013," accessed April 19, 2014, http://www.library.appstate.edu/about/budget (page now discontinued).

6. University of California Santa Cruz, University Library, "Budget Reduction Frequently Asked Questions," accessed October 9, 2015, http://library.ucsc.edu/collections/budget-reduction-frequently-asked-questions (page now discontinued).

7. MIT Libraries, "MIT Libraries Budget Information," accessed April 24, 2011, http://libraries.mit.edu/about/budget/index.html (page now discontinued).

8. Gerald R. Lowell, "Message from the Interim University Librarian," *UCI Libraries Update: A Newsletter for Faculty,* (University of California, Irvine, Libraries), Fall 2010, http://update.lib.uci.edu/fall10/index.html.

9. George W. Breslauer, Executive Vice Chancellor and Provost, and Elizabeth Deakin, Chair, Academic Senate, "Letter to the University," University of California, Berkeley, January 27, 2014. See also Connor Grubaugh, "UC Berkeley Announces $4.6 Million of Additional Funding for Library," *Daily Californian,* January 29, 2014, http://www.dailycal.org/2014/01/29/campus-officials-announce-4-6-million-additional-funding-library.

10. Karen Butter, "The Library Budget, 2010: A Letter from University Librarian Karen Butter," University of California, San Francisco, Library and Center for Knowledge Management, July 2009, http://www.library.ucsf.edu/about/planning/budget#strategic (page now discontinued).

11. Complicating matters, managerial leaders engaged in financial management and leadership

should be aware of resonant leaders and take steps to reduce the amount of stress on them. See Richard Boyatzis and Annie McKee, *Resonant Leadership* (Boston: Harvard Business School Press, 2005).

12. Herbert Snyder, *Small Change, Big Problems* (Chicago: ALA, 2006).

Bibliography

Appalachian State University, Belk Library and Information Commons. "University Library Budget Reduction Strategies FY 2012/2013." Accessed April 19, 2014. http://www.library.appstate.edu/about/budget (page now discontinued).

Boyatzis, Richard, and Annie McKee. *Resonant Leadership: Renewing Yourself and Connecting with Others through Mindfulness, Hope, and Compassion* (Boston: Harvard Business School Press, 2005).

Breslauer, George W. (Executive Vice Chancellor and Provost), and Elizabeth Deakin (Chair, Academic Senate). "Letter to the University." University of California, Berkeley, January 27, 2014.

Butter, Karen. "The Library Budget, 2010: A Letter from University Librarian Karen Butter." University of California, San Francisco, Library and Center for Knowledge Management, July 2009. http://www.library.ucsf.edu/about/planning/budget#strategic (page now discontinued).

Eastern Michigan University Library. "New @ EMU Library: Fall 2010—Faculty Edition." October 2010. http://www.emich.edu/library/users/Faculty-NewAttheLibraryFall2010.pdf (page now discontinued).

Grubaugh, Connor. "UC Berkeley Announces $4.6 Million of Additional Funding for Library." *Daily Californian,* January 29, 2014. http://www.dailycal.org/2014/01/29/campus-officials-announce-4-6-million-additional-funding-library.

Lowell, Gerald R. "Message from the Interim University Librarian." *UCI Libraries Update: A Newsletter for Faculty,* (University of California, Irvine, Libraries), Fall 2010. http://update.lib.uci.edu/fall10/index.html.

Manley, Will. "Winning the Budget Wars." *American Libraries,* May 6, 2010. https://americanlibrariesmagazine.org/2010/05/06/winning-the-budget-wars.

MIT Libraries. "MIT Libraries Budget Information." Accessed April 24, 2011. http://libraries.mit.edu/about/budget/index.html (page now discontinued).

Snyder, Herbert. *Small Change, Big Problems: Detecting and Preventing Financial Misconduct in Your Library.* Chicago, ALA, 2006.

University of California Santa Cruz, University Library. "Budget Reduction Frequently Asked Questions." Accessed October 9, 2015. http://library.ucsc.edu/collections/budget-reduction-frequently-asked-questions (page now discontinued).

University of North Carolina, Greensboro Library. "Budget Information for 2013/14 and 2014/15." Accessed April 19, 2014. http://library.uncg.edu/info/budget (page now discontinued).

Wilkinson, Pat. "Renewed Focus." *Polk Library News* (Polk Library, University of Wisconsin Oshkosh), no. 46 (October 2009.

Chapter 10[*]

Financial Leadership

This chapter moves the discussion from financial management to financial leadership, thereby viewing organizational finances from a leadership, not a management, perspective. Leadership deals with organizational transformation and keeping the library relevant to the institution and the stakeholders it serves for the long term.[1] Management focuses on staff acceptance of the importance of accomplishing stated goals and objectives, whereas leadership engages the staff to accept and work toward the accomplishment of a new organizational reality, as expressed through a vision—"a sensible and appealing picture of the future"—and strategies—"a logic for how the vision can be achieved."[2] In other words, leaders develop a vision that frames the future library. Managers create plans, which advance goals and objectives, together with steps and timetables to implement stated goals, and budgets, which convert plans into financial realities to accomplish those goals and objectives. In brief, managers focus on the mission statement, and leaders concentrate on the development of a vision and stakeholder buy-in to the future specified. Table 10.1 offers an additional comparison between financial management and financial leadership.

The purpose of leadership in financial management is to help translate the direction in which the library intends to go into an action plan, to influence service and program development, and to improve the effectiveness of services and programs for the entire library. Since libraries tend to exist in not-for-profit institutions, leadership values for financial management differ from those in the profit sector.

*The first part of this chapter draws on Peter Hernon, "Reflections on Library Leadership: An Examination of Four Leadership Theories," *Library Leadership and Management Library* 31 (August 2017): 1-12.

Table 10.1
Differences between Financial Management and Financial Leadership

Financial Management	Financial Leadership
• Deals with management (organizing, delegating, implementing, interviewing, and supervising)	• Addresses leadership (motivating others, creating enthusiasm, inspiring organizational loyalty and workforce productivity, setting a course for the organization, initiating change, and building consensus)
• Relates to the organizational mission and its accomplishment	• Relates to the institutional and organizational vision (operationalizes both)
• Ensures credibility and trust in operations and in reporting	• Focuses on the long term or the next fifteen years for the organization and its institutional role
• Is associated with the accomplishment of goals and objectives specified in planning documents	• Guides an organization to sustainability by staking out a role central to institutional growth
• Involves the collection of financial data, production of financial reports, and solution of immediate near-term (1–3 years) financial issues	• Tries to improve the current environment, undergo change (accepted or forced), or cope with a crisis (e.g., budget or disaster)
• Involves managers in matters of monitoring expenditures, evaluation, and accountability	

These values relate to accountability, partnerships, stewardship, integrity, and ethics. Accountability is a set of initiatives others take to monitor the results of institutional actions and to penalize or reward the institution based on fulfillment of stated outcomes. Accountability is a managerial responsibility with functions that include coordinating among units, inserting control mechanisms to manage inputs and outputs, and reporting (and acting on) the findings. Accountability is important when stakeholders ask if the benefits of library programs and services equal or exceed costs (as specified in the budget).[3] Taxpayers want tax-supported institutions to be accountable for the funds, time, and resources allocated to them and for the funds expended. They also want institutions to demonstrate their effectiveness through accountability (e.g., institutional fiscal efficiency), ensuring quality and making improvements (e.g., changes in users through their contact with library programs and services). Managers assume a leadership role, in part, when they champion a culture of accountability, recognize that accountability is not a fad, and initiate evaluation and assessment studies to identify problems for which decision makers can make internal improvements.

Leaders develop partnerships so that they can create an awareness of the library and its institutional role, learn what stakeholders need, communicate what the library is doing, work with external groups on common agendas, and gain buy-in to existing and new services. Partnerships must be nurtured, and the relationship established must be mutually beneficial. Using public relations, the library tells its story about what it is (its mission) and what it does for its stakeholders in terms of services and programs. Partnerships enable the library to market itself, conducting a two-way dialogue with its stakeholders to learn more about their needs in addition to the library's announcements of events. The maturation of established partnerships increases advocacy; the library builds relationships with the partners so that they will become advocates of library-related issues through a planned, deliberate, and sustained effort to raise awareness of its organizational principles and values. As a result, a library furthers the partnerships by stating that the stakeholders' agenda, be it furthering education, furthering research, or supporting the social good, is assisted by what the library offers.

Stewardship refers to the efficient administration of resources and the execution of plans for conserving and using those resources, effectively directing and controlling an organization's human and material resources, and maintaining and reporting on the custodianship of resources. Managerial leaders manage the assets entrusted to the library and their care, while they adhere to legal and regulatory standards. Any mismanagement of resources might place the library in legal jeopardy of losing its 501(c)(3) tax-exempt status or result in a critical undervaluing of library's assets. Leaders engage in best practices, keep the promises they make, and convey the cultural attitude that oversight is important and acceptable, which leads the organization to "doing the right thing."

Integrity refers to the conduct of business in ways that avoid even the appearance of a conflict of interest; communicating unfavorable, as well as favorable, information; and avoiding any conduct that reflects negatively on the organization or the library profession. Ethics, a related subject, involves adherence to the standards of ethical conduct for professional organizations, such as the Institute of Management Accountants. These standards require accountants, or, in this case, managerial leaders, to have an appropriate level of competence; perform their duties in accordance with relevant laws, regulations, and technical standards; maintain confidentiality; and exercise objectivity when communicating information. Leaders recognize the confluence between appearance and reality, intention and action, promise and performance, and desired outcome (trust and credibility). They ensure behavior that fosters ethical conduct throughout the organization ("do as I say"). They also ensure that the organization has articulated values and that managers live by them ("do as I do"), and they vigorously support organizational ethics and a culture of accountability, ethical behavior, effectiveness, and efficiency. They might even conduct anonymous surveys of employees or develop a hotline for ethics violations, and they regard character, integrity, and decision making as values to include on performance reviews. Additionally, they insert values and character in the hiring process as part of a review of personnel vitas, ensure the highest level of ethical conduct throughout the organization, and establish consistent consequences for misbehavior and violations of the organization's code of conduct.

As part of the hiring process for lower-level managers, leaders might place an interviewee in practical situations (scenarios) and ask how he or she would react. For instance,

- "What would you do if a student assistant working in the library told you that her dorm roommate is abusive?"
- "How do you deal with a student who is insisting that she returned a laptop?"
- "What do you do about a student who refuses to leave when the library is closing?"
- "How do you deal with workers you supervise who are habitually late?"
- "What do you do when you know that staff are taking books from the library without checking them out?"
- "What do you do when you know a staff colleague is taking supplies for his or her personal use?"

Within a library, senior and middle managers help to set the organizational culture, especially for their direct reports, through their communications, transparency, focus on accountability, work with other managers (their peers), and mediation. Leadership is not confined to managers, regardless of position in the organization. Non-managers, those known as followers in the leadership literature, should be encouraged to assume a leadership role when they have expertise and knowledge beneficial to the achievement of an organizational objective.[4]

Leadership

No single definition of leadership, within and beyond library and information science, dominates. A preferred definition might depend on a person's position within an organization, including a library. For directors and members of a library's senior management team, a definition might emphasize the vision they set for the organization and the buy-in of staff and stakeholders to, and the successful implementation of, that vision. Other managers in the organization might not mention the vision, except to say they agree with it; they might emphasize implementation of the vision or achievement of common goals as they cope with a changing environment.

Leadership has often been framed in terms of exerting influence, leading or orchestrating manageable change, setting an example for others to follow, or empowering and inspiring (or motivating) a group to achieve a common goal or vision. James M. Kouzes and Barry Z. Posner add that that the cornerstone of leadership is credibility, or displaying skills and abilities such as being trustworthy, demonstrating integrity, and having a reputation for honesty. Leadership, they explain, also involves the development and clarification of a set of guiding values and the alignment of one's actions with those values.[5]

Because leadership is not limited to those in managerial positions, those assigned to a team as so-called followers might display knowledge, skills, or abilities that enable them, on occasion, to guide the team to achieve assigned tasks. Barbara Kellerman provides insight into different types of followers, not all whom support change.[6] In a later work, she portrays the dark side of leadership, namely bad or negative (incompetent or unethical) leadership, and observes that the results achieved are not always positive or moral.[7] Thus, the term *leadership* is neutral; it applies to positive and negative leadership. Most often the leadership literature concentrates on positive leadership.

Leadership Theories

To be most effective, leaders must be familiar with different theories and be comfortable with those they adopt; after all, theories are about change, sustainability, and the process of influencing others.[8] Kellerman argues that leaders and followers are intertwined; followership should not be ignored in any discussion of leadership and which theory is most appropriate. The context within which both leaders and followers function, she adds, is critical to that discussion. Context goes beyond the organization or the institution overseeing that organization and refers to the national and international environment that impinges on societies and ultimately organizations. That environment encompasses such things as financial crises, terrorism, dysfunctional government, and shifting national, state, and local priorities.[9]

Leadership, a complex process, represents an evolution of theories and approaches. Perhaps one of the earliest approaches was the emphasis of leadership traits and the personal qualities that individuals should possess. Later, there was a shift from innate personality traits to skills and abilities that can be learned and developed. The style approach shifted attention to the behavior of leaders and their capabilities. Attention now focused on the actions that leaders take with subordinates or followers. From this beginning, more theories and approaches emerged.

Situational theories adapt leadership actions to meet the needs of different situations and circumstances. Such theories might focus on the identification of the ability (or competence) and willingness (commitment or motivation) of followers, and then determining the best style of leadership to adopt. They might also suggest continuums of leadership style, the broad approach adopted by a leader. A leader's style of leadership is often based on that person's beliefs, personality, and experiences and the given situation. Some leaders rely on one leadership style. Others are more flexible and adapt their style of leadership to meet the needs of different situations.

Participative leadership theories, which developed out of the concept of leadership style, focus on the relationship between the leader and the followers. In these theories, leaders empower followers, involve them in the decision-making process, build support to accomplish a shared vision and common goals, and encourage others to act.

Another perspective looks at the type of work that leaders do and the relationship between leaders and followers. Transactional leadership theory, based on transactions or exchanges between both groups, assumes that the working relationship is one where the leader issues the work, praises or criticizes, rewards or punishes. The followers have little responsibility, other than doing as they are required, correctly. Both leaders and followers are expected to carry out their part in the transactions. In transformational leadership theory, leaders see the big picture, and they inspire others to follow the vision and to take responsibility for new ideas.

The Global Leadership and Organizational Behavior Effectiveness Research Program (GLOBE) and researchers such as Geert Hofstede, the eminent Dutch psychologist, view the effectiveness of leaders as contextual or embedded in the societal and organizational norms, values, and beliefs of the people being led. They compare societies on cultural dimensions, note differences in cultural influences among different countries, and advance numerous hypotheses about the relationship between national culture and leadership.[10]

GLOBE, however, has generated criticism, such as there is no single theory about how culture relates to leadership or influences leadership processes. Existing research has not connected this framework to general leadership theories such as authentic, situational, and transformational leadership. Nonetheless, GLOBE underscores the importance of national cultures and reminds anyone engaged in the study of leadership that culture should not be ignored. "Globalization and the growing interdependence of our world community," as Juana Bordas points out, "are making the ability to lead and build community with people from very distinct cultures, nationalities, and ethnic groups fundamental to effective leadership."[11] Clearly, "leaders must have the cultural flexibility and adaptability to inspire and guide people who represent the whole rainbow of humanity."[12] Bordas is referring to multicultural leadership, which

- focuses on cultural values (e.g., fairness and equity), influences, practices, collaboration (concentrating on we as opposed to I in hierarchical leadership), differences, and the relationships among people—within and across cultures—in a multicultural society
- discourages stifling cultural identity and recognizes that nuances in the practice of multicultural leadership are likely to exist among cultures
- recognizes that leaders must earn the respect and trust of those who follow

This brief overview would not be complete without the mention of additional theories:

- authentic leadership, which address the authenticity of leaders
- contingency leadership, which suggests that the effectiveness of a leader equates to how well that person's style fits the situation or context

- ethical leadership, which sees leadership in terms of the choices leaders make and how ethics (values and morals) direct their response to a given situation
- leader-member exchange theory, which views leadership as a process centered on the interactions between leaders and followers
- path-goal theory, which presents how leaders motivate followers to accomplish organizational goals
- servant leadership, which views the leader as someone wanting to serve and who aspires to lead
- team leadership, which focuses on the effectiveness of work groups in accomplishing stated goals and objectives

One way to view leadership is through models that encompass various theories and approaches. One such model guided the Simmons College School of Library and Information Science doctoral program, Managerial Leadership in the Information Professions (MLIP). This model accommodates different leadership theories, approaches, and styles. Leaders use the theories to form their leadership approach or style. Theory explains concepts and advances one's understanding. A style, on the other hand, is based on a combination of one's beliefs, values, comfort level, personality, and preferences; it shows how individuals practice theory and focuses on what leaders do as well as on the leadership traits and behaviors they favor.

The MLIP program focused on managerial leadership predominantly for those in positions of senior management in academic and public libraries. Supported by two grants from the Institute of Museum and Library Services (IMLS), the program modified a leadership model developed by the National Center for Healthcare Leadership.[13] This competency-based model focused on three primary domains:[14]

1. **Transformation**, which refers to visioning, energizing, and stimulating a change process that coalesces communities, patrons, and professionals around new models of managerial leadership in the information professions
2. **Accomplishment**, which refers to translating vision and strategy into optimal organizational performance
3. **People**, which refers to creating an organizational climate that values employees in all their diversity and provides an energizing environment for them

Each of these domains contains a number of competences, which individuals can learn and master.

Developing a Fuller Vision

When an institution searches for a new director, the candidates, among other things, present their organizational vision. Most likely, as they make on-site visits, they observe how well that vision matches the environment, gain a more comprehensive picture of what is happening, and form an image of how they would refine that vision and what changes they might make. In conducting this review, they might be guided by Lee G. Bolman and Terrence E. Deal's four frames: a frame equates to a mental model and consists of ideas and assumptions that help managerial leaders to assemble information into a coherent pattern. With the information gathered, newly hired managerial leaders, for instance, can uncover clues as they gain a more comprehensive picture of what is happening and what to do. These frames are the

- **structural frame**, which presents ways to organize and structure groups, departments, and teams to get the desired results
- **human resource frame**, which looks at how to tailor organizations to satisfy human needs, improve human resource management, and build positive interpersonal and group dynamics
- **political frame**, which deals with how to cope with power and conflict, build coalitions, hone political skills, and deal with internal and external politics
- **symbolic frame**, which presents the organization to others through symbols such as ritual, ceremony, stories, and culture. Leaders use symbols to capture attention, portray the organization, give purpose and meaning to work, build team spirit, frame experiences by providing plausible interpretations of experiences, and communicate a vision.[15]

Once in the position, they might review the vision with stakeholders and involve senior managers in further refining it. An expanded vision statement that can serve as an action plan for the future is more detailed than the one depicted in box 1.1, which states "The Libraries will be an innovative, inspiring, and vital component in the academic life of the University," but it is derived from the original sentence. The purpose of developing a more detailed statement is to demonstrate the sustainability of the library and institutional relevance, provide a foundation for stakeholder buy-in, and place the intended transformative change in a broader context. This statement—the organizational vision—achieves one component found in many definitions of leadership, namely trying to inspire others to accept and work to achieve the projected future. As John P. Kotter explains, unless a vision can be explained within five minutes and the interest of this audience piqued, "you have more work to do in this phase of a transformation process."[16]

How to Develop the More Detailed Image of the Future

Kotter, among others, identifies the steps critical to the development of an effective vision for an organization; for him, the focus is on a for-profit organization.[17] Instead of duplicating his discussion, this section focuses on an alternative method, namely the inclusion of others in the articulation of a more expansive vision statement through the development of scenarios or scenario planning. Neither of these methods involves predictions of the future; they are about anticipation, monitoring the environment, and breaking away from conventional strategic mind-sets as components of relevant futures expressed in that statement emerge. Scenario planning, a structured process, uses stories to describe possible futures to help managers think about how surprises and discontinuities can be examined in the planning process. These stories take complex elements and weave them into coherent pictures of the future organization that are generally no more than one page. They help managers to envision possible futures and to develop strategies that will increase the chances of organizational success as the library or institution responds to a changing environment. "Scenarios can help an organization evaluate its progress and course of action, as it answers the following question: Are we headed in the right direction given the most probable scenarios and the alternative options?"[18] Scenarios might be developed independent of the scenario planning process as managers and stakeholders lay out preferred futures for the type of service organization that will be most relevant to the changing institution.

Dana Mietzner and Guido Reger recommend that the number of proposed scenarios not exceed four,[19] while forecaster Joseph P. Martino advises that a set of scenarios should project no more than fifteen years. He notes that the accuracy of what a vision offers declines dramatically with a longer time frame.[20] Setting the time limit prevents those developing the scenarios from creating "pie in the sky" futures that are meaningless to institutional and organizational planning.[21]

Scenarios can reflect one of two perspectives. The first focuses on the organization, its potential services, and how the future matches the direction in which the institution is headed, whereas the second deals with the changing institution and what it might resemble. Managers might then pursue organizational scenarios in the context of reflections about the future institution. An Internet search will quickly lead managers to examples of both perspectives, or readers might review two dissertations that lay out different choices for consideration.[22] One of the scenarios depicted in one of these dissertations portrays changes that "could impact research programs at major universities." The research examined "the question 'How will globalization and entrepreneurial approaches impact research program development in US universities over the next 15 years?' The author "identified major forces that impact research programs and produced a matrix of four plausible futures that can be identified from these driving forces."[23] Individual institutions could then select and tweak their preferred future.

Translating a Vision into an Action Plan

Any vision that an institution or organization selects must have local relevance and application; the purpose is not to develop a generic vision relevant to all types of academic institutions globally. For the sake of discussion, let us assume that a library and its stakeholders view the depiction of an organization in box 10.1 as something they want to achieve over the next fifteen years. Some components in that box might already exist or represent a logical progression from existing services. Some, however, might be relevant to what the institution wants to accomplish over the next fifteen years. Two critical questions are, "Is this vision realistic to achieve, or do we need to make some tweaks?" and "How well can the library continue to support existing services that are relevant to the future as expressed in the box while moving in new directions and capitalizing on changes already underway?" These questions lead to questions such as

- "How do managers prioritize the components in the box in terms of planning documents?"
- "How do they reallocate existing resources?"
- "What are they willing to stop doing to repurpose some existing resources?"
- "What, precisely, do they need to do to make the transformed library a reality?"
- "Where do they (and how might they) attract new resources for the next fifteen years?"

Box 10.1
Expanding Service Roles*

The library assures seamless access to needed knowledge, information, and data in an environment in which the library is a service provider. The library greatly downsizes its physical collection and traditional services, expanding its digital collections, and is a partner in teaching, learning, and research. Librarians assume a proactive, not a passive, presence with academic departments through an active, nurturing role of information discovery, supporting and advancing teaching and learning pedagogy, supporting interdisciplinary and cross-disciplinary research, and producing and preserving knowledge for the institution. Librarians may be embedded in courses alongside the instructor. The library's instruction sessions mature from orientation to library services and resources toward determining the quality of information sources through evaluation methods based on critical thinking.

Network and cooperative arrangements (e.g., through consortial memberships) provide backup support and achieve savings in bibliographic control and access to needed resources.

With the changing nature of knowledge creation and use, the library is an active partner in the institutional effort to support research projects irrespective of geographic and national boundaries. It also views scholarly communication (the process of conducting research and sharing the results: from creation to dissemination and preservation of knowledge for the purposes of teaching, research, and scholarship) as part of its core mission and engages in electronic publishing on behalf of academic departments, faculty, and graduate students.

The library emphasizes access and preservation of individual faculty educational and scholarly activities, not just those of academic departments. The institutional repository focuses on faculty members, not necessarily on disciplines and academic programs, and it concentrates on faculty scholarly activities, including presentations, video work, posters, and white papers in addition to peer-reviewed scholarly publications. To accomplish this role, the library invests in the tools necessary to engage in publishing, preferring to take a more independent role and develop both the infrastructure and expertise as an online publisher.

The library relies more on cloud-based applications than on institutionally based and locally developed applications supported through its information technology department. The physical space emphasizes group and individual study space and sharing space with selected campus support units (e.g., the writing center).

The technology provided in library spaces emphasizes collaborative work, whereas the technology in public areas emphasizes productivity. Workstation screens are larger, and workstations with dual monitors are more common. The public space furniture provided in the library varies from traditional tables and task chairs to mobile furniture and lounge seating. There is also quiet space for individual study and conversation-level areas throughout the facility.

The library uses assessment methods to demonstrate its contribution to student learning outcomes through library instruction and student interactions with library personnel. The library also shows how it adds value to aggregate student outcomes by developing methods to demonstrate its contribution to student outcomes: graduation rates, retention, and postgraduate employment.

In sum, the library intends to inspire the total individual, encouraging personal, social, and intellectual growth through the acquisition of information and knowledge, knowledge sharing, and communication among faculty, students, and other stakeholders, including library staff.

*This scenario builds extensively on the fourth and fifth ones included in Peter Hernon and Joseph R. Matthews, *Reflecting on the Future of Academic and Public Libraries* (Chicago: ALA Editions, 2013), 91-95.

Leadership focuses on the answers to these questions; for example, the benefits of partnerships and consortial memberships for the library. Licensing for information access is time-consuming for a single library. A consortium membership enables libraries to partner with others as they negotiate electronic licenses to access resources, providing contracting experience the library may lack, and saving time and money. In the past, consortial memberships were likely to be geographically based because they were structured on traditional print sharing. Now, consortial memberships are based on the member support services offered because sharing electronic resources is less geographically limited. Partnerships may be based on digital resource collection development and access, such as membership in the Center for Research Libraries and the HathiTrust.

Conclusion

Managerial leaders try to attain a more detailed vision (e.g., the one in box 10.1) and to secure (and maintain) buy-in from the staff and other stakeholders. Ultimately, the successful achievement of that vision requires effective leadership and management. This success is not confined to financial leadership and management, however.

Managers need a firm understanding of planning and the other issues discussed in previous chapters. As libraries engage in transformational change, they need individuals who are both financial managers and financial leaders and who can view financial management in terms of the proposed change. At the same time, there needs to be a realization that leadership is not confined to the director. Leadership, a shared responsibility, should be highly prized throughout the organization. As leaders, librarians engage in change within the organization but they also have an external role—ensuring the library's future is sustainability and integral to the future of the institution. Leaders accept responsibility and are personally and professionally accountable for all actions the organization undertakes. A key to leadership is gaining stakeholder buy-in to the stated vision as the library works to achieve the new future. A vision statement, after all, is not an abstract portrayal of the future; it represents a reality that the library wants to create. "That shared sense of a desirable future," Kotter notes, "can help motivate and coordinate the kinds of actions that create transformations."[24]

Exercises

1. Who is a financial leader in your library, and why do you regard this person as one?
2. For your library, whom would you involve in rewriting box 10.1? Rewrite the content of the box.
3. To accomplish this vision, list five things the library could stop doing. How much money would this save, and how might this money be used? Pick one priority item from the rewritten box that the library does not currently do, and prepare a financial plan to accomplish the priority within a set time frame. From where would the new resources come?

(Answers to these questions can be found in the appendix at the back of the book. We encourage different library managers to work together, perhaps with staff members, to answer each question and to discuss the results.)

Notes

1. For an extended discussion of the libraries and their loss of supremacy in the academic institution "due… to the impact of digital technology," see Jerry Campbell, "Changing a Cultural Icon: The Academic Library as a Virtual Destination," *EDUCAUSE Review* 41, no. 1 (January/February 2006): 16–31.
2. John P. Kotter, *Leading Change* (Boston: Harvard Business Review Press, 1996), 71.
3. Stakeholders include individual library staff, groups of staff, representatives of staff (e.g., unions), institutional representatives, individual constituents, groups of constituents (may not act as a group, such as parents of constituents [e.g., children]), organized advisory groups (informal and formal), service organizations and agencies, and library consortia members.
4. For a more complete discussion, see J. Richard Hackman, *Leading Teams* (Boston: Harvard Business School Press, 2002).
5. James M. Kouzes and Barry Z. Posner, *The Leadership Challenge*, 4th ed. (San Francisco: Jossey-Bass, 2007).
6. Barbara Kellerman, *Followership* (Boston: Harvard Business Press, 2004). "Isolates," for instance, are detached, disinterested, and reinforce the status quo, while "bystanders" do not become engaged in efforts to improve organizational effectiveness.
7. Barbara Kellerman, *Bad Leadership* (Boston: Harvard Business Press, 2013).
8. For an in-depth coverage of leadership theories, including additional theories, see Peter G. Northouse, *Leadership* (Thousand Oaks, CA: Sage, 2016); and Rose Ngozi Amanchukwu, Gloria Jones Stanley, and Nwachukwu Prince Ololub, "A Review of Leadership Theories, Principles and Styles and Their Relevance to Educational Management." *Management* 5, no. 1 (2015): 6–14.
9. Barbara Kellerman, *Hard Times* (Redwood City, CA: Stanford University Press, 2014).
10. See Peter Hernon and Niels Ole Pors, eds., *Library Leadership in the United States and Europe* (Santa Barbara, CA: Libraries Unlimited, 2013), 15–18.
11. Juana Bordas, *Salsa, Soul, and Spirit* (San Francisco: Berrett-Koehler, 2012), ix.
12. Ibid.
13. See National Center for Healthcare Leadership, *Healthcare Leadership Competency Model*, v. 2.1 (Chicago: National Center for Healthcare Leadership, 2012), http://www.nchl.org/Documents/Ctrl_Hyperlink/NCHL_Competency_Model-full_uid892012228592.pdf.
14. Simmons College, Graduate School of library and Information Science, *Managerial Leadership in the Information Professions: Models* (accessed September 1, 2017), http://web.simmons.edu/~phdml/docs/phdmlip_models.pdf.
15. Lee G. Bolman and Terrence E. Deal, *Reframing Organizations* (San Francisco: Jossey-Bass, 2013).
16. Kotter, *Leading Change*, 78.
17. Ibid., 81.
18. Joan Giesecke, "Scenario Planning," in *Shaping the Future: Advancing the Understanding of Leadership*, ed. Peter Hernon (Santa Barbara, CA: Libraries United, 2010), 155.
19. Dana Mietzner and Guido Reger, "Advantages and Disadvantages of Scenario Approaches for Strategic Foresight," *International Journal of Technology Intelligence and Planning* 1, no. 2 (2005): 233, http://www.forschungsnetzwerk.at/downloadpub/stragegicforesight2005.pdf.
20. Joseph P. Martino, "The Precision of Delphi Estimates," *Technological Forecasting* 1, no. 3 (1970): 293–99.
21. For examples of scenarios see Hernon, *Shaping the Future*; Peter Hernon and Joseph R. Matthews, *Reflecting on the Future of Academic and Public Libraries* (Chicago: ALA Editions, 2013).

22. Jon E. Cawthorne, "Viewing the Future of University Research Libraries through the Perspectives of Scenarios" (PhD dissertation, Simmons College, 2013); and Tyler Walters, "The Future of Knowledge Creation and Production in University Research Programs and Their Effect on University Libraries" (PhD dissertation, Simmons College, 2013).
23. Joan Giesecke, Jon Cawthorne, and Deb Pearson, *Navigating the Future with Scenario Planning* (Chicago: Association of College and Research Libraries, 2015), 20–21.
24. Kotter, *Leading Change*, 85.

Bibliography

Amanchukwu, Rose Ngozi, Gloria Jones Stanley, and Nwachukwu Prince Ololub. "A Review of Leadership Theories, Principles and Styles and Their Relevance to Educational Management." *Management* 5, no. 1 (2015): 6–14.

Bolman, Lee G., and Terrence E. Deal. *Reframing Organizations: Artistry, Choice, and Leadership.* San Francisco: Jossey-Bass, 2013.

Bordas, Juana. *Salsa, Soul, and Spirit: Leadership for a Multicultural Age.* San Francisco: Berrett-Koehler, 2012.

Campbell, Jerry. "Changing a Cultural Icon: The Academic Library as a Virtual Destination." *EDUCAUSE Review* 41, no. 1 (January/February 2006): 16–31.

Cawthorne, Jon E. "Viewing the Future of University Research Libraries through the Perspectives of Scenarios." PhD dissertation, Simmons College, 2013.

Giesecke, Joan. "Scenario Planning." In *Shaping the Future: Advancing the Understanding of Leadership.* Edited by Peter Hernon, 155–62. Santa Barbara, CA: Libraries United, 2010.

Giesecke, Joan, Jon Cawthorne, and Deb Pearson. *Navigating the Future with Scenario Planning: A Guidebook for Librarians.* Chicago: Association of College and Research Libraries, 2015.

Hackman, J. Richard. *Leading Teams: Setting the Stage for Great Performances.* Boston: Harvard Business School Press, 2002.

Hernon, Peter, and Joseph R. Matthews. *Reflecting on the Future of Academic and Public Libraries.* Chicago: ALA Editions, 2013.

Hernon, Peter, and Niels Ole Pors, eds. *Library Leadership in the United States and Europe: A Comparative Study of Academic and Public Libraries.* Santa Barbara, CA: Libraries Unlimited, 2013.

Kellerman, Barbara. *Bad Leadership: What It Is, How It Happens, Why It Matters.* Boston: Harvard Business Press, 2013.

———. *Followership: How Followers Are Creating Change and Changing Leaders.* Boston: Harvard Business Press, 2004.

———. *Hard Times: Leadership in America.* Redwood City, CA: Stanford University Press, 2014.

Kotter, John P. *Leading Change.* Boston: Harvard Business Review Press, 1996.

Kouzes, James M., and Barry Z. Posner. *The Leadership Challenge*, 4th ed. San Francisco: Jossey-Bass, 2007.

Martino, Joseph P. "The Precision of Delphi Estimates." *Technological Forecasting* 1, no. 3 (1970): 293–99.

Mietzner, Dana, and Guido Reger. "Advantages and Disadvantages of Scenario Approaches for

Strategic Foresight." *International Journal of Technology Intelligence and Planning* 1, no. 2 (2005): 220–39. http://www.forschungsnetzwerk.at/downloadpub/stragegicforesight2005.pdf.

National Center for Healthcare Leadership. *Healthcare Leadership Competency Model*, v. 2.1. Chicago: National Center for Healthcare Leadership, 2012. http://www.nchl.org/Documents/Ctrl_Hyperlink/NCHL_Competency_Model-full_uid892012228592.pdf.

Northouse, Peter G. *Leadership: Theory and Practice.* Thousand Oaks, CA: Sage, 2016.

Walters, Tyler. "The Future of Knowledge Creation and Production in University Research Programs and Their Effect on University Libraries." PhD dissertation, Simmons College, 2013.

Appendix

Answers to Exercise Questions

Chapter 1

1. How could a library use ACRL's *Standards for Higher Education* in a strategic planning process?

ANSWER: ACRL's *Standards* serve as a framework for library planning and assessment that can be applied to library planning. The library could map, or crosswalk, its planning objectives with ACRL's principles and performance indicators.

2. Discuss the role of regional accrediting organizations in library planning.

ANSWER: All regional accrediting organizations, to differing degrees, address the quality of library resources in their standards documents. The library should be aware of how its regional organization applies the standards and ensure that the standards are directly or indirectly addressed in its strategic plan with measurable objectives.

3. Suggest a structure and format for a library's strategic plan.

ANSWER:

Mission

Vision

Library's Values
Goal 1.0 (the first goal of one or more goals)
  – Objective 1.1 (the first objective under Goal 1.0; could be several objectives)
    + Activity 1.1.1 (the first activity under Objective 1.1)

    + Activity 1.1.2 (the second activity under Objective 1.1)

Sources of Funding
Measurements for Success, Effectiveness, and Sustainability

Chapter 2

1. How does the infrastructure align with the system model?

ANSWER: The library's infrastructure (staff, collections, technology, and facilities) is an input in the system's model; the infrastructure covers the resources available to conduct processes and produce outputs. For example, staff open the library (process) and check out books (the checking-out activity is a process; the number of books checked out is an output).

2. What is the shortest time period for a financial management cycle?

ANSWER: 367 days. The library prepares, submits, and has its budget approved the day before the fiscal year begins. The budget is implemented during the 365 days of the fiscal year. Then, on day 367 of the cycle, the library submits its final report of the expenditures and undergoes an audit, if one is required. This short time period encompasses three different fiscal years, although it consumes twelve months and two days of time.

3. Besides serving as a compilation of expenditures, what other benefits does an internal management information system provide?

ANSWER:
  – collects inputs, such as the number of titles in the collection, the number of staff by classification (e.g., librarian, staff, and student assistants), number of computer workstations available for users, and the number of user seats in the library

  – collects outputs (e.g., the number of titles checked out from the circulation desk during the fiscal year, the total number of hours worked by student assistants, the number of logins to public computer workstations, and the number of total hours the library was open)

  – produces trend analysis for two or more years of inputs and outputs

Chapter 3

1. In addition to allocating collection funds, discuss another part of a budget that may have its allocation based upon a formula.

ANSWER: Funding for a branch or campus library, for instance. Sometimes, the funding allocated to support a branch or campus library may be based on the number of students (either head counts or full-time equivalents) or as a percentage of the enrollment of an academic program (the biology department has 30 percent of its students at the branch campus, so 30 percent of the print budget allocated to biology is allocated to the branch). Another funding allocation based on a formula may be travel funds for librarians assigned to professional association committee work. For example, for all travel funds allocated, 50 percent are set aside for the expected travel expenses for librarians serving on association committees.

2. The library has been directed to submit a zero-based budget that can be implemented at the beginning the next fiscal year. What service or program would you expect to first implement? Second? Third? Also, what is the justification for this set of priorities?

ANSWER: The response depends on the library's environment. At the John C. Pace Library, University of West Florida, the first one would be staff for the circulation function because they manage the processes to open and close the library physically for use. Second would be the print and collection needs of those academic programs for which maintaining accreditation is critical to their ongoing success. And third would be at least one person in the library's business office to manage the budget and expenditure processes and to pay the circulation staff and the critically needed and acquired information resources.

3. Line-item budgets are the most common budgets in libraries. Minimally, what lines should be allocated?

ANSWER: Two: staff and all other funds for expenditures. Staff should always be a separate line item accommodating full-time personnel with benefits, part-time personnel with benefits, and part-time personnel without benefits. The second line includes all other funds for expenditures, including the collections, supplies, postage, equipment, and training and development. Incidentally, if the budget included only one line item, it would be a lump sum budget.

Chapter 4

1. Why is it important to differentiate between expenditures and costs?

ANSWER: An expenditure is a payment or disbursement of funds representing the amount of funds spent. It is a number, but it does not provide any feedback about how the library benefits from spending the funds. Costs provide feedback on a benefit from the expenditure; with costs data, managers can determine what happened with the funds spent. Both expenditures and costs are outputs, but costs provide a much more complete description of an activity. The library may have expended $100,000 on books, but the costs to develop the book collection include expenditures for staff to order the items and process the books for use once they arrive at the library, together with the supplies used to prepare the books for use.

2. Staff and collections expenditures consume most of the funds allocated to the library. Where would a library manager find data about library staff and collections?

ANSWER: Detailed past expenditures are the best source. Additionally, staff salary data appear in the salary surveys at the national level and in consortial information if the library's consortia collect the data from their members. Data about collections can be found in vendor reports, on vendor websites, and in tables in the annual edition of the *Library and Book Trade Almanac* (published by Information Today, Inc.).

3. Do you plan and implement bottom-up or top-down budgeting?

ANSWER: This depends on the library's current practices. However, the closer the budgeting process is to those responsible for implementing the services, programs, and functions, the better is the planning as the basis of the library's short-term budget plan.

Chapter 5

1. Create a program budget outline for librarian-led library instruction. In doing so, complete the following steps:
   – Use a library's existing mission statement.
   – Create a library goal that would include library instruction.
   – Create a library objective for that goal.
   – Create at least one activity to support the objective.
   – Identify the budget categories for the program's budget and the detail necessary to allocate budgeted funds.
   – List one metric each for its success, effectiveness, and sustainability. Explain how this program may be used by the library to inform the long-term plan. What can the library do with this information?

ANSWER: For example,
   – Mission Statement: The University of West Florida (UWF) Libraries' purpose is to provide information-related resources and services to

support the University of West Florida's learning, teaching, research, and community service missions. It intends to inspire the total individual, encouraging personal, social, and intellectual growth and lifelong learning through the acquisition of information and knowledge.

- Goal: Foster Environments through Which Staff Provide Resources, Services, and Programs Supporting Learning, Teaching, and Research
- Objective: Coordinate a comprehensive information literacy program that provides opportunities to demonstrate student learning outcomes in support of academic achievement, career success, and lifelong learning.
- Activity: Provide library and information literacy instruction sessions by request, tailored to courses, specific assignments, and course levels.
- Budget categories: Staff will be the largest expenditure in this activity. The budget allocation will be based upon specifically identifying the staff providing instruction and then calculating the percentage of each staff member's time conducting instruction. If the library has an instruction classroom, then other costs would include identifying the staff responsible for managing the technology in the room and the costs for the equipment maintenance agreements supporting the equipment.
- Metrics. Success: Faculty request instruction sessions supporting their specific courses; these courses are from both the lower and upper divisions of the curriculum. Effectiveness: Student learning outcomes related to the sections are achieved. Sustainability: The percentage of "repeat" faculty who request instruction for their courses whenever taught (e.g., each semester; annually).

The information may answer the following questions:

- What is the number of sessions held? Is the number increasing or decreasing from past years?
- What is the number of sessions held per student? Is the number increasing or decreasing?
- What is the number of sessions held per library staff person? Is the number increasing or decreasing?
- What is the number of faculty requesting sessions? Is the number increasing or decreasing?

2. Create a program budget outline for developing the collections. To do this, use a library's existing mission statement from this chapter's first question and then
   - Create a library goal that would include collection development.
   - Create a library objective for that goal.
   - Create at least one activity to support the objective.
   - Identify the budget categories for the program's budget and the detail necessary to allocate budgeted funds.

– List one metric for success, one for effectiveness, and one for sustainability.
Explain how this program may be used by the library to inform the long-term plan.

ANSWER: For example,

– Goal: Foster Environments through Which Staff Provide Resources, Services, and Programs Supporting Learning, Teaching, and Research.
– Objective: Develop and manage relevant intellectual content, balanced across appropriate information formats, to support teaching, research, and service regardless of geographic location.
– Activity: Annually expend 25 percent of the libraries' monographs budget for digital format.
– Budget categories: Collections. The details would be a simple ratio: the total monographs budget, which includes print and digital formats, and calculate 25 percent of the total to be allocated for e-books.
– Metrics. Success: 25 percent of the total monograph funds allocated were expended for e-books. Effectiveness: The e-books purchased supported the curriculum and were accessed or otherwise viewed. Sustainability: The e-books were purchased for permanent availability rather than as an annual subscription.

The information may answer the following questions:

– Inform the long-range plan? The success of this activity may result in the library increasing its purchase to 50 percent of the monographs purchased annually.
– Also, it may be that the library adopts an acquisition approach using a patron-driven acquisition program or evidence-based acquisition program to fulfill the objective for developing relevant intellectual content based upon "when needed" rather than "just in case it is needed."

3. Explain how the program budget for the ILL program highlighted in this chapter can be improved.

ANSWER: Use the ILL program budget template from this chapter and compile expenditures for the process of borrowing items from other libraries, and, with a second template, compile expenditures for lending items to other libraries.

Chapter 6

1. How often should the library reconcile its expenditures with the institution's budget status reports, and why?

ANSWER: The library's business office function should reconcile expenditures at least monthly. The primary reason is to find errors entered into the expenditures system either by the library or at the institutional level. Common errors include numeric transpositions or the assignment of an expenditure to the wrong expenditure category (e.g., a supply expenditure wrongly assigned as a collections expenditure).Errors become more difficult to find as the fiscal year progresses.

2. List at least one financial managerial practice concerning the business office that should be avoided.

ANSWER: Micromanaging staff, which could result in low morale and disrupt the participatory management process that actively and positively involves staff.

3. Briefly explain the benefits of "economies of scale" to a library.

ANSWER: In manufacturing, economies of scale are realized when the average cost to produce something falls as the volume of output increases. Another definition is when multiple purchasers created partnerships to purchase the same good or service at a discount. For example, economies of scale are realized when two or more libraries, or the library and another organizational unit on campus, create or use existing cooperative agreements that yield discounted prices for the library. The two most common practices in libraries include purchasing information resources through consortia or other formal partnerships, and purchasing equipment and supplies. The library and its partners may negotiate these cost-saving contracts or agreements. Such contracts and agreements may also be created by another organizational unit or entity, such as a state government, as a purchasing agreement with an office supplies vendor or a computer vendor for discounted pricing for any organizational unit within state or local government.

Chapter 7

1. What types of financial reports does your library create, and for whom?

ANSWER: The library has a multiplicity of stakeholders that have varying degrees of financial information needs and interests. Those stakeholders include internal audiences within the library and institution and those external to the library, including accrediting organizations and associations and vendors that manage surveys. Most of the reports focus on expenditures as outputs rather than budgets as inputs. The detail of the financial information varies as well; some stakeholders will want more detail, such as a breakout of collection expenditures for serials and monographs or expenditures by classification of staff such as librarians and support staff, while other stakeholders may want to know the sum of the expenditures from all budget categories as a total.

2. What content does your library present in its annual report? Who are the audiences?

ANSWER: The content of an annual report varies from library to library, and, over years, content differs because library directors hold varying perspectives concerning the importance of the report and the amount of time they want to spend on its preparation and presentation. From a financial perspective, the annual report should compare the allocated budgets for each of the budgeted categories (e.g., staff and collections) and their final expenditures. The more detail that can be included in the financial section, the better it is for creating trends analysis in the future. In addition to the expenditures, the library should also describe, via narrative, how the expenditures supported the short- and long-term objectives of the library's strategic plan. Audiences for the annual report include internal stakeholders such as senior institutional administrators and members of the institution's governing bodies. External stakeholders include peer libraries, consortia members, and library monitoring and reporting bodies such as ACRL.

3. How would the library prepare for a compliance audit?

ANSWER: Compliance audits, sometimes referred to as program audits, determine if the organization adhered to applicable rules, regulations, policies, and procedures. These audits show if funds were expended on programs as planned and reported and if the outputs and outcomes reported were, indeed, factual. In case the library is audited, it must have accurate financial records and be able to explain how the expenditures comply with the rules, regulations, policies, and procedures. For example, if the institution has a contract for office supplies from a preferred vendor, and if the library did not use that vendor, it must be able to provide a rationale (e.g., the vendor did not have the specific item available on the contract). Second, as part of the monthly reconciliation process, the library must ensure that expenditures are aligned with the appropriate budget category; a best practice is to find and resolve financial reporting errors. Third, the library ensures that output and outcome data are accurate and defensible. If the library reported X number of circulation transactions, managers must be prepared to prove it. Accountability requires accuracy, and integrity requires honesty and truthfulness. Padding an output with a higher-than-accurate number may result in a negative finding from a compliance audit, which may result in a loss of credibility and trust of the library by the institution.

Chapter 8

1. How does your library identify, measure, and report its value to stakeholders?

ANSWER: Libraries vary in their approaches. Many use financial metrics to demonstrate the return on investment and adopt derived ratios to show expenditures per FTE student, faculty, or both, such as "expended $125.00 per FTE student on collection development this past fiscal year." Another set of financial metrics relate to costs. While expenditures are useful outputs, costs provide more feedback concerning the service. For example, the ILL program expended $140,000 in staff, supplies, postage, and other direct expenditures. The cost to borrow an article from another library, however, was $15.00 per filled request. Knowing the cost per article filled can be applied to decision making in collection development.

2. How would a library calculate the cost to conduct a librarian-led instruction session?

ANSWER: Adopt the template provided in chapter 5 to calculate the costs for an ILL program that records the expenditures for librarian-led instruction sessions. Staff are the largest expenditure in this activity. Be sure to include expenditures associated with the instruction program, such as staff-based technology support and the costs for the equipment maintenance agreements supporting the equipment. Sum the expenditures. At the bottom of the template, record the number of sessions conducted and the number of participants. Divide the number of sessions conducted into the sum of the expenditures to calculate the cost per instruction session. Making a similar calculation replacing the number of instruction sessions with the number of participants produces the derived ratio of cost per participant for an instruction session.

Appendix Table 1

Instruction Program Budget Expenditures Template

Objective 3.0: Coordinate a comprehensive information literacy program that provides opportunities to demonstrate student learning outcomes in support of academic achievement, career success, and lifelong learning

Program: Library Instruction Services

- Activities
    + 3.2.1—Provide library and information literacy instruction sessions by request, tailored to courses, specific assignments, and course levels.

PERSONNEL SALARIES and WAGES	Job title	Sessions Conducted	Fiscal Year Salary	Hours per Week	Wage per Hour	Fringe Benefits	Total per Person Expended
Full-Time	Person 1		$			$	$
	Person 2		$			$	$
	Person 3		$	$	$		$
	Person 4		$	$	$		$
Part-Time	Person 1			$	$		$

		Hours of Tech Support Provided	Fiscal Year Salary	Hours per Week	Wage per Hour	Fringe Benefits	Total per Person Expended
Technology Support	Person 1			$	$		$
NON-PERSONNEL	Vendor	Description					Expended
Equipment							$
Software							$
Contractual Services							$
Supplies and Materials							$
Shipping and Postage							$
Staff Training and Development							$
Marketing / PR							$
Copyright							$
OTHER COSTS		Description					Cost Assigned
Indirect							$
Overhead							$
Depreciation							$
TOTAL EXPENDED							$
EXPECTED MEASURES of SUCCESS	**Number of Sessions and Participants Expected**	**Number of Sessions and Participants**					
Sessions	200	225					
Participants	4,000	4,728					

3. A library wants to compare its operating expenditures with its benchmarking peers. First, which libraries comprise benchmarking peers? Second, how is this determination made? Third, how would the library develop this benchmarking report? Finally, what specific derived ratios would be useful for the benchmark study?

ANSWER: The libraries at the institutions identified by your institution as peers serve for the benchmarking study. Additionally, the library may have other sets of peers, such as consortia members or libraries in a defined geopolitical area. First, compile the operating expenditures from the peer libraries. Operating expenditures could include staff, collections, and all other direct operating costs (e.g., supplies and equipment). This financial data would provide subtotals and totals for the benchmark study. To help with context, compile the number of full-time equivalent (FTE) students, faculty, or both. Using the expenditures, it is then possible for the benchmark study to calculate derived ratios for the total expenditures per FTE student, collections expenditures per FTE student, staff expenditures per FTE student, and other operating expenditures per FTE student.

Chapter 9

1. What may a library do when it learns about a budget reduction from the current year's budget level two months before the next fiscal year begins?

ANSWER: First, managers can ask some questions. Is the budget cut based on a percentage of the library, or is it a fixed amount? Will the library be able to make recommendations as to what to cut, or will those decisions come from the institution as part of the budget reductions? If the library can make recommendations, the second step is to review the library's short-term plan for the next fiscal year and to determine if any activities can be delayed a year. For example, suppose a project was planned to shift the print serials collection in the stacks to free up some shelves that could then be removed and replaced with user seating. Maybe that project can be delayed or existing furniture relocated to this area and the new seating not purchased as planned. The management decision is to determine whether one or more activities in the strategic plan can be cut or delayed. Library managers may also want to confirm if any campus site visits from accrediting organizations are planned to ensure that the program accrediting effort is not hampered. A third activity is to align the "at the moment" expenditures with the total budget to be allocated. It may be that the library's current expenditures status may be close to that of the next year's total, albeit reduced, budget allocation. If that is the case, the library may decide to use the current expenditures as the benchmark for next year's planned expenditures.

2. The library has sustained a budget rescission three months into the fiscal year. What are two strategies that should be considered for immediate implementation?

ANSWER: First, do not "trash-talk" the institution. No one really wants to implement a rescission, and it is likely that many other organizational units have sustained reductions as well. Second, once the library has made some initial decisions about how to proceed with the reductions for specific programs, services, or functions, these decisions become options or alternatives, and the library should actively inform the community and seek feedback. Library managers should make themselves available to listen, and they should hold discussions with the stakeholders.

3. A financial audit of the past fiscal year's expenditures reveals that the library overexpended its non-personnel budgeted allocation by $100,000. The library dean places the blame on the library's business office; the business office counters that it had reported to the library dean that the budget was being overspent, but nothing was done. What may happen now?

ANSWER: The cause for overexpending might be (1) an error that was not reconciled with the budget status reports, (2) the library's administration ignoring monthly reports that indicated months earlier that current expenditures and encumbrances needed to be slowed, or (3) fraudulent behavior by which someone with access to the library's financial system diverted funds for his or her own use. The institution's internal audit office or risk managers will likely initiate a step-by-step analysis to understand what happened and to identify shortcomings in the library's financial controls. While that analysis is underway, the institution will likely test its trust in the library's administration.

Chapter 10

1. Who is a financial leader in your library, and why do you regard this person as one?

ANSWER: While there are multiple responses to this question based on the local environment, a leader may not always have a formal leadership role. Leaders create a vision (or they execute an established vision), and they display the values discussed in this chapter.

2. For your library, whom would you involve in rewriting box 10.1? Rewrite the content of the box.

ANSWER: Rewrite the content of the box; identify internal and external stakeholders and stakeholder groups that would be affected by any changes.

3. To accomplish this vision, list five things the library could stop doing. How much money would this save, and how might this money be used? Pick one priority item from the rewritten box that the library does not currently do, and prepare a financial plan to accomplish the priority within a set time frame. From where would the new resources come?

ANSWER: To determine how much money will be saved and to prepare a financial plan for a new service, the library may want to use a program budgeting process (chapter 5) as well as to calculate the current costs for the existing services to stop and the expected costs for the new service (chapter 8) to be implemented.

About the Authors

Robert E. Dugan is the dean of libraries at the University of West Florida (Pensacola). Prior to assuming this position, he had been at Suffolk University, Boston; Wesley College, Dover, Delaware; and Georgetown University, Washington, DC. He has also worked in state and public libraries during his more than forty-three-year career. He is the coauthor of fourteen books, including the award-winning *Viewing Library Metrics from Different Perspectives* (2009). He has taught library financial management at the master's and doctoral levels and at library leadership workshops.

Peter Hernon is a professor emeritus at Simmons College, Boston, and was the principal (and founding) faculty member for the doctoral program, Managerial Leadership in the Information Professions. He received his PhD degree from Indiana University Bloomington, and was the 2008 recipient of the Association of College and Research Libraries' award for Academic/Research Librarian of the Year, the founding editor *of Government Information Quarterly*, past editor-in-chief of *The Journal of Academic Librarianship*, and past co-editor of *Library & Information Science Research*. He has taught, conducted workshops, and delivered addresses in twelve countries outside the United States. He is the author or coauthor of fifty-eight books, including the award-winning *Federal Information Policies in the 1980s* (1985), *Assessing Service Quality* (1998), and *Viewing Library Metrics from Different Perspectives* (2009).